# SEVEN OLD ENGLISH POEMS

# SEVEN OLD ENGLISH
# POEMS

·

CÆDMON'S HYMN

THE BATTLE OF BRUNANBURH

THE DREAM OF THE ROOD

THE BATTLE OF MALDON

THE WANDERER

THE SEAFARER

DEOR

·

EDITED WITH COMMENTARY AND GLOSSARY

*by JOHN C. POPE*

W · W · NORTON & COMPANY

*New York · London*

# Preface to the Second Edition

The present edition is an exact photographic reproduction of the seventh printing of the first edition, except that it has been possible to correct a number of minor errors that had escaped notice in earlier printings. Most of these have to do with vowel length, pronunciation of palatal *c* and *g*, punctuation, and style of type. A few corrections of the glossary could not so easily be entered. They have been reserved for the Supplement, which attempts to add major bibliographical information up to 1980 and to reconsider certain matters of interpretation in the light of recent opinion. I am grateful to the Norton editors for undertaking publication of this new edition, and to Bobbs-Merrill for turning over the copyright to me and consenting to the reproduction, with minor revision, of the first edition.

J. C. P.

*New Haven, Connecticut*
*February, 1981*

# Preface

This edition has grown out of my needs as the teacher of an elementary course in Old English for graduate students. The poems are those I have found it most profitable to read early in the year, as a preliminary to the study of *Beowulf*. They are arranged in the order in which I usually take them up with the class. There is nothing sacred about this order, except that *The Wanderer* and *The Seafarer* offer difficulties of interpretation beyond the rest, since they exhibit a more richly metaphorical and connotative use of language in accordance with their intellectually complicated themes; while *Deor*, with its allusions to heroic legends, stands in that respect closer than the others to the world of *Beowulf*.

The text and glossary have been my principal concern. The text is normalized very much according to the system of Professor F. P. Magoun, Jr., whose normalized text, *The Anglo-Saxon Poems in Bright's Anglo-Saxon Reader* (Department of English, Harvard University, 1960) has been a staple of my course for several years; and I might have rested content with this if I had not wished to include the whole of *The Dream of the Rood* and *The Seafarer*, and to treat all seven poems somewhat more intensively than his edition allowed. I have decided to adopt as my norm a somewhat less archaic version of Early West Saxon than Magoun's, which follows the spellings of Holthausen's *Altenglisches etymologisches Wörterbuch*. These spellings are excellent for the student of etymology and phonology, but in certain respects (notably the rounded *œ*, long and short, and the distinction between *io* and *eo*) they go beyond the spellings most frequently encountered in the literary manuscripts, especially those of the poetry, and beyond the spellings adopted as standard by the leading grammars. I have retained the *e* of the poetical manuscripts for the *i*-mutation of *o*, and have included what was historically *io* under the generalized *eo* of many, though by no means all, of the manuscripts. The most conspicuous mark of Early West Saxon, the *ie*, long and short, though it became archaic during the tenth century and was obsolete by the time of *The Battle of Maldon*, is too helpful to the student to be abandoned.

In a few other particulars I have departed from Holthausen and Magoun, generally in favor of less drastic alteration of the manuscript records and in accord with the forms given precedence in the grammars of Sievers-Brunner and Campbell. Here and there (like Magoun) I have allowed variant forms to stand for fear of disturbing the meter, and at least once (*sleaht* in *The Wanderer* for *slieht* in *Brunanburh*) for fear of too drastic an alteration of the phonetic pattern—though in this matter we must generally resign ourselves to the probability that our inherited texts are very far from faithful to the dialectal forms and other details of the poet's own speech. At all events the full record and cross-references of the glossary should render my few inconsistencies harmless. I have deliberately refrained from normalizing the pronominal forms *mē, þē, ūs, ēow*, so that the reader must decide whether they are dative or accusative, or consult my guesses in the glossary. Similarly, I have not normalized the endings in the manuscripts for the nominative and accusative plural of adjectives. The generalized ending *-e* is very common and is allowed to stand even if the noun modified is feminine or neuter. Consequently there is no instance in the ensuing texts of the specifically feminine *-a*, and only two of the neuter *-u* (*Wanderer* 85, *īdlu* and 100, *wæl-ġīfru*).

Partly to let the reader know precisely how I have modified these texts, and partly to keep the student aware of the irregularities he will encounter as soon as he turns to our standard editions of Old English poetry, I have put at the foot of the page the full record of the manuscript readings insofar as they differ from the normalized text. Outright emendations (most of which are the work of previous editors) are distinguished from mere variations in spelling—though sometimes a grammatical ending in the manuscript is susceptible of more than one interpretation, and the normalizer must make an editorial choice.

The glossary has been an even greater concern than the text.

It is planned for a double purpose. On the one hand, it enables the beginner to make considerable progress toward gaining a general control of the poetic vocabulary. All nominal and adjectival compounds, if distinctly recognizable as such, are separated into their two components by hyphens in the text of the poems, and each component is separately defined in its alphabetical place in the glossary. In this way the student, following a plan recommended by Professor Magoun, can learn a relatively small number of simple words out of which a rather large number of compounds are formed by the poets, and can usually understand the compounds for himself, as the poets themselves, freely compounding words as they wished, expected their audiences or readers to do. On the other hand, the student of poetry wants not only to increase his general command of the vocabulary but to understand the subtleties of his text. For this reason I have defined the compounds as well as their components, and tried as far as possible to give, for all words, the meanings most applicable to their particular occurrences.

My own practice is to return to the standard editions, with their unnormalized texts, as soon as the student has acquired a grounding in the grammar and has begun to build a substantial vocabulary. Those who wish to continue the use of normalized texts can with very slight adjustment proceed to those of Professor Magoun, which are published by the Department of English at Harvard. Besides the poems in Bright's Reader, he has normalized *Beowulf* and *Judith* in one volume (1959) and the poems of the Vercelli Book in another (1960). His own device for building vocabulary is the *Grouped Frequency Word-List of Anglo-Saxon Poetry*, prepared jointly with John F. Madden, C.S.B. (Second corrected printing, 1960). An almost essential companion to these texts is Jess B. Bessinger, Jr., *A Short Dictionary of Anglo-Saxon Poetry*, Toronto University Press: Toronto, Ontario, 1960.

NOTE TO THE REVISED EDITION: The first edition of this book was reproduced photographically from typescript for the use of my own students. In preparing it for general use I have corrected many small errors and omissions, rewritten several portions of the commentary, augmented others, and added a section on versification. The bibliographical suggestions in the commentary have been extended but remain highly selective. The older bibliography is amply represented in the special editions to which I have referred. I must rely upon teacher and student to make further exploration and to add fresh items year by year.

I am grateful to many of my present and former students for calling attention to inconsistencies and oversights. To Dr. Robert B. Burlin I am indebted for valuable bibliographical suggestions and for generously given assistance in editorial tasks. To Dr. Frances Randall Lipp, who tried out the first edition with her classes, I owe searching criticism on several matters pertaining to the interpretation of the texts and further help on bibliography.

J. C. P.

*New Haven, Connecticut*
*1966*

# CONTENTS

# AIDS TO PRONUNCIATION

Þ, þ  represent the voiceless *th* in *thin*.

Ð, ð  represent the voiced *th* in *this*.

ċ   is pronounced like *ch* in *chin*.

ċċ  is the same sound prolonged or doubled.

ġ   is pronounced like *y* in *year* or *day*.

nġ  is pronounced like the *ng* in *hinge* (but not if the *n* belongs to a separable element, as in an-ġinn or on-ġinnan).

cg  (not specially marked) is always like *dge* in *edge*.

sc  (not specially marked) when initial or final is like *sh* in *shall*, *English*; when medial, as in *āscian*, it is like *sk* in *ask*.

# TEXTS

# Cædmon's Hymn

*The Northumbrian Version of MS M, dated 737
(The Moore MS, University Library, Cambridge,
Kk. 5. 16, f. 128ᵛ)*

Nu scylun hergan   hefaenricaes uard,
metudæs maecti   end his modgidanc,
uerc uuldurfadur,   sue he uundra gihuaes,
eci dryctin,   or astelidæ.
5     He aerist scop   aelda barnum
heben til hrofe,   haleg scepen;
tha middungeard   moncynnæs uard,
eci dryctin,   æfter tiadæ,
firum foldu,   frea allmectig.

Variants in MS L (Leningrad, Public Library, MS Lat. Q. v. I. 18, f. 107, dated 746 or earlier): **1** scilun. herga. hefenricæs. **2** mehti. and. modgithanc. **3** gihuæs. **5** ærist. ældu. **6** hefen to hrofæ halig sceppend. **7** middingard. **9** allmehtig.

3

# Cædmon's Hymn

*The Hymn Normalized in West-Saxon Spelling*
*Based on the Northumbrian Version of* MSS M *and* L

Nū sculon herian    heofon-rīċes Weard,
Metodes meahta    and his mōd-ġeþanc,
weorc Wuldor-Fæder,    swā hē wundra ġehwæs,
ēċe Dryhten,    ōr astealde.
5    Hē ǣrest scōp    ielda bearnum
heofon to hrōfe,    hāliġ Scieppend;
þā middan-ġeard    mann-cynnes Weard,
ēċe Dryhten,    æfter tēode—
fīrum foldan    Frēa ælmihtiġ.

Substantive variants in MS T (Bodleian Library, Tanner
10, f. 100), the best of the West-Saxon texts, included in the
Old English version of Bede's *Historia Ecclesiastica*:
4 onstealde.  5 eorðan *for* ielda.

Spelling variants in T compared with the normalized text:
1 herigean.  2 meotodes.  meahte.  4 drihten.  5 sceop.
6 scyppend.  7 moncynnes.  8 drihten.
Among variants in some of the later copies are: 1 we
*before* sculon.  4 ord *for* or.  5 gesceop *for* scop.

4

# The Battle of Brunanburh

## (*The Anglo-Saxon Chronicle*)

Hēr Æðelstān cyning, eorla dryhten,
beorna bēag-ġiefa, and his brōðor ēac,
Ēadmund æðeling, ealdor-langne tīr
ġeslōgon æt sæċċe sweorda ecgum
5 ymbe Brūnanburh. Bord-weall clufon,
hēowon heaðu-linda hamora lāfum
eaforan Ēadweardes, swā him ġe-æðele wæs
fram cnēo-māgum þæt hīe æt campe oft
wiþ lāðra ġehwone land ealgoden,
10 hord and hāmas. Hettend crungon,
Scotta lēode and scip-flotan,
fǣġe fēollon. Feld dennode

A = Corpus Christi College, Cambridge, MS 173 (the Parker
Chronicle), ff. 26ʳ–27ʳ. B = British Museum, MS Cotton Tiberius
A. vi, ff. 31ʳ–32ʳ. C = British Museum, MS Cotton Tiberius B. i,
f. 141ʳ⁻ᵛ. D = British Museum, MS Cotton Tiberius B. iv, ff.
49ʳ–50ʳ. A was copied at Winchester soon after 955; B and C are
copies of a MS at Abingdon, now lost; B after 977, C eleventh
century. D was copied from a northern MS after 1016.

1 B æþestan. BC cing. BCD drihten. 2 ACD beah-. ABD -gifa;
C -gyfa. 3 C ealdorlagne. D tyr. 4 B geslogan. B sake; D secce.
C swurda. B ecggum. 5 BC embe. BC brunnan- (AD brunan, *but* A
*corrected to* brunnan). bord-] D heord-. AD -weal. ABD clufan.
6 ABD heowan. ABCD heaþo-. A -linde; B -lina; D -linga *altered to* -linda.
D hamera. A lafan. 7 A afaran; C aforan; D eoforan *altered to*
eaforan. D cadweardæs. 8 A from. ACD -mægum. ACD hi.
9 ACD gehwæne; B gehwane. AC ealgodon; B ealgodan; D gealgodon.
10 D heted. A crungun. 11 A sceotta. A leoda. C scyp-.
12 ABC feollan. A dænede *corrected to* dænnede; BC dennade.

secga swāte    siþþan sunne upp
on morgen-tīd,    mǣre tungol,
15    glād ofer grundas,    Godes candel beorht,
ēċes Dryhtnes,    oþ sēo æðele ġesceaft
sāg to setle.    Þǣr læġ secg maniġ
gārum aġīeted,    guma Norðerna
ofer scield scoten,    swelċe Scyttisc ēac,
20    wēriġ, wīġes sæd.
                              West-Seaxe forþ
andlangne dæġ    ēorod-cystum
on lāst leġdon    lāðum þēodum,
hēowon here-flīeman    hindan þearle
mēċum mylen-scearpum.    Mierċe ne wierndon
25    heardes hand-plegan    hæleða nānum
þāra-þe mid Anlāfe    ofer ēar-ġebland
on lides bōsme    land ġesōhton,
fǣġe to ġefeohte.    Fīfe lāgon
on þam camp-stede    cyningas ġeonge,
30    sweordum aswefede,    swelċe seofone ēac
eorlas Anlāfes,    unrīm herġes,
flotena and Scotta.    Þǣr ġeflīemed wearþ
Norþ-manna bregu,    nīede ġebǣded,
to lides stefne    lȳtle weorode;

---

13 A secgas hwate. AD up.    15 A Condel.    16 ABCD drihtnes. oþ] B þæt.
A sio; D se.    17 ABCD sah. D sætle. A mænig; CD monig.    18 ACD ageted;
B forgrunden. BCD guman. BC norðerne; D norþærne.    19 A scild;
BCD scyld. BD sceoten. AC swilce; BD swylce. A scittisc.    20 BC
wigges. D ræd. AD wesseaxe; B westsexe; C and wessexe.    21 A ondlongne.
BCD eored-. A -cistum.    22 A legdun; D lægdon. C ðeodon.    23 ABD
heowan. A herefleman; B hereflyman; C hereflymon; D heora flyman.    24 A
mylenscearpan; D mycelscearpum. ABCD myrce. ABCD wyrndon.    25 A
heeardes. A hond-.    26 þara-þe] A þæ; D þæra þe. A æra-.    27 C
liþes. A gesohtun; B gesohtan.    28 D fage. D feohte. A lægun.
29 B þæm. A cyninges; B ciningas; C cingas. A giunge; D iunga.
30 C aswefde. ABC swilce; D swylce. AD seofene; C vii.    31 unrim]
C and unrim. A heriges.    32 ABCD flotan. A sceotta. A geflemed;
BCD geflymed.    33 BCD brego. AB nede; CD neade. A gebeded.    34 D
stæfne. A litle. C werode.

35 crēad cnearr on flot, cyning ūt ġewāt
  on fealone flōd, feorh ġenerede.
  Swelċe þǣr ēac se frōda mid flēame cōm
  on his cȳþþe norþ, Constantīnus,
  hār hilde-rinc. Hrēman ne þorfte
40 mēċa ġemānan; hē wæs his māga sceard,
  frēonda ġefielled on folc-stede,
  beslæġen æt sæċċe, and his sunu forlēt
  on wæl-stōwe wundum forgrunden,
  ġeongne æt gūðe. Ġielpan ne þorfte
45 beorn blanden-feax bill-ġesliehtes,
  eald inwitta, nē Anlāf þȳ mā;
  mid hira here-lāfum hliehhan ne þorfton
  þæt hīe beadu-weorca beteran wurdon
  on camp-stede cumbol-ġehnāstes,
50 gār-mittunge, gumena ġemōtes,
  wǣpen-ġewrixles, þæs hīe on wæl-felda
  wiþ Ēadweardes eaforan plegodon.
  Ġewiton him þā Norþ-menn næġled-cnearrum,
  drēoriġ daroða lāf, on Dinges mere
55 ofer dēop wæter Dyflin sēċan,

---

35 D creat. cnearr on] BCD cnear on; A cnearen. D flod. B cing;
C cining. D *omits 35b and 36a.*  36 A fealene. CD generode.  37
AC swilce; BD Swylce.  38 A costontinus.  39 har] D hal. A hildering;
D hylderinc. D hryman.  40 meca] A mæcan; B mecea; D mecga. he]
BC her. AD mæga.  41 ABCD gefylled. on] C on his.  42 beslægen]
A beslagen; C beslegen; B forslegen. B sace; D sæcge. D forlæt.
43 A wundun. A fergrunden.  44 A giungne. A gelpan; BCD gylpan.
45 BC -fex. A bil-. A geslehtes; B geslyhtes; CD geslihtes.  46 A
inwidda; D inwuda. þy] BD þe.  47 AB heora; CD hyra. D -leafum.
A hlehhan; BC hlihhan; D hlybban. AC þorftun; BD þorftan.  48 A
heo; CD hi. BCD beado-. A wurdun; B wurdan.  49 A culbod-,
cumbel- *over line.* A -gehnades.  50 ABC -mittinge.  51 þæs] D þæs þe.
ACD hi.  52 AD afaran; C aforan. AB plegodan.  53 AB gewitan.
C hym. A normen *altered to* norþmen; D norðmen. C negledcnearrum;
D dæg gled on garum.  54 C dreori. A daraða; C dareþa; D dareða.
B dynges; D dyniges.  55 D deopne. A difelin; B dyflen; D dyflig.
B secean.

eft Īra land    ǣwisc-mōde.
Swelċe þā ġebrōðor    bēġen ætsamne,
cyning and æðeling,    cȳþþe sōhton,
West-Seaxna land,    wīġes hrēmġe.

60   Lēton him behindan    hrǣw bryttian
sealwiġ-pādan,    þone sweartan hræfn
hyrned-nebban,    and þone hasu-pādan,
earn æftan hwīt,    ǣses brūcan,–
grǣdiġne gūþ-hafoc,    and þæt grǣġe dēor,

65   wulf on wealda.

                    Ne wearþ wæl māre
on þȳs īġ-lande    ǣfre ġīeta
folces ġefielleð    beforan þissum
sweordes ecgum,    þæs-þe ūs secgaþ bēċ,
ealde ūþwitan,    siþþan ēastan hider

70   Engle and Seaxe    upp becōmon,
ofer brād brimu    Britene sōhton,
wlance wīġ-smiðas,    Wēalas ofercōmon,
eorlas ār-hwǣte    eard beġēaton.

---

56 eft] A and eft, *the* and *added later above the line*. Ira] A hira;
CD yra.    57 AC swilce; B Swylce; D swylce. A gebroþer; C broðor.
D bege.    BC ætsomne; D æt runne.    58 BC cing. D eaðeling. B sohtan.
59 A wesseaxena; C wessexena. BC wigges. A hramige *altered to*
hremige; BCD hremige.    60 AB letan; D læton. C hym. C behindon.
A hræ *with* w *added over line;* B hraw; CD hra. B bryttigean; C brittigan;
D bryttinga.    61 A saluwig; BCD salowig. C hrefn.    62 D hyrnet-.
A þane. A hasewan-; B haso-. D -wadan.    64 D cuðheafoc. D grege.
65 ABCD wealde.    66 A þis; D þisne. A eiglande; B eglande. A æfer.
BC gyta; D gita.    67 ACD gefylled; B afylled. BCD þyssum.
68 C swurdes. B secggeaþ.    69 B syþþan.    70 B sexan; C sexe. AD up. AB
becoman.    71 BCD brade. AB brytene; C bretene. AB sohtan.    72 A
weealles. AB ofercóman.    73 ABC arhwate. A begeatan.

# The Dream of the Rood

(*Vercelli Book,* ff. 104ᵛ–106ʳ)

    Hwæt, iċ swefna cyst   secgan wille,
hwæt mē ġemætte   to midre nihte,
siþþan reord-berend   reste wunodon.
Þūhte mē þæt iċ ġesāwe   seldlīcre trēo
5    on lyft lǣdan   lēohte bewunden,
bēama beorhtost.   Eall þæt bēacen wæs
begoten mid golde;   ġimmas stōdon
fæġere æt foldan sċēatum,   swelċe þǣr fīfe wǣron
uppe on þam eaxl-ġespanne.   Behēoldon þǣr enġel-dryhta fela,
10    fæġere þurh forþ-ġesceaft;   ne wæs þǣr hūru fracuðes ġealga,
ac hine þǣr behēoldon   hālġe gāstas,
menn ofer moldan   and eall þēos mǣre ġesceaft.
Seldlīċ wæs se siġe-bēam,   and iċ synnum fāg,
forwundod mid wammum.   Ġeseah iċ wuldres trēo
15    wǣdum ġeweorðod   wynnum scīnan,
ġeġiered mid golde;   ġimmas hæfdon
bewriġen weorþlīċe   Wealdendes trēo.
Hwæðre iċ þurh þæt gold   onġietan meahte
earmra ǣr-ġewinn,   þæt hit ǣrest ongann
20    swǣtan on þā swīðran healfe.   Eall iċ wæs mid sorgum ġedrēfed;
forht iċ wæs for þǣre fæġeran ġesihþe.   Ġeseah iċ
                            þæt fūse bēacen

Emendations: 2 hwæt] MS hæt.   9 eaxl] MS eaxle.  engel-dryhta fela]
MS engel dryhtnes ealle.  15 geweorðod] MS geweorðode.  17 bewrigen]
MS bewrigene.  Wealdendes] MS wealdes.  20 sorgum] MS surgum.

Variant spellings in the MS: 1 wylle.  3 syðþan. wunedon.
4 syllicre. treow.  8 swylce.  10 fracodes.  11 halige.  12 men.
13 Syllic. fah.  14 forwunded. wommum. treow.  16 gegyred.  17 treow.
18 ongytan.  19 gewin. ongan.  21 fægran. gesyhðe.

wendan wǣdum and blēoum:   hwīlum hit wæs mid wǣtan
bestīemed,

beswiled mid swātes gange,   hwīlum mid since ġeġierwed.

   Hwæðre iċ þǣr licġende   lange hwīle

25     behēold hrēow-ċeariġ   Hǣlendes trēo,

     oþ-þæt iċ ġehīerde   þæt hit hlēoðrode;

     ongann þā word sprecan   wudu sēlesta:

       "Þæt wæs ġēara ġeō   —iċ þæt ġīeta ġeman—

     þæt iċ wæs ahēawen   holtes on ende,

30 astyred of stefne mīnum.   Ġenāmon mē þǣr strange fēondas,

   ġeworhton him þǣr to wǣfer-sīene,   hēton mē hira
weargas hebban.

Bǣron mē þǣr beornas on eaxlum,   oþ-þæt hīe mē on
beorg asetton;

ġefæstnodon mē þǣr fēondas ġenōge.   Ġeseah iċ þā
Frēan mann-cynnes

efstan elne miċle   þæt hē mē wolde on ġestīgan.

35     Þǣr iċ þā ne dorste   ofer Dryhtnes word

     būgan oþþe berstan   þā iċ bifian ġeseah

     eorðan scēatas.   Ealle iċ meahte

     fēondas ġefiellan,   hwæðre iċ fæste stōd.

   Onġierede hine þā ġeong Hæleþ   —þæt wæs God ælmihtiġ—,

40 strang and stīþ-mōd;   ġestāg hē on ġealgan hēanne,

   mōdiġ on maniġra ġesihþe,   þā hē wolde mann-cynn līesan.

Bifode iċ þā mē se Beorn ymbclypte;   ne dorste iċ
hwæðre būgan to eorðan,

feallan to foldan scēatum.   Ac iċ scolde fæste standan.

   Rōd wæs iċ arǣred;   ahōf iċ rīċne Cyning,

45     heofona Hlāford;   hieldan mē ne dorste.

---

Variant spellings: 22 bleom. bestemed. 23 beswyled. gegyrwed. 25 treow.
26 gehyrde. 27 ongan. 28 geo] iu. gyta. 30 genaman. 31 -syne.
heora. wergas. 33 man-. 34 mycle. 37 mihte. 38 gefyllan.
39 Ongyrede. 40 Gestah. 41 gesyhðe. mancyn. lysan. 43 sceolde. 45 hyldan.

Þurhdrifon hīe mē mid deorċum næġlum:   on mē sindon
                                    þā dolg ġesīene,
opene inwitt-hlemmas;   ne dorste iċ hira ǣnigum scieþþan.
Bismerodon hīe unc bū-tū ætgædere.   Eall iċ wæs mid
                                    blōde bestīemed,
begoten of þæs Guman sīdan   siþþan hē hæfde his
                                    gāst onsended.
50      Fela iċ on þam beorge   ġebiden hæbbe
        wrāðra wyrda.   Ġeseah iċ weoroda God
        þearle þenian.   Þīestru hæfdon
        bewriġen mid wolcnum   Wealdendes hrǣw,
        scīrne scīman;   scadu forþ ēode
55      wann under wolcnum.   Wēop eall ġesceaft,
        cwīðdon Cyninges fiell;   Crīst wæs on rōde.
        "Hwæðre þǣr fūse   feorran cōmon
        to þam Æðelinge.   Iċ þæt eall behēold.
Sāre iċ wæs mid sorgum ġedrēfed,   hnāg iċ hwæðre þam
                                    secgum to handa,
60      ēaþ-mōd, elne miċle.   Ġenāmon hīe þǣr ælmihtiġne God,
        ahōfon hine of þam hefigan wīte.   Forlēton mē þā hilde-rincas
        standan stēame bedrifenne;   eall iċ wæs mid strǣlum forwundod.
        Aleġdon hīe þǣr lim-wēriġne;   ġestōdon him æt his
                                    līċes hēafdum;
        behēoldon hīe þǣr heofones Dryhten,   and hē hine þǣr
                                    hwīle reste,
65      mēðe æfter þam miċlan ġewinne.   Ongunnon him þā
                                    mold-ærn wyrċan
        beornas on banan ġesihþe,   curfon hīe þæt of beorhtan stāne;

---

Emendations: **47** ænigum] MS nænigum.   **59** sorgum] *not in* MS.

Variant spellings: **46** -drifan. hi. deorcan. syndon.   **47** inwid-.
sceððan.   **48** Bysmeredon. bestemed.   **50** Feala.   **51** weruda.
**52** Þystro.   **54** sceadu.   **55** eal.   **56** fyll.   **57** Hwæðere. cwoman.
**60** mycle.   **61** hefian.   **63** Aledon.   **64** heofenes.   **65** moldærn
*altered to* moldern.   **66** gesyhðe.

ġesetton hīe þǣr-on sigora Wealdend.   Ongunnon him þā
                                  sorg-lēoþ galan,
earme on þā ǣfen-tīde,   þā hīe woldon eft sīðian,
mēðe fram þam mǣran þēodne;   reste hē þǣr mǣte weorode.
70        Hwæðre wē þǣr grēotende   gōde hwīle
         stōdon on staðole.   Stefn upp ġewāt
         hilde-rinca.   Hrǣw cōlode,
         fǣġer feorh-bold.   Þā ūs man fiellan ongann
         ealle to eorðan.   Þæt wæs eġeslīċ wyrd!
75   Bedealf ūs man on dēopan sēaðe.   Hwæðre mē þǣr
                                  Dryhtnes þeġnas,
      frēondas ġefrugnon   *  *  *
        ġieredon mē   golde and seolfre.
      "Nū þū meaht ġehīeran,   hæleþ mīn se lēofa,
      þæt iċ bealu-wara weorc   ġebiden hæbbe,
80        sārra sorga.   Is nū sǣl cumen
        þæt mē weorðiaþ   wīde and sīde
        menn ofer moldan   and eall þēos mǣre ġesceaft,
        ġebiddaþ him to þissum bēacne.   On mē Bearn Godes
        þrōwode hwīle;   for-þon iċ þrymm-fæst nū
85        hlīfie under heofonum,   and iċ hǣlan mæġ
        ǣghwelċne ānra,   þāra-þe him biþ   eġesa to mē.
        Ġeō iċ wæs ġeworden   wīta heardost,
        lēodum lāðost,   ǣr-þon iċ him līfes weġ
        rihtne ġerȳmde,   reord-berendum.
90        Hwæt, mē þā ġeweorðode   wuldres Ealdor
        ofer holt-wudu,   heofon-rīċes Weard,
        swelċe swā hē his mōdor ēac,   Mārian selfe,
        ælmihtiġ God,   for ealle menn

---

Emendations: **70** greotende] MS reotende.   **71** stefn] MS syððan.
**91** holt-] MS holm-.

Variant spellings: **67** sorh-.   **70** Hwæðere.   **71** up.   **73** feorg-. fyllan.
ongan.   **76** gefrunon.   **77** gyredon.   **78** miht. gehyran.   **83** þyssum.
**84** forþan. þrym-.   **85** hlifige. heofenum.   **86** æghwylcne.   **87** Geo] Iu.
**88** ærþan.   **92** swylce. sylfe.

ġeweorðode   ofer eall wīfa cynn.

95    "Nū iċ þē hāte,   hæleþ mīn se lēofa,
þæt þū þās ġesihþe   secge mannum;
onwrēoh wordum   þæt hit is wuldres bēam,
sē-þe ælmihtiġ God   on þrōwode
for mann-cynnes   manigum synnum
100   and Ādames   eald-ġewyrhtum.
Dēaþ hē þǣr bieriġde;   hwæðre eft Dryhten arās
mid his miċlan meahte   mannum to helpe.
Hē þā on heofonas astāg.   Hider eft fundaþ
on þisne middan-ġeard   mann-cynn sēċan
105   on dōm-dæġe   Dryhten selfa,
ælmihtiġ God   and his englas mid,
þæt hē þonne wile dēman,   sē āg dōmes ġeweald,
ānra ġehwelċum,   swā hē him ǣror hēr
on þissum lǣnan   līfe ġe-earnaþ.
110   Ne mæġ þǣr ǣniġ   unforht wesan
for þam worde   þe se Wealdend cwiþ:
friġneþ hē for þǣre meniġe   hwǣr se mann sīe,
sē-þe for Dryhtnes naman   dēaðes wolde
biteres onbierġan,   swā hē ǣr on þam bēame dyde.
115   Ac hīe þonne forhtiaþ,   and fēa þenċaþ
hwæt hīe to Crīste   cweðan onġinnen.
Ne þearf þǣr þonne ǣniġ   anforht wesan
þē him ǣr on brēostum bereþ   bēacna sēlest.
Ac þurh þā rōde sceal   rīċe ġesēċan
120   of eorþ-weġe   ǣghwelċ sāwol,
sēo-þe mid Wealdende   wunian þenċeþ."

Emendation: 117 anforht] MS unforht *(either a misleading spelling or an error)*.

Variant spellings: **96** gesyhðe.   **99** man-.   manegum.   **100** Adomes.
**101** byrigde.   hwæðere.   **102** mihte.   **103** heofenas.   **104** þysne.   man-.
**105** sylfa.   **107** ah.   **108** gehwylcum.   ærur.   **109** þyssum.   lænum.
**111** cwyð.   **112** frineð.   mænige.   man.   **114** onbyrigan.   **118** on] in.
**120** æghwylc.   sawl.

Ġebæd iċ mē þā to þam bēame    blīðe mōde,
elne miċle,    þǣr iċ āna wæs
mǣte weorode;    wæs mōd-sefa
125    afȳsed on forþ-weġ;    fela ealra ġebād
langung-hwīla.    Is mē nū līfes hyht
þæt iċ þone siġe-bēam    sēċan mōte,
āna oftor    þonne ealle menn
wēl weorðian;    mē is willa to þām
130    miċel on mōde,    and mīn mund-byrd is
ġeriht to þǣre rōde.    Nāg iċ rīċra fela
frēonda on foldan.    Ac hīe forþ heonan
ġewiton of weorolde drēamum,    sōhton him wuldres Cyning;
libbaþ nū on heofonum    mid Hēah-Fædere,
135    wuniaþ on wuldre;    and iċ wēne mē
daga ġehwelċe    hwonne mē Dryhtnes rōd,
þē iċ hēr on eorðan    ǣr scēawode,
on þissum lǣnan    līfe ġefeċċe,
and mē þonne ġebringe    þǣr is bliss miċel,
140    drēam on heofonum,    þǣr is Dryhtnes folc
ġeseted to symble,    þǣr is singāl bliss;
and mē þonne asette    þǣr iċ siþþan mōt
wunian on wuldre,    wēl mid þam hālgum
drēames brūcan.    Sīe mē Dryhten frēond,
145    sē-þe hēr on eorðan    ǣr þrōwode
on þam ġealg-trēowe    for guman synnum:
hē ūs onlīesde,    and ūs līf forġeaf,
heofonlīċne hām.    Hyht wæs ġenīewod

---

Emendations: **125** -weg] MS -wege.    **142** me] MS he.

Variant spellings: **122** þan.    **123** mycle.    **124** werede.    **128** men.
**129** well.    **130** mycel.    **131** Nah. feala.    **132** heonon.    **133** worulde.
**134** lifiaþ. heofenum.    **136** gehwylce. hwænne.    **138** þysson. gefetige.
**139** blis. mycel.    **141** symle. blis.    **142** syþþan.    **143** well.
**144** Si.    **147** onlysde.    **148** Hiht. geniwad.

mid blǣdum and mid blisse,   þām-þe þǣr bryne þolodon.
150  Se Sunu wæs sigor-fæst   on þam sīþ-fǣte,
mihtïġ and spēdiġ,   þā hē mid meniġe cōm,
gāsta weorode,   on Godes rīċe,
Anwealda ælmihtiġ,   englum to blisse,
and eallum þam hālgum   þām-þe on heofonum ǣr
155  wunodon on wuldre,   þā hira Wealdend cōm,
ælmihtiġ God,   þǣr his ēðel wæs.

Variant spellings: 149 bledum. þolodan.   150 -fate.   151 manigeo.
155 wunedon. heora. cwom.

# The Battle of Maldon

(*Bodleian Library, MS Rawlinson B.* 203, pp. 7–12,
a transcript made about 1724 by John Elphinston
from the incomplete eleventh-century manuscript,
Cotton Otho A. xii, burned in 1731.)

\* \* \* brocen wurde.
Hēt þā hyssa hwone    hors forlǣtan,
feorr afȳsan    and forþ gangan,
hycgan to handum    and to hyġe gōdum.
5  Þā þæt Offan mǣġ    ǣrest onfunde,
þæt se eorl nolde    iergþe ġeþolian,
hē lēt him þā of handum    lēofne flēogan
hafoc wiþ þæs holtes    and to þǣre hilde stōp;
be þām man meahte oncnāwan    þæt se cniht nolde
10  wācian æt þam wīġe    þā hē to wǣpnum fēng.
Ēac him wolde Ēadrīċ    his ealdre ġelǣstan,
frēan to ġefeohte,    ongann þā forþ beran
gār to gūðe.    Hē hæfde gōd ġeþanc
þā hwīle þe hē mid handum    healdan meahte
15  bord and brād sweord;    bēot hē ġelǣste
þā hē ætforan his frēan    feohtan scolde.

    Þā þǣr Byrhtnōþ ongann    beornas trymian,
rād and rǣdde,    rincum tǣhte
hū hīe scoldon standan    and þone stede healdan,

Emendations and restorations (E = Elphinston's transcript):
4b to] E t.  5 Þa] E þ.  10 wige] E w . . . ge.

Variant spellings: 2 hwæne.  3 feor.  4 hicgan. hige  6 yrhðo.
7 handon.  9 mihte.  10 w(ig)ge.  12 ongan.  14 mihte.  15 swurd.
16 sceolde.  17 ongan.  19 sceoldon.

20 and bæd þæt hira randas   rihte héolden
   fæste mid folmum   and ne forhtoden nā.
   Þā hē hæfde þæt folc   fægere ġetrymed,
   hē līehte þā mid lēodum   þǣr him lēofost wæs,
   þǣr hē his heorþ-weorod   holdost wisse.

25 Þā stōd on stæðe,   stīþlīċe clipode
   wīċinga ār,   wordum mǣlde,
   sē on bēot abēad   brim-līðendra
   ǣrende to þam eorle   þǣr hē on ōfre stōd:
   "Mē sendon to þē   sǣ-menn snelle,
30 hēton þē secgan   þæt þū mōst sendan hræðe
   bēagas wiþ ġebeorge;   and ċow betere is
   þæt ġē þisne gār-rǣs   mid gafole forġielden
   þonne wē swā hearde   hilde dǣlen.
   Ne þurfe wē ūs spillan   ġif ġē spēdaþ to þām;
35 wē willaþ wiþ þam golde   griþ fæstnian.
   Ġif þū þæt ġerǣdest,   þe hēr rīċost eart,
   þæt þū þīne lēode   līesan wille,
   sellan sǣ-mannum   on hira selfra dōm
   feoh wiþ frēode   and niman friþ æt ūs,
40 wē willaþ mid þam sceattum   ūs to scipe gangan,
   on flot fēran,   and ēow friðes healdan."
   Byrhtnōþ maðelode,   bord hafenode,
   wand wācne æsc,   wordum mǣlde
   ierre and anrǣd,   aġeaf him andsware:
45 "Ġehīerst þū, sǣ-lida,   hwæt þis folc sæġeþ?
   Hīe willaþ ēow to gafole   gāras sellan,

Emendations and restorations: 20 randas] E randan.  33 þonne] E þon.
hilde] E . .ulde.  36 þæt] E þat.

Variant spellings: 20 hyra. heoldon.  21 folman. forhtedon.  22 getrymmed.
23 lihte. leodon.  24 -werod. wiste.  25 clypode.  28 ærænde.  29 -men.
30 raðe.  32 forgyldon.  33 dælon.  36 Gyf.  37 leoda. lysan.  38 syllan.
hyra. sylfra.  40 scype.  44 yrre.  45 Gehyrst. segeð.  46 Hi. syllan.

ǣtrenne ord   and ealde sweord,
þā here-ġeatwe   þe ēow æt hilde ne dēag.
Brim-manna boda,   abēod eft onġēan,
50  sæġe þīnum lēodum   miċle lāðre spell,
þæt hēr stent unforcūþ   eorl mid his weorode,
þe wile ealgian   ēðel þisne,
Æðelrēdes eard   ealdres mīnes,
folc and foldan.   Feallan sculon
55  hǣðne æt hilde.   Tō hēanlīċ mē þynċeþ
þæt ġē mid ūrum sceattum   to scipe gangen
unbefohtne,   nū ġē þus feorr hider
on ūrne eard   inn becōmon.
Ne scule ġē swā sōfte   sinc ġegangan;
60  ūs sceal ord and ecg   ǣr ġesēman,
grimm gūþ-plega,   ǣr wē gafol sellen."
     Hēt þā bord beran,   beornas gangan
þæt hīe on þam ēa-stæðe   ealle stōden.
Ne meahte þǣr for wætere   weorod to þam ōðrum;
65  þǣr cōm flōwende   flōd æfter ebban,
lucon lagu-strēamas.   Tō lang hit him þūhte
hwonne hīe togædere   gāras bǣren.
Hīe þǣr Pantan strēam   mid prasse bestōdon,
East-Seaxna ord   and se æsc-here.
70  Ne meahte hira ǣniġ   ōðrum derian
būtan hwā þurh flānes flyht   fiell ġenāme.
     Se flōd ūt ġewāt.   Þā flotan stōdon ġearwe,
wīċinga fela,   wīġes ġeorne.
Hēt þā hæleða hlēo   healdan þā brycge

---

Emendations and restorations: **61** we] E þe

Variant spellings: **47** ættrynne. swurd.   **48** -geatu. deah.   **50** sege.
miccle.   **51** stynt. werode.   **52** gealgean. þysne.   **54** sceolon.
**55** hæþene. þinceð.   **56** scype. gangon.   **57** unbefohtene. feor   **58** in.
**59** sceole.   **61** grim. gofol. syllon.   **63** hi. -steðe. stodon.   **64** mihte. werod.
**67** hwænne. hi. beron.   **68** Hi.   **69** -seaxena.   **70** mihte. hyra.   **71** buton. fyl.
**72** gearowe.   **74** bricge.

75  wigan wīġ-heardne  —sē wæs hāten Wulfstān—
    cāfne mid his cynne;  þæt wæs Ċēolan sunu,
    þe þone forman mann  mid his francan ofscēat
    þe þǣr bealdlīcost  on þā bryċge stōp.
    Þǣr stōdon mid Wulfstāne  wigan unforhte,
80  Ælfhere and Maccus,  mōdġe twēġen;
    þā noldon æt þam forda  flēam ġewyrċan,
    ac hīe fæstlīċe  wiþ þā fīend weredon
    þā hwīle þe hīe wǣpna  wealdan mōston.

    Þā hīe þæt onġēaton  and ġeorne ġesāwon
85  þæt hīe þǣr bryċg-weardas  bitere fundon,
    ongunnon lytiġian þā  lāðe ġiestas,
    bǣdon þæt hīe upp-gang  āgan mōsten,
    ofer þone ford faran,  fēðan lǣdan.

    Þā se eorl ongann  for his ofermōde
90  alīefan landes tō fela  lāðre þēode.
    Ongann ċeallian þā  ofer ċeald wæter
    Byrhthelmes bearn  —beornas ġehlyston—:
    "Nū ēow is ġerȳmed;  gāþ recene to ūs,
    guman to gūðe.  God āna wāt
95  hwā̆ þǣre wæl-stōwe  wealdan mōte."

    Wōdon þā wæl-wulfas  —for wætere ne murnon—
    wīċinga weorod,  west ofer Pantan,
    ofer scīr wæter  scieldas wǣgon,
    lid-menn to lande  linda bǣron.
100 Þǣr onġēan gramum  ġearwe stōdon
    Byrhtnōþ mid beornum;  hē mid bordum hēt

    Emendations: **87** upp-gang] E upgangan.
    **97** west] E pest (?—*Dobbie thinks* west *was intended*).

    Variant spellings: **77** man. **78** baldlicost. briċge. **80** Ælfere.
    modige. **82** hi. fynd. **83** hi. **84** hi. **85** hi. briċg-.
    **86** lytegian. gystas. **87** hi. moston. **89** ongan. **90** alyfan.
    laþere. **91** ongan. cald. **92** Byrhtelmes. **93** ricene. **97** werod.
    **98** scyldas. wegon. **99** -men. linde. **100** gearowe.

wyrċan þone wīġ-hagan   and þæt weorod healdan
fæste wiþ fēondum.   Þā wæs feohte nēah,
tīr æt ġetohte.   Wæs sēo tīd cumen
105 þæt þǣr fǣġe menn   feallan scoldon.
Þǣr wearþ hrēam ahafen,   hræfnas wundon,
earn ǣses ġeorn.   Wæs on eorðan ċierm.
Hīe lēton þā of folmum   fēol-hearde speru,
grimme ġegrundne   gāras flēogan.
110 Bogan wǣron bisiġe,   bord ord onfēng.
Biter wæs se beadu-rǣs,   beornas fēollon
on ġehwæðere hand,   hyssas lāgon.
Wund wearþ Wulfmǣr,   wæl-reste ġeċēas,
Byrhtnōðes mǣġ;   hē mid billum wearþ,
115 his sweostor sunu,   swīðe forhēawen.
Þǣr wearþ wīċingum   wiðerlēan aġiefen.
Ġehīerde iċ þæt Ēadweard   ānne slōge
swīðe mid his sweorde,   swenġes ne wiernde,
þæt him æt fōtum fēoll   fǣġe cempa;
120 þæs him his þēoden   þanc ġesæġde,
þam būr-þeġne,   þā hē byre hæfde.
Swā stefnetton   stīþ-hycgende
hyssas æt hilde,   hogodon ġeorne
hwā þǣr mid orde   ǣrest meahte
125 on fǣġan menn   feorh ġewinnan,
wigan mid wǣpnum;   wæl fēoll on eorðan.
Stōdon stede-fæste;   stihte hīe Byrhtnōþ,
bæd þæt hyssa ġehwelċ   hogode to wīġe,

Emendations: **103** feohte] E fohte.   **109** grimme] *not in* E.
**113** wearþ] E weard.   **116** wearþ] E wærd.

Variant spellings: **102** wi-. werod.   **103** neh.   **105** men. sceoldon.
**106** hremmas.   **107** cyrm.   **108** Hi. folman.   **109** gegrundene.
**110** bysige.   **113** -ræste.   **115** swuster-.   **116** agyfen.   **117** gehyrde.
**118** swurde. wyrnde.   **120** gesæde.   **121** -þene.   **122** stemnetton.
-hicgende.   **123** hysas.   **124** ærost. mihte.   **125** fægean. men.   **126** feol.
**127** stæde-. hi.   **128** gehwylc.

þe on Denum wolde   dōm ġefeohtan.

130   Wōd þā wīġes heard,   wǣpen upp ahōf,
bord to ġebeorge,   and wiþ þæs beornes stōp.
Ēode swā anrǣd   eorl to þam ċeorle,
ǣġðer hira ōðrum   yfeles hogode.
Sende þā se sǣ-rinc   sūðerne gār,

135   þæt ġewundod wearþ   wiġena hlāford.
Hē sċēaf þā mid þam sċielde   þæt se sceaft tobærst
and þæt spere sprenġde   þæt hit sprang onġēan.
Ġegremed wearþ se gūþ-rinc;   hē mid gāre stang
wlancne wīċing   þe him þā wunde forġeaf.

140   Frōd wæs se fierd-rinc;   hē lēt his francan wadan
þurh þæs hysses heals,   hand wīsode
þæt hē on þam fǣr-scaðan   feorh ġerǣhte.

Þā hē ōðerne   ofostlīċe sċēat
þæt sēo byrne tobærst;   hē wæs on brēostum wund

145   þurh þā hring-locan,   him æt heortan stōd
ǣterne ord.   Se eorl wæs þȳ blīðra,
hlōg þā mōdiġ mann,   sæġde Metode þanc
þæs dæġ-weorces   þe him Dryhten forġeaf.

Forlēt þā drenga sum   daroþ of handa

150   flēogan of folman,   þæt sē tō forþ ġewāt
þurh þone æðelan   Æðelrēdes þeġn.
Him be healfe stōd   hyse unweaxen,
cniht on ġecampe,   sē full cāflīċe
bræġd of þam beorne   blōdiġne gār,

155   Wulfstānes bearn,   Wulfmǣr se ġeonga
forlēt forheardne   faran eft onġēan;
ord inn ġewōd   þæt sē on eorðan læġ
þe his þēoden ǣr   þearle ġerǣhte.

---

Variant spellings: **129** Denon.   **130** up.   **133** hyra.   **136** scylde.
**138** Gegremod.   **140** fyrd-.   **141** hals.   **142** -sceaðan.   **143** ofstlice.
**146** ætterne. þe.   **147** hloh. modi. man. sæde.   **148** Drihten.
**151** þegen.   **154** bræd.   **157** in.

Ēode þā ġesierwed  secg to þam eorle;
160 hē wolde þæs beornes  bēagas ġefecċan,
rēaf and hringas  and ġereġnod sweord.
Þā Byrhtnōþ bræġd  bill of scēaðe,
brād and brūn-ecg,  and on þā byrnan slōg.
Tō hræðe hine ġelette  lid-manna sum
165 þā hē þæs eorles  earm amierde.
Fēoll þā to foldan  fealu-hilte sweord,
ne meahte hē ġehealdan  heardne mēċe,
wǣpnes wealdan.  Þā-ġīet þæt word ġecwæþ
hār hilde-rinc,  hyssas bielde,
170 bæd gangan forþ  gōde ġefēran;
ne meahte þā on fōtum lenġ  fæste ġestandan.
Hē to heofonum wlāt:
"Iċ ġeþancie þē,  þēoda Wealdend,
ealra þāra wynna  þe iċ on weorolde ġebād.
175 Nū iċ āg, milde Metod,  mǣste þearfe
þæt þū mīnum gāste  gōdes ġe-unne,
þæt mīn sāwol to þē  sīðian mōte
on þīn ġeweald,  Þēoden engla,
mid friðe ferian.  Iċ eom frymdiġ to þē
180 þæt hīe hell-scaðan  hīenan ne mōten."
Þā hine hēowon  hǣðne scealcas,
and bēġen þā beornas  þe him bī stōdon,
Ælfnōþ and Wulfmǣr  bēġen lāgon,
þā on-efen hira frēan  feorh ġesealdon.

Emendations: **171** gestandan] E ge stundan.  **173** Ic geþancie] E ge
þance (*but there is probably a considerable loss here*).

Variant spellings: **159** gesyrwed.  **160** gefecgan.  **161** gerenod.  swurd.
**162** brǣd.  sceðe.  **163** -eccg.  sloh.  **164** raþe.  **165** amyrde.
**166** fealo-.  swurd.  **167** mihte.  **168** -gyt.  **169** bylde.  **171** mihte.
**172** heofenum.  **173** Waldend.  **174** þæra.  worulde.  **175** ah.
**177** sawul.  **179** frymdi.  **180** hi.  helsceaðan.  hynan.  moton.  **181** hæðene.
**182** big.  **183** Wulmær.  **184** onemn.  hyra.

85    Hīe bugon þā fram beadwe  þe þǣr bēon noldon.
    Þǣr wearþ Oddan bearn  ǣrest on flēame,
    Godrīc fram gūðe,  and þone gōdan forlēt
    þe him maniġne oft  mearh ġesealde;
    hē ġehlēop þone eoh  þe āhte his hlāford,
90    on þām ġerǣdum  þe hit riht ne wæs,
    and his brōðru mid him  bēġen ærndon,
    Godwine and Godwīġ,  gūðe ne ġīemdon,
    ac wendon fram þam wīġe  and þone wudu sōhton,
    flugon on þæt fæsten  and hira feore burgon,
95    and manna mā  þonne hit ǣniġ mǣþ wǣre,
    ġif hīe þā ġe-earnunga  ealle ġemunden
    þe hē him to duguðe  ġedōn hæfde.
    Swā him Offa on dæġ  ǣr asæġde
    on þam mæðel-stede  þā hē ġemōt hæfde,
00    þæt þǣr mōdiġlīċe  maniġe sprǣcon
    þe eft æt þearfe  þolian noldon.

    Þā wearþ afeallen  þæs folces ealdor,
    Æðelrēdes eorl;  ealle ġesāwon
    heorþ-ġenēatas  þæt hira hearra læġ.
05    Þā þǣr wendon forþ  wlance þeġnas,
    unearge menn  efston ġeorne;
    hīe woldon þā ealle  ōðer twēġa:
    līf forlǣtan  oþþe lēofne ġewrecan.
    Swā hīe bielde forþ  bearn Ælfrīċes,
10    wiga wintrum ġeong,  wordum mǣlde;
    Ælfwine þā cwæþ,  hē on ellen sprǣc:

Emendations: **186** wearþ] E wurdon.    **191** ærndon] E ærdon.
**192** Godwine] E godrinc.  **201** þearfe] E þære.  **208** forlǣtan] E for
lætun.

Variant spellings: **185** Hi. beaduwe.  **188** mænigne. mear.  **192** gymdon.
**194** hyra.  **196** gyf. hi. gemundon.  **198** asæde.  **199** meþel-.  **200** modelice.
manega.  **204** hyra. heorra.  **205** þegenas.  **206** men.
**207** hi.  **209** hi. bylde.

"Ġemunaþ þāra mǣla    þe wē oft æt medu sprǣcon,
þonne wē on benċe    bēot ahōfon,
hæleþ on healle,    ymbe heard ġewinn;
215    nū mæġ cunnian    hwā cēne sīę.
Iċ wille mīne æðelu    eallum ġecȳðan,
þæt iċ wæs on Mierċum    miċles cynnes;
wæs mīn ealda fæder    Ealhhelm hāten,
wīs ealdor-mann    weorold-ġesǣliġ.
220    Ne sculon mē on þǣre þēode    þeġnas ætwītan
þæt iċ of þisse fierde    fēran wille,
eard ġesēċan,    nū mīn ealdor liġeþ
forhēawen æt hilde.    Mē is þæt hearma mǣst;
hē wæs ǣġðer mīn mǣġ    and mīn hlāford."
225    Þā hē forþ ēode,    fǣhþe ġemunde,
þæt hē mid orde    ānne ġerǣhte
flotan on þam folce,    þæt sē on foldan læġ
forweġen mid his wǣpne.    Ongann þā winas manian,
frīend and ġefēran,    þæt hīe forþ ēoden.
230    Offa ġemǣlde,    æsc-holt ascōc:
"Hwæt þū, Ælfwine, hafast    ealle ġemanode
þeġnas to þearfe.    Nū ūre þēoden liġeþ,
eorl on eorðan,    ūs is eallum þearf
þæt ūre ǣġhwelċ    ōðerne bielde
235    wigan to wīġe,    þā hwīle þe hē wǣpen mæġe
habban and healdan,    heardne mēċe,
gār and gōd sweord.    Ūs Godrīċ hafaþ,
earg Oddan bearn,    ealle beswicene.
Wēnde þæs formaniġ mann,    þā hē on mēare rād,
240    on wlancan þam wicge,    þæt wǣre hit ūre hlāford.

Emendations: 212 Ġemunaþ þara] E ge munu þa.    224 ægðer] E ægder.
Variant spellings: 212 meodo. 215 sy. 216 wylle. æþelo. 217 Myrcon.
miccles. 218 Ealhelm. 219 -mann. woruld-. 220 sceolon. þegenas.
221 fyrde. 228 Ongan. 229 frynd. hi. eodon. 230 asceoc. 232 þegenas.
lið. 234 æghwylc. bylde. 237 swurd. hæfð. 238 earh.
239 formoni. man.

For-þon wearþ hēr on felda    folc totwǣmed,
scield-burg tobrocen.    Abrēoðe his anġinn,
þæt hē hēr swā maniġne    mann aflīemde!"
    Lēofsunu ġemǣlde    and his linde ahōf,
245  bord to ġebeorge;    hē þam beorne oncwæþ:
" Iċ þæt ġehāte,    þæt iċ heonan nylle
flēon fōtes trem,    ac wille furðor gān,
wrecan on ġewinne    mīnne wine-dryhten.
Ne þurfon mē ymbe Stūrmere    stede-fæste hæleþ
250  wordum ætwītan,    nū mīn wine ġecrang,
þæt iċ hlāford-lēas    hām sīðie,
wende fram wīġe;    ac mē sceal wǣpen niman,
ord and īren."    Hē full ierre wōd,
feaht fæstlīċe,    flēam hē forhogode.
255      Dunnere þā cwæþ,    daroþ acweahte,
unorne ċeorl,    ofer eall clipode,
bæd þæt beorna ġehwelċ    Byrhtnōþ wrǣce:
"Ne mæġ nā wandian    sē-þe wrecan þenċeþ
frēan on folce,    nē for feore murnan."
260      Þā hīe forþ ēodon,    feores hīe ne rōhton;
ongunnon þā hīred-menn    heardlīċe feohtan,
grame gār-berend,    and God bǣdon
þæt hīe mōsten ġewrecan    hira wine-dryhten
and on hira fēondum    fiell ġewyrċan.
265      Him se ġīsel ongann    ġeornlīċe fylstan;
hē wæs on Norþ-Hymbrum    heardes cynnes,
Ecglāfes bearn;    him wæs Æscferhþ nama.
Hē ne wandode nā    æt þam wīġ-plegan,
ac hē fȳsde forþ    flān ġeneahhe;

Variant spellings: 241 -þan.    242 scyldburh.    angin.    243 man.    aflymde.
246 heonon.    nelle.    247 trym.    248 -drihten.    249 embe.    hælæð.
250 gecranc.    253 ful.    yrre.    255 acwehte.    256 clypode.    257 gehwylc.
260 hi.    hi.    261 -men.    263 hi.    moston.    hyra.    -drihten.    264 hyra.    fyl.
265 gysel.    ongan.    266 Norðhymbron.    267 Æscferð.    269 genehe.

270 hwīlum hē on bord scēat, hwīlum beorn tǣsde,
ǣfre ymbe stunde hē sealde sume wunde
þā hwīle þe hē wǣpna wealdan mōste.

Þā-ġīet on orde stōd Ēadweard se langa,
ġearu and ġeornfull, ġielp-wordum sprǣc
275 þæt hē nolde flēogan fōt-mǣl landes,
ofer bæc būgan, þā his betera læġ.
Hē brǣc þone bord-weall and wiþ þā beornas feaht
oþ-þæt hē his sinc-ġiefan on þam sǣ-mannum
weorþlīċe wrǣc ǣr hē on wǣle lāge.
280 Swā dyde Æðelrīċ, æðele ġefēra,
fūs and forþ-ġeorn feaht eornoste;
Siġebyrhtes brōðor and swīðe maniġ ōðer
clufon cellod bord, cēne hīe weredon.

\* \* \* \*

Bǣrst bordes læriġ, and sēo byrne sang
285 gryre-lēoða sum. Þā æt gūðe slōg
Offa þone sǣ-lidan þæt hē on eorðan fēoll,
and þǣr Gaddes mǣġ grund ġesōhte.
Hrǣðe wearð æt hilde Offa forhēawen;
hē hæfde þēah ġeforðod þæt hē his frēan ġehēt,
290 swā hē bēotode ǣr wiþ his bēag-ġiefan,
þæt hīe scolden bēġen on burg rīdan
hāle to hāme oþþe on here cringan,
on wæl-stōwe wundum sweltan;
hē læġ þeġnlīċe þēodne ġehende.
295 Þā wearþ borda ġebrǣc. Brim-menn wōdon,
gūðe ġegremede; gār oft þurhwōd
fǣġes feorh-hūs. Forþ þā ēode Wīstān,

Emendations: **283** *No sign of loss after this line in E, but the context indicates that some lines describing a viking's attack on Offa are missing.* **292** cringan] E crintgan (*for* crincgan). **297** Forþ þa] E forða.

Variant spellings: **270** hwilon. hwilon. **271** embe. **273** -gyt. **274** gearo. geornful. gylp-. **276** leg. **278** -gyfan. **279** wurðlice. wrec. læge. **282** Sibyrhtes. mænig. **283** hi. **285** sloh. **288** raðe. **290** beahgifan. **291** hi. sceoldon. burh. **294** ðegenlice. **295** -men. **296** gegremode.

Þurstānes sunu,  wiþ þās secgas feaht;
hē wæs on ġeþrange  hira þrēora bana
300  ǣr him Wīġhelmes bearn  on þam wæle lāge.
Þǣr wæs stīþ ġemōt;  stōdon fæste
wigan on ġewinne,  wiġend crungon
wundum wērġe.  Wæl fēoll on eorðan.

Ōswold and Ēadwold  ealle hwīle,
305  bēġen þā ġebrōðru,  beornas trymedon,
hira wine-māgas  wordum bǣdon
þæt hīe þǣr æt þearfe  þolian scolden,
unwāclīċe  wǣpna nēotan.

Byrhtwold maðelode,  bord hafenode—
310  sē wæs eald ġenēat—  æsc acweahte;
hē full bealdlīċe  beornas lǣrde:
"Hyġe sceal þȳ heardra,  heorte þȳ cēnre,
mōd sceal þȳ māre  þȳ ūre mæġen lȳtlaþ.
Hēr liġeþ ūre ealdor  eall forhēawen,
315  gōd on grēote.  Ā mæġ gnornian
sē-þē nū fram þȳs wiġ-plegan  wendan þenċeþ.
Iċ eom frōd feores;  fram iċ ne wille,
ac iċ mē be healfe  mīnum hlāforde,
be swā lēofum menn  licgan þenċe."
320  Swā hīe Æðelgāres bearn  ealle bielde,
Godrīċ to gūðe.  Oft hē gār forlēt
wæl-spere windan  on þā wīċingas;
swā hē on þam folce  fyrmest ēode,
hēow and hīende,  oþ-þæt hē on hilde ġecrang.
325  Næs þæt nā sē Godrīċ  þe þā gūðe forbēag  *  *  *

Emendations: **299** geþrange] E geþrang.  **300** Wighelmes]
E wigelines (*defended as a name by Dobbie, but very
likely a misreading of* wigelmes).  **324** oþ-] E od.  **325** guðe] E gude.

Variant spellings: **298** suna.  **299** hyra.  **300** lǣge.  **302** cruncon.
**303** werige. feol.  **306** hyra. wordon.  **307** hi. sceoldon.  **310** acwehte.
**311** ful. baldlice.  **312** Hige. þe. þe.  **313** þe. þe.  **314** lið.
**316** þis.  **319** leofan. men.  **320** hi. bylde.  **324** hynde. gecranc.
**325** forbeah.

# The Wanderer*

(*Exeter Book*, ff. 76ᵛ–78ʳ)

    Oft him ān-haga   āre ġebīdeþ,
    Metodes mildse,  þēah-þe hē mōd-ċeariġ
    ġeond lagu-lāde  lange scolde
    hrēran mid handum  hrīm-ċealde sǣ,
5   wadan wrǣc-lāstas.  Wyrd biþ full arǣd.
    —Swā cwæþ eard-stapa  earfoða ġemyndiġ,
    wrāðra wæl-sleahta,  wine-māga hryre.—
    "Oft iċ scolde āna  ūhtna ġehwelċe
    mīne ċeare cwīðan;  nis nū cwicra nān
10  þe iċ him mōd-sefan  mīnne durre
    sweotule asecgan.  Iċ to sōðe wāt
    þæt biþ on eorle  indryhten þēaw
    þæt hē his ferhþ-locan  fæste binde,
    healde his hord-cofan,  hycge swā hē wille.
15  Ne mæġ wēriġ-mōd  wyrde wiþstandan
    nē se hrēo hyġe  helpe ġefremman.
    For-þon dōm-ġeorne  drēoriġne oft
    on hira brēost-cofan  bindaþ fæste.
    "Swā iċ mōd-sefan  mīnne scolde,
20  oft earm-ċeariġ,  ēðle bedǣled,
    frēo-māgum feorr,  feterum sǣlan,

Emendations: 14 healde] MS healdne.

Variant spellings in the MS: 2 metudes. miltse.  3 longe. sceolde.
4 hondum.  5 ful.  6 earfeþa.  7 -mæga.  8 sceolde. gehwylce.  12 in.
13 ferð-.  15 -stondan.  18 in. hyra.  19 sceolde.  20 bidæled.
21 -mægum. feor.

* The quotation marks at line 57 (explained below, p. 79) should be dis-
regarded for the reading as a monologue recommended in the Supplement,
p. 221. Quotation marks surrounding lines 1–5 in the first edition have been
removed in accordance with the note in the Supplement, p. 222.

siþþan ġēara ġeō   gold-wine mīnne
hrūsan heolstre bewrāh,   and iċ hēan þanan
wōd winter-ċeariġ   ofer waðuma ġebind,
25   sōhte sele-drēoriġ   sinces bryttan
hwǣr iċ feorr oþþe nēah   findan meahte
þone-þe on medu-healle   mīne wisse
oþþe meċ frēond-lēasne   frēfran wolde,
wēman mid wynnum.—   Wāt sē-þe cunnaþ
30   hū slīðen biþ   sorg to ġefēran
þam-þe him lȳt hafaþ   lēofra ġeholena.
Waraþ hine wrǣc-lāst,   nealles wunden gold,
ferhþ-loca frēoriġ,   nealles foldan blǣd.
Ġeman hē sele-secgas   and sinc-þeġe,
35   hū hine on ġeoguðe   his gold-wine
wenede to wiste.   Wynn eal ġedrēas.

"For-þon wāt sē-þe sceal   his wine-dryhtnes
lēofes lār-cwidum   lange forþolian,
þonne sorg and slǣp   samod ætgædere
40   earmne ān-hagan   oft ġebindaþ,
þynċeþ him on mōde   þæt hē his mann-dryhten
clyppe and cysse   and on cnēo lecge
handa and hēafod,   swā hē hwīlum ǣr
on ġēar-dagum   ġïef-stōles brēac.
45   Þonne onwæcneþ eft   wine-lēas guma,
ġesiehþ him beforan   fealwe wǣgas,
baðian brim-fuglas,   brǣdan feðra,
hrēosan hrīm and snāw   hæġle ġemenġed.

"Þonne bēoþ þȳ hefiġran   heortan benna,
50   sāre æfter swǣsne.   Sorg biþ ġenīewod

Emendations: 22 minne] MS mine.   24 waðuma] MS waþena.
28 -leasne] MS -lease.

Variant spellings: 22 geo] iu.   23 biwrah.   þonan.   26 feor.   27 in.
meodu-.   32 nales.   33 ferð-.   nalæs.   34 gemon.   36 wyn.   eal.
38 longe.   39 somod.   ætgædre.   40 anhogan.   41 þinceð.   mon-.
43 honda.   44 in.   -stolas.   46 gesihð.   biforan.   wegas.   48 hagle.
49 benne.   50 geniwad.

þonne māga ġemynd mōd ġeondhweorfeþ;
grēteþ glēo-stafum, ġeorne ġeondscēawaþ
secga ġeseldan. Swimmaþ eft on-weġ.
Flēotendra ferhþ nā þǣr fela bringeþ
55 cūðra cwide-ġiedda. Cearu biþ ġenīewod
þam-þe sendan sceal swīðe ġeneahhe
ofer waðuma ġebind wēriġne sefan."

"For-þon iċ ġeþenċan ne mæġ ġeond þās weorold
for-hwon mōd-sefa mīn ne ġesweorce
60 þonne iċ eorla līf eall ġeondþenċe,
hū hīe fǣrlīċe flett ofġēafon,
mōdġe magu-þeġnas. Swā þes middan-ġeard
ealra dōgra ġehwǣm drēoseþ and fealleþ;
for-þon ne mæġ weorðan wīs wer, ǣr hē āge
65 wintra dǣl on weorold-rīċe.— Wita sceal ġeþyldiġ,
nē sceal nā tō hāt-heort nē tō hræd-wyrde
nē tō wāc wīga nē tō wan-hyġdiġ
nē tō forht nē tō fæġen nē tō feoh-ġīfre
nē nǣfre ġielpes tō ġeorn ǣr hē ġeare cunne.
70 Beorn sceal ġebīdan, þonne hē bēot spriċeþ,
oþ-þæt collen-ferhþ cunne ġearwe
hwider hreðra ġehyġd hweorfan wille.

"Onġietan sceal glēaw hæle hū gǣstlīċ biþ
þonne eall þisse weorolde wela wēste standeþ,
75 swā nū missenlīċe ġeond þisne middan-ġeard
winde bewāwne weallas standaþ,
hrīme behrorene, hrīðġe þā eodoras.

Emendations: 53 eft] MS oft. 59 mod-sefa min ne] MS modsefan minne.
74 eall] MS ealle.

Variant spellings: 52 gliw-. 54 ferð. no. 55 cearo. geniwad.
57 waþema. 58 woruld. 59 forhwan. 60 eal. 61 hi. flet.
63 gehwam. 64 wearþan. 65 in. woruld. 66 no. 67 -hydig.
71 -ferð. 74 worulde. stondeð. 76 biwaune. stondaþ.
77 bihrorene. hryðge. ederas.

Wōriaþ þā wīn-salu,   wealdend licgaþ
drēame bedrorene,   duguþ eall ġecrang
80    wlanc be wealle.   Sume wīġ fornam,
     ferede on forþ-weġ;   sumne fugol oþbær
     ofer hēanne holm,   sumne se hāra wulf
     Dēaðe ġedælde,   sumne drēoriġ-hlēor
     on eorþ-scræfe   eorl ġehȳdde.
85    "Ieðde swā þisne eard-ġeard   ielda Scieppend,
     oþ-þæt burg-wara   breahtma lēase,
     eald enta ġeweorc   īdlu stōdon.
     Sē þonne þisne weall-steall   wīse ġeþōhte
     and þis deorce līf   dēope ġeondþenċeþ,
90    frōd on ferhþe,   feorr oft ġeman
     wæl-sleahta worn   and þās word acwiþ:
     'Hwǣr cōm mearh? Hwǣr cōm magu?   Hwǣr cōm
                                      māðum-ġiefa?
     Hwǣr cōm symbla ġesetu?   Hwǣr sindon sele-drēamas?
     Ēa-lā beorht bune!   Ēa-lā byrn-wiga!
95    Ēa-lā þēodnes þrymm!   Hū sēo þrāg ġewāt,
     ġenāp under niht-helm,   swā hēo nā wǣre!
     Standeþ nū on lāste   lēofre duguðe
     weall wundrum hēah,   wyrm-līcum fāg.
     Eorlas fornāmon   æsca þrȳðe,
100   wǣpen wæl-ġīfru,   wyrd sēo mǣre,
     and þās stān-hliðu   stormas cnyssaþ,
     hrīþ hrēosende   hrūsan bindeþ,
     wintres wōma,   þonne wann cymeþ,
     nīpeþ niht-scua,   norðan onsendeþ

Emendations: 81 -weg] MS -wege.   89 deorce] MS deornce.
102 hrusan] MS hruse.

Variant spellings: 78 -salo. waldend.   79 bidrorene. eal. gecrong.
80 wlonc. bi. fornom.   81 in. fugel.   84 in.   85 yþde. ælda. scyppend.
88 weal-steal.   90 in. ferðe. feor. gemon.   92 cwom. mearg. cwom.
mago. cwom. maþþum-gyfa.   93 cwom.   95 þrym.   96 no.   97 Stondeð.
98 weal. fah.   99 fornoman. asca.   101 hleoþu.   103 won.

105    hrēo hæġl-fære,  hæleðum on andan.
Eall is earfoþlīċ  eorðan rīċe,
onwendeþ wyrda ġesceaft  weorold under heofonum.
Hēr biþ feoh lǣne,  hēr biþ frēond lǣne,
hēr biþ mann lǣne,  hēr biþ mǣġ lǣne,
110    eall þis eorðan ġesteall  īdel weorðeþ.' "

Swā cwæþ snottor on mōde,  ġesæt him sundor æt rūne.
Til biþ sē-þe his trēowe ġehealdeþ,  nē sceal nǣfre his
torn tō recene
beorn of his brēostum acȳðan,  nefne hē ǣr þā bōte cunne
eorl mid elne ġefremman.  Wēl biþ þam-þe him āre sēċeþ,
115    frōfre to Fæder on heofonum,  þǣr ūs eall sēo
fæstnung standeþ.

Variant spellings: 105 -fare.  107 weoruld.  109 mon.  110 eal.
gesteal.  112 rycene.  113 nemþe.  115 eal.  stondeð.

# The Seafarer *

(*Exeter Book*, ff. 81ᵛ–83ʳ)

1ST SEAF.  "Mæġ iċ be mē selfum   sōþ-ġiedd wrecan,
  sīðas secgan,   hū iċ ġeswinċ-dagum
  earfoþ-hwīle   oft þrōwode,
  bitre brēost-ċeare   ġebiden hæbbe,
5  ġecunnod on ċēole   ċear-selda fela,
  atol ȳða ġewealc,   þǣr meċ oft beġeat
  nearu niht-wacu   æt nacan stefnan,

  þonne hē be clifum cnossaþ.   Ċealde ġeþrungen
  wǣron mīne fēt,   forste ġebunden
10  ċealdum clammum,   þǣr þā ceara seofodon
  hāt' ymb heortan;   hungor innan slāt
  mere-wērġes mōd.   Þæt se mann ne wāt
  þe him on foldan   fæġrost limpeþ,
  hū iċ earm-ċeariġ   īs-ċealdne sǣ
15 † winter wunode   wreċċan lāstum,
  wine-māgum bedroren,
  behangen hrīm-ġicelum;   hæġl scūrum flēag.
  Þǣr iċ ne ġehīerde   būtan hlimman sǣ,
  īs-ċealdne wǣġ.   Hwīlum ielfete sang

For the marginal directions and the punctuation see the notes. A dagger indicates a corrupt passage which the editor hesitates to emend. For suggestions see the notes.

Variant spellings in the MS: 1 sylfum.  -gied.  3 þrowade.
5 gecunnad.  in.  6 bigeat.  7 nearo.  -waco.  8 calde.  10 caldum.
clommum.  ceare.  seofedun.  12 mon.  15 wunade.  wræccan.
16 -mægum.  bidroren.  17 bihongen.  18 gehyrde.  19 -caldne.
ylfete.  song.

* All quotation marks and marginal directions (explained below, pp. 84 f.) should be disregarded for the reading as continuous monologue recommended in the Supplement, p. 224.

20      dyde iċ mē to gamene,   ganotes hlēoðor
and hwilpan swēġ   fore hleahtor wera,
mǣw singende   fore medu-drince.
Stormas þǣr stān-clifu bēoton,   þǣr him stearn oncwæþ,
īsiġ-feðra;   full oft þæt earn beġeall,
25  †  ūriġ-feðra;   nǣniġ hlēo-māga
fēa-sceaftiġ ferhþ   frēfran meahte.
    "For-þon him ġelīefeþ lȳt,   sē-þe āg līfes wynn
ġebiden on burgum,   bealu-sīða hwōn,
wlanc and wīn-gāl,   hū iċ wēriġ oft
30      on brim-lāde   bīdan scolde.
Nāp niht-scua,   norðan snīwde,
hrīm hrūsan band,   hæġl fēoll on eorðan,
corna ċealdost."

2ND SEAF.              "For-þon cnyssaþ nū
heortan ġeþōhtas   þæt iċ hēan strēamas,
35      sealt-ȳða ġelāc   self cunnie;
manaþ mōdes lust   mǣla ġehwelċe
ferhþ to fēran,   þæt iċ feorr heonan
el-þēodiġra   eard ġesēċe.
For-þon nis þæs mōd-wlanc   mann ofer eorðan,
40      nē his ġiefena þæs gōd,   nē on ġeoguðe to þæs hwæt,
nē on his dǣdum to þæs dēor,   nē him his dryhten
                            to þæs hold,
þæt hē ā his sǣ-fōre   sorge næbbe,
to hwon hine Dryhten   ġedōn wille.
Nē biþ him to hearpan hyġe   nē to hring-þeġe—

Emendation: 26 frefran] MS feran.

Variant spellings: 20 gomene. ganetes.  21 huilpan.  22 medo-.
23 beotan. 24 feðera. ful. bigeal. 25 -mæga. 26 ferð. 27 gelyfeð. ah.
wyn.  28 in. bealo-.  29 wlonc.  30 in. sceolde.  32 bond. feol.
33 caldast.  35 sylf. cunnige.  36 monað. gehwylce.  37 ferð.
feor.  39 -wlonc. mon.  40 gifena. in.  41 in.

45       nē to wīfe wynn   nē to weorolde hyht—
          nē ymbe āwiht elles   nefne ymb ȳða ġewealc;
          ac ā hafaþ langunge   sē-þe on lagu fundaþ.

          "Bearwas blōstmum nimaþ,  byriġ fæġriaþ,
          wangas wlitiġiaþ;  weorold ōnetteþ;
50       ealle þā ġemaniaþ  mōdes fūsne
          sefan to sīðe  þam-þe swā þenċeþ
          on flōd-wegas  feorr ġewītan.

          Swelċe ġēac manaþ  ġeōmran reorde;
          singeþ sumores weard,  sorge bēodeþ
55       bitre on brēost-hord.  Þæt se beorn ne wāt,
          sēft-ēadiġ secg,  hwæt þā sume drēogaþ
          þe þā wræc-lāstas  wīdost lecgaþ.

          "For-þon nū mīn hyġe hweorfeþ  ofer hreðer-locan,
          mīn mōd-sefa  mid mere-flōde,
60       ofer hwæles ēðel  hweorfeþ wīde,
          eorðan sċēatas,  cymeþ eft to mē
          ġīfre and grǣdiġ;  ġielleþ ān-floga,
          hweteþ on hwæl-weġ  hreðer unwearnum
          ofer holma ġelagu;—  for-þon mē hātran sind
65       Dryhtnes drēamas  þonne þis dēade līf
          lǣne on lande.

                "Iċ ġelīefe nā
          þæt him eorþ-welan  ēċe standaþ.
          Simble þrēora sum  þeġna ġehwelċum
          ǣr his tīd-dæġe  to twēon weorðeþ:
70       ādl oþþe ieldu  oþþe ecg-hete
          fǣgum framweardum  feorh oþ-þringeþ.

Emendations: 52 gewitan] MS gewitað.   56 seft-eadig] MS eft
eadig.   63 hwæl-weg] MS wælweg.   67 standaþ] MS stondeð.
68 þegna gehwelcum] MS þinga gehwylce.   69 tid-dæge] MS tide ge.

Variant spellings: 45 wyn. worulde.  46 owiht.  47 longunge.
49 wongas. wlitigað. woruld.  50 gemoniað.  52 feor.  53 swylce.
monað.  54 sumeres.  55 bitter (*perhaps an elided form of* bittere).  in.
66 londe. gelyfe. no.  68 simle.  70 yldo.  71 from-.

For-þon biþ eorla ġehwǣm    æfter-cweðendra,
lof libbendra    lāst-worda betst.

Þæt hē ġewyrċe,    ǣr hē on-weġ scyle,
75    fremum on foldan    wiþ fēonda nīþ,
dēorum dǣdum    dēofle toġēanes,
þæt hine ielda bearn    æfter herien,
and his lof siþþan    libbe mid englum
āwa to ealdre,    ēċan līfes blǣd,
80    drēam mid duguðum.

          "Dagas sind ġewitene,
ealle anmēdlan    eorðan rīċes;
nearon nū cyningas    nē cāseras
nē gold-ġiefan    swelċe ġeō wǣron,
þonne hīe mǣst mid him    mǣrða ġefremedon
85    and on dryhtlīċestum    dōme lifdon.

Ġedroren is þēos duguþ eall,    drēamas sind ġewitene;
wuniaþ þā wācran    and þās weorold healdaþ,
brūcaþ þurh bisgu.    Blǣd is ġehnǣged,
eorðan indryhtu    ealdaþ and sēaraþ,
90    swā nū manna ġehwelċ    ġeond middan-ġeard.

Ieldu him on fareþ,    ansīen blācaþ,
gamol-feax gnornaþ,    wāt his ġeō-wine,
æðelinga bearn    eorðan forġiefene.

Ne mæġ him þonne se flǣsc-hama,    þonne him
                              þæt feorh losaþ,
95    nē swēte forswelgan    nē sār ġefēlan
nē hand onhrēran    nē mid hyġe þenċan.

Þēah-þe græf wille    golde strēġan
brōðor his ġeborenum,    byrġan be dēadum

---

Emendations: 72 biþ] MS þæt.     75 fremum] MS fremman.     79 blæd]
MS blæð.     82 nearon] MS næron.

Variant spellings: 72 gehwam.     73 lifgendra.     77 ælda. hergen.
78 lifge.     80 dugeþum.     81 onmedlan.     83 swylce. iu.     84 hi.
86 eal.     87 woruld.     88 bisgo.     89 indryhto.     90 monna. gehwylc.
91 yldo. onsyn.     92 gomel-. iuwine.     94 -homa. feorg.     96 hond.

máðmum mislícum, þæt hine mid nyle;
100 ne mæġ þære sáwle þe biþ synna full
gold to ġéoce for Godes eġesan,
þonne hé hit ǽr hýdeþ þenden hé hér leofaþ."

EPIL. Miċel biþ sē Metodes eġesa, for þon híe séo
molde onċierreþ;
sē ġestaðolode stíðe grundas,
105 eorðan sċéatas and upp-rodor.
Dol biþ sē-þe him his Dryhten ne ondrǽdeþ: cymeþ
him se déaþ unþinġed.
Éadiġ biþ sē-þe éaþ-mód leofaþ;
cymeþ him séo ár of heofonum.
Metod him þæt mód ġestaðolaþ, for-þon hé on his
meahte ġelíefeþ.
Stíeran man sceal strangum móde, and þæt on
staðolum healdan,
110 and ġewiss wǽrum, wísum clǽne.
Scyle manna ġehwelċ mid ġemete healdan
lufan wiþ léofne and wiþ láðne bealu,
† þéah-þe hé ne wille w——— fulne
oþþe on bǽle forbærnedne
115 his ġeworhtne wine: wyrd biþ swíðre,
Metod mihtiġra, þonne ǽnġes mannes ġehyġd.
Wuton wé hycgan hwǽr wé hám ágen,
and þonne ġeþenċan hú wé þider cumen;
and wé þonne éac tilien þæt wé tó móten

Emendations: **99** nyle] MS wille. **109** man] MS mod. **112** lufan]
*not in* MS. **113** ne] MS hine. w——— (*some noun beginning with* w,
*in the genitive*)] MS fyres. **115** swiðre] MS swire. **117** hwær we]
MS. hwær se.

Variant spellings: **100** ful. **101** egsan. **103** meotudes. egsa. hi.
oncyrreð. **104** gestaþelade. **105** up-. **108** meotod. gestaþelað.
in. gelyfeð. **109** strongum. staþelum. **110** gewis. werum.
**111** monna. gehwylc. **112** bealo. **116** meotud. meahtigra. monnes.
**117** Uton.

120     on þā ēċan    ēadiġnesse
       þǣr is līf ġelang   on lufan Dryhtnes,
       hyht on heofonum.   Þæs sīe þam Halgan þanc,
       þæt hē ūsiċ ġeweorðode,   wuldres Ealdor,
       ēċe Dryhten,   on ealle tīd.

Amen.

Variant spellings: **120** in.    **121** gelong. in.    **122** in. sy. þonc.
**123** geweorþade.    **124** in.

# Deor

(*Exeter Book*, f. 100ʳ⁻ᵛ)

Wēland him be wearnum   wræces cunnode,
anhyġdiġ eorl,   earfoðu drēag,
hæfde him to ġesīðe   sorge and langoþ,
winter-ċealde wræce,   wēan oft onfand
5   siþþan hine Nīþhād on   nīeda leġde,
swancre sinu-benda,   on sēlran mann.
      Þæs oferēode;   þisses swā mæġ.

Beaduhilde ne wæs   hire brōðra dēaþ
on sefan swā sār   swā hire selfre þing,
10   þæt hēo ġearulīċe   onġieten hæfde
þæt hēo ēacen wæs;   æfre ne meahte
þrīste ġeþenċan   hū ymb þæt scolde.
      Þæs oferēode;   þisses swā mæġ.

Wē þæt Mæþhilde   māna ġefrugnon
15   wurdon grund-lēase,   Ġēates frīġe,
þæt hīe sēo sorg-lufu   slǣp' ealle benam.
      Þæs oferēode;   þisses swā mæġ.

Þēodrīċ āhte   þrītiġ wintra
Mǣringa burg;   þæt wæs manigum cūþ.

Emendations: 1 wearnum] MS wurman.   14 mana] MS monge.

Variant spellings in the MS: 1 Welund. cunnade.   2 anhydig.
earfoþa. 3 gesiþþe. longaþ.   4 onfond.   5 nede.   6 swoncre.
seonobende. syllan. monn. 8 Beado-. hyre. 9 hyre. sylfre.
10 gearo-. 12 sceolde. 16 hi. slæp. binom. 19 monegum.

20      Þæs oferēode;    þisses swā mæġ.


We ġe-āscodon    Eormanrīċes
wylfenne ġeþōht;    āhte wīde folc
Gotena rīċes;    þæt wæs grimm cyning.
Sæt secg maniġ    sorgum ġebunden,
25      wēan on wēnum,    wȳscte ġeneahhe
þæt þæs cyne-rīċes    ofercumen wǣre.
Þæs oferēode;    þisses swā mæġ.


Siteþ sorg-ċeariġ,    sǣlum bedǣled,
on sefan sweorceþ,    selfum þynċeþ
30      þæt sīe ende-lēas    earfoða dǣl,
mæġ þonne ġeþenċan    þæt ġeond þās weorold
wītiġ Dryhten    wendeþ ġeneahhe,
eorle maniġum    āre ġescēawaþ,
wislīċne blǣd,    sumum wēana dǣl.


35      Þæt iċ be mē selfum    secgan wille,
þæt iċ hwīle wæs    Hedeninga scop,
dryhtne dīere;    mē wæs Dēor nama.
Āhte iċ fela wintra    folgoþ tilne,
holdne hlāford,    oþ-þæt Heorrenda nū,
40      lēoþ-cræftiġ mann,    land-riht ġeþeah
þæt mē eorla hlēo    ǣr ġesealde.
Þæs oferēode;    þisses swā mæġ.


Emendations: **25** wenum] MS wenan *(leveled ending or error)*.
**30** earfoða] MS earfoda.

Variant spellings: **21** geascodan.    **23** grim.    **24** monig.    **28** bidæled.
**29** sylfum. þinceð.    **30** sy.    **31** woruld.    **33·** monegum.    **35** bi.
sylfum.    **36** heodeninga.    **37** dyre. noma.    **38** folgað.    **40** monn.
londryht. geþah.

# COMMENTARY

Old English poetry is descended from a preliterary stock once common to the Germanic tribes of the European continent. Its basic alliterative verse form appears with minor modifications in the oldest poetical remains of other Germanic peoples, High German and Saxon on the one hand, Scandinavian (chiefly Icelandic) on the other. Certain features of its diction, even verse formulas, besides many of its themes and stories, are similarly shared and betray a common inheritance supplemented now and then by early borrowing. In England itself the earliest poetry of the Anglo-Saxon settlers was necessarily composed orally, like that of their ancestors; and Bede's story of Cædmon indicates that even in his time it was often if not always sung or chanted to the accompaniment of the traditional Germanic instrument, the harp. It is probable that oral composition was practiced throughout the Anglo-Saxon period in spite of the introduction of writing; for writing was an art restricted to a relatively small portion of the population. How much of the output of unlettered singers may have found its way into books by dictation or by memorial reconstruction we have no reliable means of discovering; but it is evident from the style of the surviving poetry, with its use of a common verse form and its ready acceptance of a host of verse formulas, that the art of the oral practitioners has left its mark on even the most learned of the literary poets.

Writing as a literary art, in contrast to the old half-magical runic writing—confined to brief inscriptions—of the primitive Germanic peoples, was introduced among the Anglo-Saxons in the course of the seventh century by missionaries from the Mediterranean world and from Ireland. Englishmen were engaged in literary pursuits, writing in Latin or English, prose or verse, from about the middle of the seventh century onwards, so that we have some four centuries to reckon with before the Norman Conquest brought about the subversion of the old aristocracy and the beginnings of a new era. Culturally these were centuries marked by astonishing intellectual advances and sudden retrogressions, by sharp contrasts between the learned few, chiefly though not exclusively clerics, and the rest of society, but also in some quarters by a fruitful blending and assimilation. Old English poetry shows at times the collision, but often the harmonious fusion, of Christianity and a submerged paganism, Mediterranean civilization and a more primitive but not always inferior Germanic heritage.

Some thirty thousand lines of Old English poetry have come down to us out of an incalculably larger quantity.[1] Much of the best of it belongs, so far as we can tell, to the eighth and ninth centuries, but its broad characteristics are little changed from beginning to end; and the older works were still prized, as our manuscripts show, on the eve of the Conquest. The longest and finest of all the surviving poems is the three-thousand-line *Beowulf*, but there are many smaller pieces of distinction, among which the seven in this volume hold a high place. They very nearly span the four literary centuries. Cædmon's Hymn should have been composed about 665; *The Battle of Maldon*, shortly after 991. The others, some of which can be dated only within wide limits, fall between these extremes.

Among the numerous histories of Old English literature, the most recent and one of the most helpful is Stanley B. Greenfield's *A Critical History of Old English Literature* (New York University Press, 1965). For the poetry alone, a stimulating guide is Charles W. Kennedy's *The Earliest English Poetry* (New York: Oxford University Press, 1943). The great bulk and variety of writings that survive from the period, in both prose and verse, make it difficult for the student to get his bearings while he is still struggling with the language. A work of the first importance

---

[1] The standard collective edition is *The Anglo-Saxon Poetic Records* in six volumes, each with its own special title, edited by G. P. Krapp and E. V. K. Dobbie (New York: Columbia University Press, 1931–1953).

for both beginners and advanced students is *English Historical Documents*, Volume I, *ca.* 500–1042, edited by Dorothy Whitelock (London: Eyre and Spottiswood, 1955). This contains a very broad selection of documents, from laws and charters to letters, histories, sermons, and poems, admirably translated into modern English from Latin, Old English, and occasionally Old Norse. The introductions, notes, and bibliographies are of the highest quality. There could be no better guide to the general cultural background of Old English poetry.

## Cædmon's Hymn

This little hymn has a peculiar importance among the relatively abundant relics of Old English poetry, an importance by no means limited to its modest charm or its supposedly miraculous origin. It has come down to us as the maiden effort of the first English poet to treat the major themes of the Christian religion, and although he is described as the author of a great many poems, this is the only surviving composition that can with any degree of assurance be attributed to him. Even the copies of it are notable, for the two oldest are our earliest manuscript records of Old English poetry. The hymn itself has a further interest: as the work of a man who had never learned to read and write, it affords a brief yet precious example of that orally composed poetry, largely unrecorded, by which the written poems were preceded and in all probability surrounded.

All our ancient copies of the hymn have been preserved in the manuscripts of Bede's *Ecclesiastical History of the English Nation*, either in its original Latin form [1] or in the Old English

[1] *Historia Ecclesiastica Gentis Anglorum*, best edited by Charles Plummer, *Venerabilis Bedae Opera Historica*, 2 vols. (Oxford: The Clarendon Press, 1896).

version produced more than a century later; [2] and our knowledge
of Cædmon himself depends entirely on a single chapter of that
work. Bede completed the history about 731, some four years
before his death. Cædmon had died long before, probably while
Bede was still a boy, and there is nothing in Bede's account to
suggest that the two had ever met; but they were both Northum-
brians, and Cædmon's monastery at *Streoneshealh* (the modern
Whitby) was only sixty or seventy miles to the south of Bede's at
Jarrow. Bede, who was assiduous in gathering information for
the history and received some of it from much more distant re-
gions, would have had ready access to the records of Cædmon's
monastery, and had probably talked with persons who had been
well acquainted with the poet.

According to Bede, the beginning of Cædmon's poetical career
and the greater part at least of his subsequent achievement
belonged to the period between 657 and 680, when Hild, having
built the monastery, governed it as abbess. This remarkable
woman, whom Bede celebrates in the previous chapter of the
history, was a grand-niece of Edwin, the first Christian king of
Northumbria. Having taken the veil in middle life and
acquired some experience as abbess at another foundation, she
ruled at Streoneshealh with wisdom and vigor. The monastery,
which was of the double type not uncommon at this period, with
separate houses for men and women, soon became renowned for
learning as well as devotion. It was chosen as the meeting place
of the great synod of 663, where Roman authority prevailed over
Irish. Several of its monks were afterwards bishops; but Cædmon,
a simple herdsman on the monastic estate at the time of the
miracle, was to become the most distinguished of all the

[2] Edited with modern English translation by Thomas Miller, *The Old Eng-
lish Version of Bede's Ecclesiastical History of the English People* (Early
English Text Society, London, 1890–1899); reprinted for the society by the
Oxford University Press, London, 1959 (Part I, text and translation) and 1963
(Part II, collation of the MSS.). This version has sometimes been attributed,
though mistakenly, to King Alfred, and was probably produced in or about
his time if not at his instigation.

brotherhood. Bede's account of him is too rich and too skillfully wrought to be summarized without loss. The greater part of it runs as follows: [3]

> In the monastery of this abbess there was a certain brother made notable by a grace of God specially given, for that he was wont to make songs fit for religion and godliness; insomuch that, whatsoever of the divine writings he learned by them that expounded them, he set it forth after a little time with poetical language, put together with very great sweetness and pricking of the heart, in his own, that is to say, the English tongue. With whose songs the minds of many men were oft inflamed to the contempt of the world and desire of the heavenly life. And indeed other too among the English people after him assayed to make religious poems; but no man could match his cunning. For he himself learned the art of singing without being taught of men nor of men's help; [4] but he received the gift of singing freely by the aid of God. And therefore he could never make any fond or vain poem, but only such as belong to religion befitted his religious mouth. For as long as he was settled in secular life, until he was well stricken in age, [5] he had at no time learned any songs. And so it was that at the table, [6] when the company was set to be merry and had agreed that each man should sing in his course, he, when he saw the harp to be coming near him, would rise up at midst of supper and going out get him back to his own house.
>
> And as he did so on a certain time, and leaving the house of feasting had gone out to the stable of the beasts which had been appointed him to look to that night, and there at the fitting hour had bestowed his limbs to rest, there stood by him

[3] Book IV, chapter 24 of the history. By kind permission of the Harvard University Press, I quote from the translation by R. E. King in the Loeb Library edition, *Baedae Opera Historica*, 2 vols. (Cambridge, Mass., Harvard University Press, and London, William Heinemann Ltd., 1930; reprinted 1954, 1962), II, 141 ff. King's translation is based on that of Thomas Stapleton, made in 1565.

[4] This echoes St. Paul's reference to his calling as an apostle in Galatians 1:1.

[5] The Latin, *usque ad tempora provectioris aetatis*, might suggest any time past the prime of life, perhaps no more than forty, though both the Old English and the modern translators seem to think of a greater age.

[6] Bede's expression, *in convivio*, is rendered as *on beorscipe*, "at a beer-drinking" in the Old English version.

a certain man in a dream and bade him God speed, and calling him by his name said to him: "Caedmon, sing me something!" Whereupon he answering said: "I know not how to sing; for that too is the matter why I came out from the table to this place apart, because I could not sing." "But yet," quoth he again that spake with him, "thou hast to sing to me." "What," quoth he, "should I sing?" Whereupon the other said: "Sing the beginning of the creatures!" At which answer he began forthwith to sing in praise of God the Creator verses which he had never heard before, of which the sense is this: "Now ought we to praise the Maker of the heavenly kingdom, the power of the Creator and His counsel, the acts of the Father of glory; how He, being God eternal, was the author of all miracles; Which first created unto the children of men heaven for the top of their dwelling-place, and thereafter the almighty Keeper of mankind created the earth." [7] This is the sense but not the selfsame order of the words which he sang in his sleep: for songs, be they never so well made, cannot be turned of one tongue into another, word for word, without loss to their grace and worthiness.

Now on rising from slumber he remembered still all the things that he had sung in his sleep, and did by and by join thereto in the same measure more words of the song worthy of God. And coming on the morrow to the town reeve under whom he was, he showed unto him what gift he had received; and being brought to the abbess, he was commanded in the presence of many learned men to tell his dream and rehearse the song, that it might by the judgment of them all be tried what or whence the thing was which he reported. And it seemed to them all, that a heavenly grace was granted him of the Lord. And they recited unto him the process of a holy story or lesson, bidding him, if he could, to turn the same into meter and verse. Whereupon he undertaking so to do went his way, and on the morrow came again and brought the same which they had required of him, made in very good verse. Wherefore by and by the abbess embracing the grace of God in the man, instructed him to forsake the secular habit and take upon him the monastical vow, and when he had so done she placed him in the company of the brethren with all them that were with her,

[7] It is important here to have Bede's exact words: "Nunc laudare debemus auctorem regni caelestis, potentiam Creatoris, et consilium illius, facta Patris gloriae; quomodo ille, cum sit aeternus Deus, omnium miraculorum auctor exstitit; qui primo filiis hominum caelum pro culmine tecti, dehinc terram custos humani generis omnipotens creavit."

and gave commandment for him to be instructed in the regular
course of holy history. But he by thinking again with himself
upon all that he could hear and learn, and chewing thereon as
a clean beast cheweth the cud, would turn it into very sweet
song; and by melodiously singing the same again would make
his teachers to become in their turn his hearers. [8]

Now he sang of the creation of the world, and beginnings of
mankind, and all the glory of Genesis, of the going of Israel out
of Egypt, and their entering in the land of promise, and of very
many other histories of Holy Scripture, of the incarnation of
the Lord, of His passion, resurrection and ascension into
heaven, of the coming of the Holy Ghost, and the teaching of
the apostles. Also he would make many songs of the dread of
judgment to come, of the terror of the pains of hell, and of the
sweetness of the kingdom of heaven; moreover, many other
songs of the divine benefits and judgments, in all which his
endeavor was to pull men away from the love of wickedness
and stir them up to the love and readiness to do well. For he
was a man very devout and humbly obedient to the discipline
of the rules; but very zealous and fervently inflamed against
them that would do otherwise: wherefore too he closed his life
with a goodly end. [9]

Although Bede did not include the hymn itself in his account
of Cædmon, the scribes of the original Latin version of his history
frequently added it marginally, and the author of the Old English
version substituted it for the Latin paraphrase. In this way
all seventeen of our surviving copies of the hymn came into
being. Since there are substantive variations in these copies,
there have been differences of opinion about the best readings,
for it is conceivable that certain variations are attributable to
Cædmon himself or to those closest to him. It has seemed best to
select the oldest Northumbrian version for our text, since this is
the one with which Bede's paraphrase most nearly agrees, and to

[8] The Old English translator says that they wrote at his dictation. Was
this simply the translator's notion of the proper way to learn, or was he
familiar with written poems that were thought to be Cædmon's? Bede's
description suggests the possibility that many of the poems were recorded by
dictation, but we cannot prove it by the surviving records.

[9] The remainder of Bede's chapter tells an affecting story of Cædmon's
last hours. Whether he died before or after Hild is not known.

present it first with its original Northumbrian spellings as they appear in the two oldest copies, then in the normalized West Saxon spellings adopted for the other poems in this edition. A sampling of the actual West Saxon versions is given at the foot of the page below the normalized text. [10]

The manuscripts containing the two oldest copies are essentially of Bede's own time. The Moore manuscript, dated 737, contains the Northumbrian version at the top of its last page rather than where one would expect it, in the margin near Bede's paraphrase. It is followed by the identifying statement, *primo cantauit caedmon istud carmen*, and by three glosses, alphabetically arranged, of Latin words that appear in the history. Apparently the scribe of the manuscript was gathering together at this spot certain items from the margins of his exemplar which he had passed over while he was copying the text. In the Leningrad manuscript, of which the main text may be some years earlier than the chronological notations dated 746, the Northumbrian version of the hymn is at the foot of the page that contains Bede's paraphrase of it. [11]

Bede's well-established respect for documentary evidence, together with the inconsistently archaic spelling in these copies (especially the copy in the Moore MS.), suggests that he had in

[10] The fullest study of the text and its manuscripts is by E. V. K. Dobbie, *The Manuscripts of Cædmon's Hymn and Bede's Death Song* (New York: Columbia University Press, 1937). Dobbie's later edition of it in *The Anglo-Saxon Minor Poems* (*Anglo-Saxon Poetic Records*, VI), Columbia University Press, 1942, pp. 105 and 106, presents the Northumbrian and West Saxon versions with very full collations of other manuscripts. The Northumbrian text, with discussion of its background, is edited by A. H. Smith, *Three Northumbrian Poems: Cædmon's Hymn, Bede's Death Song and the Leiden Riddle* (London: Methuen's Old English Library, 1933).

[11] Both these manuscripts are now available in facsimile, with valuable introductions, in the series *Early English Manuscripts in Facsimile*, under the general editorship of Bertram Colgrave and his successor Peter Clemoes, published by Rosenkilde and Bagger, Copenhagen: *The Moore Bede*, with preface by P. Hunter Blair and a contribution by R. A. B. Mynors, 1959; *The Leningrad Bede*, edited by O. Arngart, 1952.

his possession a considerably older copy from which these two were made. Since Bede makes it plain that Cædmon was unable to read and write when he entered the monastery, and gives no indication that he learned to do so later, we may assume that the hymn was first recorded by someone else, quite possibly during Cædmon's lifetime if not on the occasion of the alleged miracle.

In spite of Cædmon's supposed incompetence as a singer before the moment when this hymn came into being, it exhibits the characteristic meter and style of Old English poetry under skill-ful control. The individual half-lines or verses have the typical range in number of syllables and stress patterns, the alliteration linking each pair of verses is placed according to the rules—no easy task for the novice—and the sequence of verses has, for so short and simple a piece, a surprisingly varied yet expressive movement. One would not expect, and does not find, the rhyth-mical elaborations of the finest passages in the longer poems, for these require more room and more complicated matter; but with-in its limits this is an accomplished piece of versification. Con-spicuous also is the familiar stylistic device of variation, the delib-erate dwelling on different aspects of an important subject by partially synonymous repetition. In these nine lines there are seven different epithets for God, only one of them repeated. Among these epithets, moreover, we recognize a number that appear in other poems. If they were not already verse formulas of the type essential to the oral composition of long poems and by no means distasteful to the literary poets of the period, they were soon to become so, perhaps as much by Cædmon's subse-quent repetition of them as by the currency of the hymn. Docu-mentary evidence for the formulas and formulaic expressions in the hymn has been presented very fully by F. P. Magoun, Jr., "Bede's Story of Cædman: The Case History of an Anglo-Saxon Oral Singer," *Speculum*, XXX (1955), 49–63, an article which raises questions of great interest about oral singers, and needs pondering. Tentative discussion of these and other points will be found in the somewhat earlier Gollancz Memorial Lecture by C. L. Wrenn, "The Poetry of Cædmon," *Proceedings of the British Academy*, XXXII (1946), 277–296. Magoun's suggestion that some of the expressions in the hymn had already been coined for Cædmon by earlier religious poets has been vigorously opposed by Kemp Malone, "Cædmon and English Poetry," *Modern Language Notes*, LXXVI (1961), 193–195.

In one respect the structure of the hymn is unusual. In most Old English poems the pairs of verses constituting what we print as lines are loosely organized in verse paragraphs of uneven length. Here we find a tendency toward stanzaic structure. The first four lines, celebrating God's divine powers and the unspecified wonders of the Creation, introduce him as the guardian of the heavenly kingdom. The next four direct attention to his care for the human race and call him the guardian of mankind. The two sets of four are marked and balanced by the one repeated epithet, *ēce Dryhten,* in lines 4 and 8. The ninth line partly offsets this symmetry, because it is technically a mere variation of the statement in lines 7 and 8 and to this extent differentiates the second part from the first. But the closing epithet, *Frēa ælmihtiġ,* harks back to the magnificence of God as he is described in the first section. Hence this final line sums up the essential meaning of the whole poem. Bede's prose paraphrase, by deliberately avoiding the repetition and shortening the second section, sacrifices all such structural interest.

Although the formal elements of the hymn, like its language, are of native origin and representative of an age-old tradition, its sentiment is obviously Biblical. Attention has recently been called to its close dependence on the Psalms, not only for the very notion of praising God but for the specific powers and functions assigned to him as creator and governor of heaven and earth, magnificent in the heavens yet mindful of the children of men. The very expression "children of men," the *ielda bearnum* of line 5, occurs in an appropriate context in Psalm 115:15–16: "Ye are blessed of the Lord which made heaven and earth. The heaven, even the heavens, are the Lord's: but the earth hath he given to the children of men." (Vulgate, 113:23–24: *Benedicti vos a Domino, qui fecit cælum et terram. Cælum cæli Domino: terram autem dedit filiis hominum.*) [12] The varied epithets for God probably owe something, as a stylistic device, to royal panegyrics and even, perhaps, to the praise of pagan gods; but their substance is fully justified by the Psalms, and the naming itself, as has often been observed, is enjoined in one of the most famous of the prophetic passages, Isaiah 9:6: "For unto us a child is born: . . . and his name shall be called Wonderful, Counsellor, The mighty God, The everlasting Father, The Prince of Peace."

It is perhaps idle to speculate on the origins of a miracle. Dream-visions have been credited to other poets, from Hesiod on, to account for their inspiration, and legends quickly acquire ideal shapes that baffle all attempts to isolate some kernel of fact. Yet it may not be irrelevant to consider the impact, on a simple man of strong feelings and powerful imagination, of a new religion planted so impressively in the very soil to which he had been attached for a great part of his life. The building of Hild's monastery, the sudden aggregation of monks and nuns, the mysterious liturgy, possibly (if it came before the dream) the great synod attended by the king himself as well as the ecclesiastical dignitaries—all these things, given some curiosity on Cædmon's part and some reflection on what he learned, could have played a part in preparing him to receive that seemingly instantaneous gift of song.

## Notes

2. *meahta*, "powers." The distinctively plural ending -*a* of the feminine ō-stem nouns has been chosen for the normalized text in view of the *maecti* of the Moore MS. and the *mehti* of the

[12] See N. F. Blake, "Cædmon's Hymn," *Notes and Queries*, CCVII (1962), 243–246.

Leningrad MS. The word *meaht* or *miht* was originally a feminine *i*-stem with no ending in the accusative singular and *-i* in the accusative plural, but in West Saxon it came to be declined like the *ō*-stems with *-e* in the accusative singular and *-a* in the accusative plural. The spelling *meahte* in the West Saxon Tanner MS. may represent either the old plural or the new singular. Bede's choice of the singular *potentiam* in his paraphrase may be due to his sense of Latin usage.

3, 4. *swā hē wundra ġehwæs, /ēċe Dryhten, ōr astealde.* The expression *wundra gehwæs*, "of each of wonders," goes together as if it were a compound, and the genitive *ġehwæs* depends on *ōr*, the direct object of *astealde*: "as he, eternal Lord, established the beginning of every wondrous thing."

7. By putting the object, *middanġeard*, ahead of the subject, *Weard*, the poet not only solves a metrical problem but adds a syntactical contrast to his parallel clauses.

9. The verb *tēode* is to be understood as repeated from the previous line.

# The Battle of Brunanburh

The victory of the English forces at Brunanburh under the command of Athelstan and his brother Edmund was the military climax of a movement by which Alfred the Great and his immediate successors, having first freed their hereditary West Saxon kingdom from the threat of a Danish conquest, gradually gained power over the whole of England and made themselves secure against their enemies abroad.[1] The poem describing the battle

[1] The historic significance of the battle is carefully assessed by Sir Frank Stenton, *Anglo-Saxon England*, 2nd ed. (Oxford: The Clarendon Press, 1947). See especially chapter X and, on the battle itself, pp. 338–339.

was early put on record as chief witness to the event. Accordingly it has survived in four manuscripts of the *Anglo-Saxon Chronicle*, appearing in each of them as the sole entry for the year 937.[2]

In spite of this association, the exact time and circumstances of the composition of the poem are uncertain. In our earliest manuscript (A), it is included in a block of texts that were not transcribed till about 955. We cannot tell how much earlier it was entered in the master copy from which A is derived, or how long before that it was composed. Neither do we know whether the author intended it for a place in the *Chronicle*. Its length and elaboration, no less than its poetic form, distinguish it sharply from the otherwise meagre and perfunctory annals of Athelstan's reign. Its ardor suggests that the battle had occurred very recently; its self-sufficiency, that it was designed as an independent piece; yet its perspective and its concerns are not far removed from those that govern the *Chronicle* as it had taken shape under Alfred and Edward.

Although this is perhaps the most familiar of all Old English poems through Tennyson's translation—a brilliant and thoroughly Tennysonian performance for good and for ill—it is not altogether easy to evaluate in its tenth-century form and setting. Critics have been able to show, by comparing it with earlier Old

---

[2] The manuscripts are listed above, in the headnote below the text of the poem. The readings of a fifth manuscript, destroyed by fire in 1731, have been reconstructed from earlier transcriptions by Campbell in Appendix I of the edition mentioned below, but have no independent value as witnesses to the text of the poem, for the manuscript was a direct copy of A. MS. A. is available in facsimile: *The Parker Chronicle and Laws*, edited by Robin Flower and Hugh Smith (London: Oxford University Press, 1941). The various versions of the *Chronicle* are printed, with translation in a second volume, by B. Thorpe, *The Anglo-Saxon Chronicle*, Rolls Series (London, 1861). Of great importance for its annotation is Charles Plummer's edition, *Two of the Saxon Chronicles Parallel*, 2 vols. (Oxford: The Clarendon Press, 1892 and 1899; reprinted 1952 with two notes by D. Whitelock). The clearest and most up-to-date presentation of the work in its various versions is in *The Anglo-Saxon Chronicle, A Revised Translation*, edited by Dorothy Whitelock with David C. Douglas and Susie I. Tucker (London: Eyre and Spottiswoode, 1961).

English poetry, that it is highly conventional, even archaic, in meter and diction. What is likely to escape us is its no less remarkable originality in design and vision. Nothing quite like it in genre has survived from earlier periods, nor are there close parallels in the poetry of other Germanic peoples. It does indeed have partial parallels, and it probably had antecedents, insofar as it can be classified as a royal panegyric; but it is much more than a panegyric by reason of its strong national feeling. This feeling depends in part, doubtless, on the long antecedent years of humiliation by Scandinavian ravagers and invaders and in part on the consolidation of England that had been achieved under West Saxon leadership since the time of Alfred. Likewise original, though now it seems a matter of course, is the author's historical perspective, not quite the same thing as the knowledge of heroic tradition of which the Norse panegyrists made use. He has been reading Bede and the *Chronicle* and (to judge by his connoisseurship in the diction and phraseology of battle poetry) several of the older poems in manuscript, as well as keeping his ears open. He places the battle historically within a firmer frame of reference than an unbookish author might be expected to supply, and even in treating the conflict itself maintains a distant view, surveying the scene as from a height and noting armies and battalions rather than individuals. He had some precedent for this in the battle scenes of Cynewulf and the Biblical poets, but a more traditional method of describing a battle in poetry is to be seen in *The Battle of Maldon*, where the originality, equally notable and doubtless of a higher poetic order, lies in a different sphere.

A thorough edition of the poem from all the manuscripts, with full historical introduction and notes, has been produced by Alistair Campbell, London, Heinemann, 1938. See also the edition by E. V. K. Dobbie, *The Anglo-Saxon Minor Poems* ("Anglo-Saxon Poetic Records," VI), Columbia University Press, 1942, pp. 16–20. Dobbie's full presentation of the text is followed by that of the other conventionally composed poems of the *Chronicle*, which celebrate later events and are poetically of less importance. I have depended on these editions for my report, slightly abridged, of the manuscript readings, except for those of MS. A, which are taken from the facsimile.

The main facts about the battle as presented in the poem are confirmed by a number of later accounts, partially or wholly independent. Among those cited in Campbell's edition are Irish and Scottish annals, a Norse saga, and Latin histories produced in England. Yet the location of Brunanburh is still uncertain. Of the various sites proposed, those that seem most probable lie near the west coast of England between Chester and southern Scotland. According to the poem, the opposing army consisted of two main forces: Scots under their king *Constantinus* (Constantine III, king of the combined Picts and Scots), and Norse vikings, the *scip-flotan* of line 11, who had come by sea from Ireland under the command of a certain *Anlaf*. Other reports make it clear that this Anlaf, a son of Guthfrith,[3] ruled a viking settlement in and around Dublin. His uncle Sihtric had held sway in York, but Guthfrith, claiming the succession after Sihtric's death, had been driven out of England by Athelstan and had ruled for a few years in Ireland before he died and left his kingdom there to Anlaf. The Scottish forces were apparently supported by their neighbors and allies, the Welsh of Strathclyde, who held the coastal region west of Northumbria.

Brief treatments of some of the puzzling details, such as the problematical *dennode* of line 12 and the body of water called *Dinges mere* in line 54, will be found in the glossary and the index of proper names, where also are identifications of the chief persons. For full discussion of such matters the reader must be guided by the notes and bibliographies of Campbell and Dobbie.

---

[3] This Anlaf, the later form of whose name is *Olaf*, appears in a seventeenth-century English version of some Irish annals (quoted by Campbell, p. 159) as *Awley McGodfrey*.

# Notes

1. The word *Hēr*, "Here," introduces each annal in the *Anglo-Saxon Chronicle* directly after the number of the year. Hence it takes on the temporal meaning, "In this year." It is probably not a genuine part of the poem, which makes perfect sense and correct meter without it. The later poems of the *Chronicle* also begin with *Hēr*, and in one of them, *The Coronation of Edgar*, it is clearly required by the meter. Perhaps some or all of these later poems were written specifically for the *Chronicle*, as *The Battle of Brunanburh* in all likelihood was not.

6. The expression *hamora lāfum*, "with swords," literally "with leavings of hammers," is a familiar poetic periphrasis of a type cultivated by the ancient Germanic poets and especially popular in Norse poetry, where it received the name "kenning," from the verb *kenna*, "to call, name." The term is often applied to any periphrasis consisting of two or more words or a compound even if the meaning is obvious, but there is frequently something metaphorical or recondite about a kenning. Here, although a sword is in fact left on the anvil after a smith's hammer has forged it, there is probably a latent comparison to a human warrior as the survivor of a battle. In line 54 we find the expression *daroða lāf*, "what was left by the spears," applied to the bedraggled remnant of Anlaf's army.

7–9. *swā . . . ealgoden*, "as befitted the nobility they got from their ancestors, that they should often defend the land in battle against every foe." Instead of the distinctively subjunctive ending *-en* of the normalized *ealgoden* the manuscripts have *-on* or *-an*, which at this period can be either indicative or subjunctive. Campbell recommends the subjunctive, which yields a more plausible meaning and firmer syntax.

22. *on lāst leġdon lāðum þēodum*, "pursued the hostile peoples." Since *lecgan*, "to lay," is normally transitive, the ex-

pression *on lāst leġdon* is evidently elliptical: probably, as Camp-bell has suggested, for *on lāst leġdon lāstas*, "they laid tracks on the track." It is probably too early for Shakespeare's idiom, "Lay on, Macduff," which implies "lay blows on, strike vigorously"; but this would surely be appropriate. The phrase *lāðum þēodum* goes with *on lāst*, "on the track of the hostile peoples," the dative being used with possessive force instead of the genitive, a usage that is customary with nouns closely associated with parts of the body, as *lāst*, "footprint, track," is evidently felt to be.

51. The demonstrative *þæs* is here used as a relative, "which," agreeing with the last of its series of antecedents, each of which is in the genitive singular, and serving also as object of *plegodon*, which normally takes the accusative (Campbell's ex-planation). MS. D has substituted the more usual compound relative, *þæs þe,* where *þæs* agrees with the antecedent and the indeclinable *þe* serves as object of the verb.

54. *drēoriġ.* Campbell maintains that the meaning "bloody" attributed to this word in addition to "dejected" cannot be sub-stantiated from its use in Old English poems; but since *drēor,* as he admits, means "blood," it is difficult to see how *drēoriġ* can fail to suggest "bloody" in the context of a battle. That is not its most frequent meaning, however, and it need not be domin-ant even here.

60–65. In this enumeration of the creatures that prey on corpses after a battle—a familiar motif in Old English poetry—one may choose to combine the words in several ways. I prefer to take *sealwiġ-pādan* as a noun, "dark-coated ones," applicable to all the creatures that are then enumerated, each being credited with a slightly different shade of the common darkness: "the black raven with horny beak, and the dusky-coated one, the eagle white from behind—greedy war hawk—and that grey beast, the wolf in the forest." Campbell suggests that *gūþ-hafoc* is not the name of some unknown kind of hawk but a kenning for the

white-tailed eagle previously mentioned. Raven, eagle, and wolf
are the usual trio. It is true that the *earn* is separated from the
*gūþ-hafoc* by the verse *āses brūcan*, but this is only a variation
of *hrǣw bryttian* above and may well be followed by a variation
of *earn æftan hwīt*. The uninflected *hwīt* is metrically necessary
and may, as Campbell suggests, be excused if the verse is felt to
be parenthetical.

65b–68a. "No greater number of people was ever yet slain in
this island before this by sword's edges." Campbell points out
that *wæl*, in its frequent sense "number of slain," governs the
genitive *folces*, and that *wearþ* goes with *ġefielled* to form the
preterite passive of *ġefiellan*.

68b. Here *þæs-þe* is used as a conjunction, "according to what,
as." This use is found in other poems, for instance in *Beowulf*
1341, *þæs þe þincean mæg þegne monegum*, "as it may seem to
many a thane."

# The Dream of the Rood

This, the earliest extant example of a dream-vision poem to
emerge from Western Europe, has been elaborately edited by A.
S. Cook, Oxford, 1905, and later (with greater authority in some
matters) by Bruce Dickins and Alan S. C. Ross, Methuen's Old
English Library, 1934; fourth edition, 1954, reprinted with
further additions and corrections, 1963. The manuscript is
available in facsimile, *Il Codice Vercellese*, ed. Max Förster,
Rome, 1913; the poem stands on ff. 104ᵛ–106ʳ, being the fifth of
six religious poems interspersed in the volume among twenty-
three homilies.

That the poem was first composed before A.D. 750 (even, as
some think, before 700) is attested by the presence of the central

part of the rood's speech, somewhat abridged and in some places obliterated, in the runic inscription on the monumental cross at Ruthwell in Dumfriesshire, southwestern Scotland. Dickins and Ross believe that the character of the runes points to a date not later than about 750. On the monument itself, see especially G. Baldwin Brown, *The Arts in Early England*, Vol. V, London, 1921, pp. 102–317; Fritz Saxl, "The Ruthwell Cross," *Journal of the Warburg and Courtauld Institutes*, VI (1943), 1–19; Meyer Shapiro, "The Religious Meaning of the Ruthwell Cross," *Art Bulletin*, XXVI (1944), 232–245; and Eric Mercer, "The Ruthwell and Bewcastle Crosses," *Antiquity*, XXXVIII (1964), 268–276. The runic inscription and a transliteration of it are included in Dickins and Ross, and again in Dobbie, *Anglo-Saxon Minor Poems*, pp. 114–115. The poem may have been considerably revised, especially at beginning and end, before making its appearance in the Vercelli Book late in the tenth century; but of such revision, apart from mere modernization of forms and spellings, there is no substantial evidence.

The emergence of a dream-vision poem in the latter part of the seventh century or the beginning of the eighth harmonizes very well with the story behind Cædmon's hymn and with the religious visions attributed to a number of Irish and English persons, several of which are reported with delight and sympathy by Bede. What is remarkable about this vision is, on the one hand, the depth and subtlety of its understanding; on the other, the art and imagination with which the speeches of dreamer and cross are invented, complexities of meaning and emotion are conveyed, order is maintained, and a significant progression is unfolded from beginning to end.

The presentation of the cross as a person able to address the dreamer—a device that gives the poet opportunity for his highly original account of the crucifixion—may owe less to the talking trees of classical poetry than to the technique illustrated in many of the riddles of the Exeter Book, a few of which go back to

Latin originals composed by Aldhelm before the end of the seventh century. Aldhelm learned something from the Latin riddles of Symphosius, but he was probably familiar with a native tradition of riddles as well. It should be added, however, that there was a much broader basis for the device in classical and post-classical Latin poetry and rhetoric. This is admirably set forth by Margaret Schlauch, "The 'Dream of the Rood' as Prosopopoeia," *Essays and Studies in Honor of Carleton Brown* (New York University Press, 1940), pp. 23–34.

Equally important in the background of the poem is the devotional and doctrinal literature accorded to the cross. Its discovery by St. Helena, the mother of Constantine the Great, was celebrated in the feast of the Invention of the Cross on the third of May. Two Latin hymns on the cross, composed by Venantius Fortunatus, an Italian who spent most of his life in Merovingian Gaul, became bishop of Poitiers in 599, and died about 610, show an equal fervor and some of the same concepts. They are reprinted conveniently in the *Oxford Book of Medieval Latin Verse*, ed. F. J. E. Raby (Oxford: The Clarendon Press, 1959), pp. 74–75. On such matters as these see, besides the editions mentioned, Howard R. Patch, "Liturgical Influence in *The Dream of the Rood*," *PMLA*, XXXIV (1919), 233–257. The theological background is significantly illuminated by Rosemary Woolf, "Doctrinal Influences on *The Dream of the Rood*," *Medium Ævum*, XXVII (1958), 137–153.

A brief but discerning critical study of the poem, with incidental comparisons to some Middle English treatments of the theme, has been published by J. A. Burrow, "An Approach to the *Dream of the Rood*," *Neophilologus*, XLIII (1959), 123–133.

## Notes

4. *seldlicre*, "exceedingly rare," an absolute use of the comparative somewhat like what we find in Latin. Compare the old expression, "passing rare."

5. *on lyft lǣdan*, "extending into the air; rising aloft." It is tempting to think there may have been some confusion with the rare verb *lēodan*, "spring up," since this would be appropriate to a tree, but since *lǣdan* can readily mean "extend" there is no occasion to emend.

8. *æt foldan scēatum*, "at the surface of the earth"—that is, at the base of the cross—a natural conception if the poet was thinking in part of ornamental crosses he had seen. Dickins and Ross quote Patch's very different notion: "*Foldan sceatas* are the corners of the earth, to which the cross reaches as it spreads over the sky," and compare the tree in Nebuchadnezzar's vision as described in the Old English poem, *Daniel*, 497–503. This interpretation of *scēatas* is entirely legitimate, but the meaning "surface" fits better at 37 and is imperative at 43; and the image proposed by Patch seems confused and improbable even for a dream. Cook, following Sweet, gave "surface" as the meaning throughout the poem.

9. *enġel-dryhta fela*, "many hosts of angels." I first proposed this emendation in *The Rhythm of Beowulf*, New Haven: Yale University Press, 1942, p. 101. The reading of the manuscript, *engel dryhtnes ealle*, does not make sense and violates the syllabic and alliterative scheme characteristic of hypermetric verses in this poem and elsewhere. Two other proposed emendations, *englas Dryhtnes* (Sievers) and *engeldryhte* (Dickins and Ross), give acceptable sense and sound meter, but they do not account for the presence of *ealle* in the manuscript. It was my notion in proposing *engeldryhta fela* that the sequence *dryhta feala* (a common spelling of *fela*), if the words were written rather close together, might look enough like *dryhtnes ealle* to produce the error. In the insular script *f* and *s* have forms that are easily confused. The compound *enġel-dryht* does not, to be sure, occur elsewhere and its genitive plural form strains the verse-type (a hypermetric verse with a close resembling type E in the Sievers scheme) unless we treat *enġel*, as I think we may, as nearly equivalent to one syllable on the analogy of historically mono-

syllabic words like *tācn* and *ādl*. It is of no great moment which of the three emendations one chooses, but the one here adopted forms a more grandiose image, which seems appropriate.

10. *fægere þurh forþ-ġesceaft*, "fair by their pre-ordained condition," or more freely, "fair by eternal decree," with reference to the angels who were destined not to fall but to maintain their original brightness. The word *forþ-ġesceaft* occurs in five other poems (never in prose) with two apparently diverse meanings: the nature of things or the created world on the one hand, future destiny or the future state or condition on the other. These meanings can be reconciled by taking *ġesceaft* in the basic sense, "that which has been created or ordained," and *forþ*, "forth, onward," as indicating its perpetuation if it is already present or its prospective existence if it is not. Thus the combination means "that which has been created or ordained to be," either for all time (the nature of things, the created world, or some preordained condition) or in the future. This explanation slightly modifies the interpretations of Cook and of Dickins and Ross without changing the basic concept. A minor problem is the gender of the nominative plural adjective *fægere*, which obviously refers to the angels or the angelic hosts, and modifies the subject of *behēoldon* in the previous line, either *fela* according to the chosen reading or *engeldryhte* or *englas* according to the readings mentioned above. If it modifies *englas* it is masculine, as we expect; but if *engeldryhte* or *fela*, it is feminine, with the generalized ending *-e* that prevails in most of the manuscripts; for the indeclinable *fela* becomes implicitly feminine in agreement with *dryhta*. It is plural as subject of the verb. A similar construction, where *fela* is treated as nominative plural masculine, occurs in the Old English *Genesis*, 2335–2336, *bregowearda fela rōfe arīsað*, "many valiant princes will arise."

15. *wǣdum ġeweorðod*, literally "worthily adorned with garments," but perhaps the phrase means no more than "splendidly

appareled." Cook suggested that the *wǣdum* were some kind of streamers such as those with which processional crosses were decorated, and this seems possible. Yet when *wǣdum* is repeated at 22, it seems primarily to refer to the contrasted costumes, gold and jewels on the one hand, blood on the other. In that context streamers are either superfluous or positively distracting.

19. *earmra ǣr-ġewinn*, literally "the former agony of wretched (ones)." The dreamer associates the blood not only with Christ but, typically, with the many wretches who have endured this form of punishment. Note that the cross itself, at line 31, says it was commanded by its makers to lift up their criminals (plural *weargas*), though it actually served for Christ alone. It is true that the dreamer has already identified the cross as the Lord's (*Wealdendes trēo*, 17), and that the blood issuing from its right side is calculated to recall the wound inflicted by the centurion, as the next note explains more fully; but the vague generality of the plural *earmra* is appropriate not merely to dream psychology but to the implicit doctrine of the poem. The cross is later to say (lines 83 ff.) that the Son of God has transformed it by his suffering from the hardest of punishments to a glorious instrument of salvation. It is unique, but it typifies all crosses. Similarly, the suffering endured by Christ in his human nature is unique, but it may typify the suffering of the sinful wretches for whose punishment crosses were devised. The alternative interpretation advocated by Cook, that *earmra ǣr-ġewinn* refers to the former strife against Christ of the wretches who were responsible for the crucifixion, seems less in accord with the train of thought in the passage and less closely related to the central themes of the poem. In line 65 the meaning of *ġewinn* is shifted and enlarged, but still closely related to that which is here recommended.

20. The cross bleeds *on þā swiðran healfe*, "on the right side," because, according to post-Biblical tradition, it was Christ's right side that was opened by the centurion's lance (John 19:34). This

tradition is mentioned by the modern authorities cited in Cook's note, and also by Bede in his treatise on the temple of Solomon. He interprets a certain door on the right of the temple (I Kings 6:8) as a type of the wound in Christ's side, "because," he says, "holy Church believes it was his right side that was opened by the soldier." (*De Templo Salomonis Liber*, chap. viii, in *Patrologia Latina*, ed. J. P. Migne, XCI, 753.)

22. *blēoum.* The uncontracted form is metrically desirable.

31, 32. *þǣr.* Dickins and Ross urge very plausibly that the word here means "at that juncture; at that; on that occasion; then" (*Oxford English Dictionary, there* adv. 5, earliest quotation *c.* 1400). See the glossary, where these and other instances (at 30, 57, 60) are listed tentatively under the definition "thereupon, then."

39–49, 56–64. These are the lines partially preserved and somewhat abridged on the Ruthwell Cross. See Dickins and Ross or Dobbie. At 39–40 the corresponding passage on the Cross consists of a single pair of hypermetric verses, running as follows in normalized spelling:

Onġierede hine God ælmihtiġ     þā hē wolde on ġealgan ġestīgan.

The greater regularity of the form suggests that the inscription may at this point be giving us an earlier reading rather than an abridgment; but it is certainly inferior, for the *ġeong hæleþ* of the Vercelli Book text brings out much more imaginatively the heroic aspect of the action, an aspect which the poet is all along at pains to emphasize as proper to Christ in his divine nature. Cook cites classical parallels to the notion that Christ here strips himself as for battle, and Miss Woolf quotes Ambrose, who makes the stripping voluntary and heroic, saying, "Most rightly, when he was about to ascend the cross, he laid aside his royal garments." (*Pulchre ascensurus crucem regalia vestimenta deposuit.* Quoted by Miss Woolf, p. 146 of her article, from

*Patrologia Latina*, XV, 1830–1831). The next few words of the inscription, corresponding to lines 41–42 of our text, are partially defaced, but what remains looks like an unmetrical abridgment. All the other remnants of the inscription show verse-by-verse correspondence with our text, with only minor verbal variations.

55. *Wēop eall ġesceaft*, "all creation wept." The sympathy of inanimate nature, familiar in classical elegy, lies close at hand in Matthew's account of the crucifixion, and the theme was developed by some of the church fathers. There may, however, be a coalescence of two traditions. The weeping of all creatures, animate and inanimate, for the dead Balder seems by no means irrelevant. Unfortunately we cannot be certain that the myth was known in England at the time the poem was composed. See the note in Dickins and Ross.

63. *ġestōdon him æt his līċes hēafdum*. The interpretation of *him* is somewhat problematical. One might take it as a possessive dative singular, proper to the simple phrase *him æt hēafdum* but rendered unnecessary by *his līċes*. If so we might either leave it untranslated or, to give it some slight recognition, say, "They stood by him at the head of his body." But *him* is more probably a "reflexive" or "ethical" dative plural, suggesting deliberate action on the part of the subject: "they took their stand" or "they came and stood." For what may be a comparable instance see the note on *Maldon* 300.

65. The word *ġewinn* here refers most directly and obviously to Christ's agony on the cross, but the military connotations of the word are also appropriate. In his divine nature Christ has waged war against the devil and all the forces of evil.

66. *banan*, probably the cross itself as the agent of death; the word *bana* is applied to one who has killed another even if unintentionally. Possibly, however, this is an error for, or a Late West Saxon levelled form of, the genitive plural *banena*, as Cook

and others have thought. The reference would then be to the human agents of the crucifixion. It is slightly more difficult, however, to accept their presence at this juncture than to suppose that the cross is alluding once more to its own unwilling participation in the affair.

69. *mǽte weorode*, literally "with limited company," meaning "alone"; a characteristic example of ironic understatement. So also in line 124.

71. *stefn.* Most editors, noting the lack of sense and alliteration, have followed Kluge in inserting this word; but Kluge substituted it for the *syððan* of the manuscript, as did Sweet and Craigie after him; whereas Cook, Krapp, and Dickins and Ross retain *syððan* and add *stefn* after it. The sense thus produced is good, but the meter is defective, for *syððan* becomes "anacrusis" before a verse of the type Sievers called D, which ordinarily does not admit even one such preliminary syllable in the second half-line. Since there is no real need for the conjunction here it seems better to follow Kluge.

76–77. The reference here to St. Helena's discovery of the cross and its adornment under her direction is surprisingly brief, and since the meter is defective we may suppose that several verses have been accidently omitted by a scribe.

79. *bealu-wara weorc*, "the work (or deeds) of dwellers in iniquity (wicked men)." If we take the expression so, as Dickins and Ross recommend, it would seem that *sārra sorga* in the next line must depend directly on *ġebiden hæbbe*, even though this means that the verb (usually governing the accusative) must govern two different cases in sequence. One might possibly excuse this on the ground that *sārra sorga* is almost partitive in feeling, "(a number of) sore sorrows"—compare the French use of *des*. Alternatively we might take *bealuwara* as a miswriting of *bealuwa* or *bealwa*, genitive plural of *bealu* and directly parallel

to *sorga*, both nouns depending on *weorc*, which would then mean "pain" or "working, effect." Cook argues persuasively for this emendation on the strength of meter as well as meaning, and it is with considerable doubt that I have allowed the manuscript reading to stand.

93. The meaning of *for ealle menn* is best taken, perhaps, as "for the sake of all men." In choosing Mary for his mother God honored her above all womankind, and he did this for the sake of all men, in that his ultimate purpose was their redemption.

112. The word *sīe* has the metrical value here (as in some other poems, especially the older ones) of two syllables, and may be pronounced accordingly (*sī-e*).

125. *on forþ-weġ*. The accusative form is substituted for the dative here and at *Wanderer* 81 on the analogy of several parallels: *on forþ-weg* at *Beowulf* 2625, *Exodus* 129, *Menologium* 218, *Guthlac* 801 and 945; *on forþ-wegas* at *Exodus* 32, 350, and [*on*] *forþ-wegas* at *Genesis* 2814. In all these instances, as here, motion is implicit, and *on* (or Anglian *in* in *The Wanderer*) would be expected to govern the accusative. Here and at *Wanderer* 81, substitution of the accusative gives a sound verse of type A instead of a very unusual instance of A with final resolution or expanded D. This is a small matter, however, and it is possible that poets differed.

146. *guman*. Dickins and Ross defend this as a generic singular, "man" in the sense "mankind," genitive "man's," and I have let it stand on that assumption, though Cook's emendation to *gumena*, genitive plural, may be right. C. L. Wrenn, wishing to interpret *wyrsan* at *Beowulf* 525 as genitive plural of the comparative, as had been suggested earlier, cites both *guman* here and *banan* at 66 as examples of a Late West Saxon genitive plural in *-an*. If this is the right explanation we ought to normalize the words as *gumena* and *banena*, since these are not Late

West Saxon poems; but neither *wyrsan* in *Beowulf* (as Klaeber explains in his note) nor these words in the *Rood* are necessarily to be interpreted as, or emended to, genitive plurals. Late West Saxon *-an* for *-ena*, if it exists, is very rare.

148–151a. The allusion in these lines is to the harrowing of hell: Christ's descent into hell, his effortless victory over Satan, and his redemption (in some versions of the story from limbo, but here from hellfire itself) of all the virtuous men of old, from Adam onward. The adverb *þǣr* in 149 points to hell, as implied by *bryne* and the context as a whole. Dickins and Ross put a period after *spēdiġ*, 151, in order to make *þam sīþ-fǣte*, 150, "that expedition," refer exclusively to the harrowing; but I have reverted to Cook's punctuation because it seems essential to maintain a parallel between the two clauses introduced by *þā* in 151b and 155b. With this punctuation, *þam sīþ-fǣte* must refer not simply to the harrowing but also to the subsequent entry into heaven, even though this was delayed for forty days until the Ascension. Both Bede's hymn on the Ascension and the poem on the subject by Cynewulf associate the harrowing with the Ascension in the same way. The procession that advances toward the gates of heaven includes an escort of angels and a vast throng of the redeemed led by Christ. For hymn and poem see *The Christ of Cynewulf*, ed. A. S. Cook (Boston: Ginn and Co., 1900; reprinted from the second impression of 1909 by Archon Books, 1964, with a new preface by J. C. Pope), pp. 22–23 and 116–118.

# The Battle of Maldon

In the *Anglo-Saxon Chronicle* for 991 the battle of Maldon figures as a comparatively small though ill-starred engagement between Byrhtnoþ, ealdorman of Essex, at the head of the local

levy, and a band of vikings, part of a large Scandinavian—
mainly Norwegian—army under the general direction of Anlaf
(Olaf) Tryggvason, who later became king of Norway. The series
of harryings and invasions that began in 991, after half a century
of comparative tranquillity, continued with occasional inter-
mission under several different Scandinavian leaders, some
Norwegian, some Danish, until Cnut the Dane became king of
England in 1016. The poem presents this battle in far greater
detail than we find in any other account of it, but not in histori-
cal perspective; rather as a self-contained little tragedy, a revela-
tion of men's strength and weakness under duress. Thus it resem-
bles such legendary encounters as we read of in the fragmentary
Old English lay, *The Fight at Finnsburg*, or, on a much greater
scale, the unavailing last stand of the Burgundians in the hall of
Attila the Hun. But it is the poet's distinction to have made us
feel the contrast between those carefully shaped, heroic old
stories and this vividly actual battle, enacted by everyday men,
many of them untrained for war, many of them but dimly aware
of the seriousness of the occasion, who nevertheless find them-
selves put to a test as absolute as any that the heroes of legend
encountered. In his poetic style, as in his basic conception, he
holds the ideal and the actual in balance, letting us see the im-
perfect, sometimes haphazard quality that belongs to most events
as we experience them, and nevertheless the emergence of a
pattern, the partial reenactment of something long familiar to the
imagination but larger than life. The result is a document a
good deal less reliable for its fact than a sober newspaper report,
as we have properly enough been warned in a recent article; [1]
but there would have been no occasion for the warning if the
poet had not deliberately, for his greater purpose, tempted us
into overliteral responses by making important use of fact. We
must suppose that the general setting, still more the named per-

[1] J. B. Bessinger, Jr., "*Maldon* and the *Óláfsdrápa*: an Historical Caveat,"
*Comparative Literature* XIV (1962), 23–35.

sons, great and small, are altogether actual, for without this kind
of local fidelity the poet could not have persuaded his contem-
poraries to take him seriously. Indeed his own inspiration clearly
depended in great measure on his belief in these men and their
sudden emergence from nonentity into tragic splendor. What he
has given us, however, is not the petty external truth of chronicle,
but the higher truth that Aristotle discerned in the best fiction,
a truth which is hardly to be attained without some perception
of a significant relation between fiction and reality. For an ex-
cellent study of this aspect of the poem as revealed by its style,
see E. B. Irving, Jr., "The Heroic Style in *The Battle of Maldon*,"
*Studies in Philology*, LVIII (1961), 457–467.

It has always been difficult to assess the exact blend of feelings
with which the poet regards the leader, Byrhtnoþ; for although
at most points his admiration is unequivocal, he makes Byrhtnoþ
fully responsible for the decision that constitutes the turning-
point of the action and costs both his own life and the lives of his
loyal retainers. It is possible to argue that the historical Byrhtnoþ
had very good reason to accept the challenge of the vikings, for
he may have thought there was no other way to prevent them
from evading the battle and attacking some other undefended
part of the coast; [2] but the poet does not consider this aspect of
the problem. For him, the decision is simply catastrophic in the
light of its tragic consequences, and the motives that provoke it
reside in the character of Byrhtnoþ and the cunning with which
the vikings take advantage of it. It is partly his integrity they
count on, the certainty that he will not break his word when he
gives them leave to cross the ford; but it is also his pride, his
readiness to take a dare. The poet seems very clearly to recognize
this trait in the phrase *for his ofermōde* in line 89. I have allowed
Gordon's definition of *ofermōd*, "great pride, overconfidence," to
stand in the glossary because I think that whatever moral blame

2 See W. A. Samouce, "General Byrhtnoth," *Journal of English and Ger-
manic Philology*, LXII (1963), 129–135.

the poet attaches to Byrhtnoþ is not very severe and is mingled with admiration for a magnanimity that is almost inseparable from this imperfection. Yet no doubt it is an imperfection. The case against a too complacent acceptance of Byrhtnoþ as hero has been put by Tolkien in a brief but penetrating essay which reveals his abiding sympathy for the heroism of the little man.[3]

For a grasp of the action it is useful to accept the hypothesis first advanced by E. D. Laborde, *English Historical Review*, XL (1925), 161–162, that the vikings had sailed up the estuary of the river Blackwater, then called the Pante, in Essex, to a small island called Northey near the village of Maldon, evidently planning to use the island as their base for raids on the neighboring countryside. This island was cut off from the mainland at high tide, but at low tide a ford gave access to the shore on the Maldon side of the river. When the poet says at line 97 that the vikings bore their shields *west ofer Pantan* he is approximately correct: the exact direction is said to be southwest.

For the setting, the identification of persons, the general historical background, and many particular notes, an indispensable guide is the edition by E. V. Gordon, Methuen's Old English Library, 1937; second edition, 1949. The general appraisal of the poem in the introduction is likewise of value. For the text alone and some helpful notes, the edition by Dobbie, *Anglo-Saxon Minor Poems*, 7–16, should also be consulted. In my presentation of the fragmentary text, based on John Elphinston's transcription of the burnt Old English manuscript, I have depended entirely on Gordon's and Dobbie's reports. My glossary of proper names gives only a digest of the much richer informa-

---

[3] J. R. R. Tolkien, "The Homecoming of Beorhtnoth Beorhthelm's Son," *English Association Essays and Studies*, New Series VI (1953), 1–18. The central part of this is an imaginary dialogue on the field of Maldon after the battle. The essay on *ofermod* is at the end, pp. 13–18. See also a more limited comment in support of Tolkien by F. S. Battaglia, "Notes on *Maldon*: Toward a definitive *ofermod*," *English Language Notes*, II (1965), 247–249.

tion in Gordon's edition, and at several points I have referred to
his notes in support or illustration of definitions in the main
glossary.

## Notes

4. *hycgan to handum,* "be intent on (the work of) hands"—
that is, "on deeds of arms" (Gordon).

5. The pronoun *þæt* is the object of *onfunde,* anticipating the
clause in line 6. It need not be translated. The same construction
appears in lines 36, 84, and 246.

23. *þær him lēofost wæs,* literally, "where it was most pleasing
to him"—that is, "where he was most pleased to be" (Gordon).

34. *ġif ġē spēdaþ to þām,* " 'if you are prosperous to that ex-
tent,' i.e. if you are wealthy enough to meet our demand."
(Gordon's tentative explanation; the idiom is not found else-
where.)

45. *sǣ-lida.* If this word is correct, the alliteration of the second
half-line is irregular, falling on *sæġeþ,* which should yield prece-
dence to *folc.* The line runs too smoothly to invite rearrange-
ment, but it seems possible that *sǣ-lida* is a scribal substitution
for a less familiar compound with the same meaning, such as
*flot-lida,* which would alliterate in orthodox fashion with *folc.*
There are several departures in this poem from the strict metrical
practice of earlier poets, but this particular departure looks more
radical than most.

48. *here-ġeatwe.* Most editors have retained the manuscript
reading, *-geatu,* interpreting it as accusative singular even though
other feminine *wō*-stem nouns have accusative singular *-we.*
Retention of *-geatu* in an unnormalized text is defensible, espe-
cially since the recorded instances of the compound show some-

what irregular endings and a tendency to use the plural rather than the singular; but since I am normalizing I have followed Kluge's *Lesebuch* (to which Dobbie draws attention) in reading -*geatwe*. The general meaning "war-equipment" makes good sense, as Dobbie maintains, but I agree with Gordon in accepting the richer meaning "heriot," first proposed by C. Brett, *Modern Language Review*, XXII, 260. See the glossary.

51. *unforcūþ eorl*. Gordon points out that the phrase is traditional, occurring in reverse order at *Andreas* 475 and again at 1263, both times with reference to Andrew himself. Gordon thinks the meaning of the adjective in *Andreas* is primarily "dauntless" with some connotation of nobility, but the most recent editor of that poem, K. R. Brooks, contents himself with the more literal interpretation, "not notorious; of unstained reputation"; and this seems nearer the mark in *Maldon* also. The negative expression allows Byrhtnoþ to say in effect that he has not yet suffered disgrace and does not intend to suffer it now, without claiming to be a paragon of nobility or courage.

75. *sē wæs hāten Wulfstān*. This parenthesis has a prosaic look, though it may be intentional. The orthodox verse-formula here would be simply *Wulfstān hāten*, with alliteration where it belongs, on the first lift.

115. *sweostor sunu*. A sister's son was traditionally dear among the Germanic peoples. Gordon quotes Tacitus in illustration of the antiquity of the sentiment. The poet shows his consciousness of the tradition as well as his sense of design by opening his account of the slain with the death of the sister's son and the quick reprisal for it.

136-137. As Gordon points out, Byrhtnoþ breaks the spear-shaft by thrusting the edge of his shield against it, and this action imparts a strain to the fragment carrying the spearhead—springs it—so that it quivers and flies out of the wound. Note the

play on transitive *sprengde* and intransitive *sprang*. The subject
of *sprengde* can be either Byrhtnoþ or the shaft, which in burst-
ing imparts a spring to the fragment.

143. *ōðerne*, "another (viking)."

170 ff. I have adopted Dobbie's punctuation for 170 and 171,
which enables us to hold together lines 166–171 as a progression
from Byrhtnoþ's dropping of his sword to his sinking to the
ground. The half-line at 172 introducing the prayer is clearly in
need of a mate, either before or after it, and there may have been
a greater loss; but in any event the prayer should be set apart
from the exhortation to the retainers in 168–170, which is
uttered by Byrhtnoþ as he makes a last effort not to fall.

183. Like Gordon and Dobbie I have allowed this obviously
faulty line to stand because I do not know how to correct it.

212. *ġemunaþ þāra mǣla*. Dobbie emends differently. Keeping
*þa mǣla* of the manuscript as a correct accusative plural of *mǣl*,
"speech," on the assumption that this word (not elsewhere
recorded) is feminine, he emends *ge munu* to *gemunan*, calling
this a first person plural imperative (which I should prefer to
call a hortatory subjunctive), on the analogy of *Christ and Satan*
207. He maintains that the loss of *n* is more likely than the loss
of *þ*. But since the next word begins with *þ* the odds would ap-
pear to be at least even. Furthermore the *gemunan* of *Christ and
Satan* 207 is made clear by the explicit *gemunan we* in 202 at
the head of the series of subjunctives. On the whole, therefore,
Grein's form, *gemunaþ*, seems better. The choice between *þä*
(supported by the manuscript) and *þāra* (the emendation
adopted by Sweet, Wyatt, and Gordon) is not so clear. The
gender of *mǣl* may be feminine, as Dobbie assumes, following the
deduction made by Bosworth-Toller and Holthausen, among
others, from this particular passage. But the Old Norse *mál*,
"speech," is neuter, and so is Old English *mæðel*, which is simply

an alternative form of the same word *mǣl*. Again, though *gemunan* often takes the accusative, and does so in this poem at 196, examples with the genitive in Bosworth-Toller include several that have to do with being mindful of words or speeches. Perhaps the choice between genitive and accusative depended somewhat on the shade of meaning and the object governed. If *mǣla* is genitive, its gender can as well be neuter as feminine. Consequently I have rather hesitantly retained the emendation favored by Gordon.

224. *hē wæs ǣġðer mīn mǣġ and mīn hlāford.* It is tempting to read this line in total disregard of the customary verse-rhythm, with the following major stresses:

hē wæs ǽġðer mīn mǽġ and mīn hláford

That is the ordinary way to say it. But by sticking to the rhythm indicated by the metrical form, with its alliteration on *m* and its apparent adherence to the familiar verse-types classified as A3 and C by Sievers, we get an unexpected but significant shade of meaning. In the following notation I use ′ for primary accent, ` for secondary, and I double these marks, ″ and ‶ , for the syllables that are most prominent by the combined testimony of meter and meaning. Vertical bars indicate the limits of the approximately isochronous measures:

hé wæs | ǽġðer | mín″ mǽ̋ġ and | mín″ hlá̋fòrd |

The double primary accent on *mǣġ* modifies the customary rhythm slightly in order to bring out the parallelism of *mǣġ* and *hlāford,* and this can be further emphasized by a slight pause at the cæsura; but the really surprising feature of this reading is the emphasis on *mīn,* and if we take careful note of Ælfwine's whole speech and remember that the poet has chosen him as the first speaker, we shall see that this is a calculated emphasis. Ælfwine's affliction is the greatest possible, as he has said, because for him (but not for everyone among the retainers) the loss is double. Presumably he is the closest of Byrhtnoþ's kinsmen, now that Wulfmær, the sister's son mentioned in line 113, is dead. Since no subsequent speaker claims kinship we may assume that most of the other members of the group, if not all, are unrelated. Because Ælfwine is aware of this difference, he sets the example of sacrifice and puts a certain emphasis on *mīn*. We do not need to exaggerate this emphasis to the point of turning the gesture into an uncalled-for assertion of superiority to his less well-connected associates, some of whom may in fact be equally noble. The distinction is one of kinship, not rank, and the privilege it carries is simply the obligation to die first. As one man after another follows his example, the poet shows us in everyone, high and low, an equal nobility of spirit.

230 ff. Offa's approval of Ælfwine's exhortation, his use of the first person plural, his explanation of the disastrous mistake made by some who had followed Godric in flight, and the fact that unlike the other speakers he does not immediately go forth to die—all point to the assumption that he was second in command to Byrhtnoþ and has now assumed the leadership.

283. The meaning of *cellod* remains unknown.

284. It has not, I think, been observed by previous editors that something is missing before this line. The antecedent implied by *þone* in 286 does not appear, and if we look more narrowly at the passage with this hint to guide us we see that the account of Offa's death is incomplete. There should have been mention of a viking's assault upon Offa, for it is the *lærig* of Offa's shield that bursts and his corselet that sings a terrible song. He has been fatally wounded, and though he manages to kill his assailant, he falls in the very act of doing so and is cut to pieces at once by other vikings.

300. For a desperate attempt to resolve the confusion of names

here, see the glossary of proper names under *Wistan* and *Wīghelm*. The reflexive datives *him* in this line and *mē* in 318 mark a distinction of meaning for the verb *licgan*. At all other places in the poem it refers to someone who is already lying prostrate or to an enemy who is caused to lie dead. At the two places mentioned, the person who is the subject of the verb is felt to be sacrificing himself voluntarily and so to be deliberately assuming a prostrate position. The sense indicated by the pronoun can be conveyed by translating the verb as "lie down". See the note on *The Dream of the Rood* 63 for a possible though less interesting parallel.

## The Wanderer *

The quotation marks in this edition are so placed as to imply that the poem consists principally of two complementary speeches, the first (1–5 and 8–57) uttered by the *eardstapa* or wanderer of line 6, the second (58–110) by the philosophical person who is described as *snottor on mōde* in line 111, and that the poet, as master of ceremonies, after identifying the second speaker, supplies a bit of sage advice by way of epilogue (112–115). The main body of the poem (8–110, with or without 1–5) has ordinarily been regarded as a monologue spoken by the *eardstapa*, who after speaking of his own experiences and the sufferings of others like himself philosophizes more broadly and thus earns the descriptive epithet of line 111. This is a perfectly possible way to read the poem, and anyone who wishes to read it so still can readily do so by ignoring the closing quotation mark after line 57. I prefer to think that the *eardstapa* and the *snottor on mōde* are different chiefly because the characterization becomes much sharper if the poem is read in that way; but its total meaning as a sequence of ideas and emotions is very little

* See Supplement, p. 221, for the editor's retraction of the dialogue theory.

altered. I have given a full exposition of my reading in an essay, "Dramatic Voices in *The Wanderer* and *The Seafarer*," in *Franciplegius: Medieval and Linguistic Studies in honor of Francis Peabody Magoun, Jr.,* edited by J. B. Bessinger, Jr. and Robert P. Creed, New York University Press, 1965, pp. 164–193. This same essay will serve as a guide to a number of articles published since the edition by Krapp and Dobbie in *The Exeter Book* ("Anglo-Saxon Poetic Records," III), Columbia University Press, 1936. For a good presentation of the poem as essentially a monologue, see S. B. Greenfield, "*The Wanderer*: A Reconsideration of Theme and Structure," *Journal of English and Germanic Philology*, L (1951), 451–465. Working on the same assumption, J. L. Rosier has made an interesting study of the imagery in "The Literal-Figurative Identity of *The Wanderer*," *PMLA*, LXXIX (1964), 366–369. An important new edition, separately edited by R. F. Leslie with introduction, notes, and glossary, has been published by the University Press, Manchester, England, 1966. Unfortunately it appeared too late to be of service here.

The poem has many elements of elegiac lament interspersed with philosophic meditation, and can be seen, in the last analysis, as somewhat akin to the type of consolation developed on the grand scale in the *Consolatio Philosophiae* of Boethius, one feature of such consolations being the effort to alleviate a personal sorrow by recognition of the instability of all earthly values and the necessity of seeking for lasting satisfactions in another realm. Two critics comment pertinently on this aspect of the poem: R. M. Lumiansky, "The Dramatic Structure of the Old English *Wanderer*," *Neophilologus*, XXXIV (1950), 104–112, and J. E. Cross, "On the Genre of *The Wanderer*," *Neophilologus* XLV (1961), 63–75. Yet it seems clear that the poet was a good deal less interested in the possible medicinal virtue of his discourse than in the imaginative realization of loss and loneliness in this unstable world.

Almost equally interesting, and more sharply evident if there are two speakers, is the interplay of traditional attitudes of the heroic, pre-Christian tradition with the ideas and feelings made available by Christian, largely Mediterranean, learning. The author and his chief speaker or speakers are Christians in the conventional sense, but the poem is full of tensions of a sort that are still with us, if with some change of costume.

The Exeter Book, an anthology written in an unusually handsome script of about A.D. 975, containing the unique copies of this and the next two poems, is available in facsimile: *The Exeter Book of Old English Poetry*, with introductory chapters by R. W. Chambers, Max Förster, and Robin Flower. London, 1933.

## Notes

1. *ān-haga*, "solitary one." This word is used to describe Beowulf when he has lost his uncle Hygelac and all his former comrades in the battle with the Franks and Frisians and is forced to swim home alone. Thus it has no necessary connection with the religious recluse, and is certainly not so used here.

7. On the puzzling grammatical form of *hryre*, see the glossary.

15. *wēriġ-mōd*. This has often been taken as two words, "a dejected spirit," but several editors from Sweet to Magoun have printed it as a compound adjective with the force of a noun, "a disheartened (man)." This reading sharpens the distinction between the clause to which it belongs and the varied clause in the next line with its impersonal *se hrēo hyġe*, where such a distinction may possibly be indicated by the use of *se*.

17. The masculine noun *hyġe*, which occurs in the preceding line, is apparently to be understood after *drēoriġne*.

23. *heolstre.* This reading, that of the manuscript, seems better than Bright's emendation to the nominative *heolstor*, since it makes the wanderer the subject. He himself has buried his lord. In 84–85 a similar situation is imagined.

25. *sōhte sele-drēoriġ sinces bryttan.* If, as previous editors have assumed, *sele* and *drēoriġ* are separate words, the line means "Dejected, I sought the hall of a giver of treasure." But this interpretation conflicts with the order of words and the meter. The order is awkward because *drēoriġ*, modifying the subject of the verb, is sandwiched between the object, *sele*, and *sinces bryttan*, which has to be taken as a genitive phrase limiting the object. To convey this intricate structure orally requires a peculiar emphasis on *drēoriġ* and a pause after it. Such a reading, difficult at best, runs counter to the metrical pattern, which subordinates *drēoriġ* to the bearers of the alliteration, *sōhte* and *sele*. The difficulty is overcome by reading *sele-drēoriġ*, "sad for want of a hall," and taking *sinces bryttan* as the object of *sōhte*: "sad for want of a hall, I sought a giver of treasure." [1] The compound here postulated occurs nowhere else. It exhibits a rare but not unexampled relation between its two members, being almost exactly paralleled by the modern "homesick" and by Old English *wine-ġeōmor*, "mournful for loss of friends," which occurs at Beowulf 2239. The idea of deprivation that must be supplied for the understanding of all these compounds is readily suggested by their second members. (The OED derives *homesick* from *homesickness*, apparently a translation of German *Heim-weh*. The same German word appears to have given rise, as early as 1678, to neo-Latin *nostalgia*, formed from Greek elements.)

27. *mine wisse*, "might know of my (people)." There are several parallels in Old English to this use of *min* without a

---

[1] This reading was first suggested by Walther Fischer, *Anglia*, LIX (1935), 300. It has now been adopted independently by R. F. Leslie in the edition cited above.

specified noun, of which the following occur in verse: *hēold mīn tela,* "I held well (what was) mine," *Beowulf* 2737; *ġif ic mōt for þē mīne wealdan,* "if I am permitted by you to rule (her who is) mine," *Genesis* 2253; *þæt þū mundbora mīnum wǣre,* "that you would be a protector to my (people, followers?)," *Descent into Hell* 75. One must take *wisse* as "might know of," not "might know, be acquainted with," which would presumably have been expressed by *cūðe.* The traditional emendation, *mīn myne wisse,* "might feel affection for me," is adapted from a passage of uncertain meaning, *Beowulf* 169, and seems unnecessary if *mīne wisse* is interpreted as here suggested.

37. The verb *wāt* is used elliptically, "knows (how)," to introduce the entire passage in lines 39–48, where the main clauses begin with *þynċeþ,* 41, and *Ponne,* 45. Translate: "Indeed he that must long be deprived of his beloved lord's counsel knows how, when sorrow and sleep joined together bind the wretched solitary, as they often do, it seems to him. . . . Then. . . ." What starts as a rather vague generalization becomes particularized as the passage advances. (See Leslie's note for a more elaborate discussion of the grammar.)

53. *secga ġeseldan.* Usually interpreted as "men's companions in the hall," where *secga* seems superfluous; but see glossary, and the article by Vivian Salmon, "*The Wanderer* and *The Seafarer,* and the Old English Conception of the Soul," *Modern Language Review,* LV (1960), 1–10.

53. *eft.* This traditional emendation is better than the MS *oft,* if I understand the passage as a whole, because it sticks to a single imagined situation instead of generalizing.

58 ff. If we suppose that a second speaker begins here, we can give extra force to *mīn* as implying "my mind too." Indeed if the wanderer is still speaking it may seem odd that he should talk of the darkening of his mind at this point, as if he had not al-

ready known darkness enough in his own experience. A new speaker can properly counterbalance the wanderer's experience with reflections on the general human condition, viewing what has seemed the special plight of a few exiles as a much more general affliction, and deriving his melancholy from contemplation rather than from any personal sorrow. The opening "Forþon" can be taken as something vaguely connective, "As to that," or just "Indeed."

80b. The *Sume* of the manuscript is probably correct, referring with understatement to *many* who fell in battle. The singulars that follow suggest the varying fate of individual corpses left on the battlefield: one is carried off by a bird of prey, another eaten by a wolf, a third buried by a sad-faced survivor.

81. *forþ-weġ*. On this minor emendation, see the note on *The Dream of the Rood* 125.

83. *Dēaðe ġedǣlde*, "shared with Death." This seems the most satisfactory interpretation, since the victim is already dead when the wolf devours him. The poet imagines Death and the wolf as rival scavengers, dividing the spoils.

88. *Sē* can best be taken as equivalent to *Sē-þe*, indefinite "he who; whoever."

92. *Hwǣr cōm*, "where is; what has become of?" On the theme expressed by this formula, see J. E. Cross, " 'Ubi Sunt' Passages in Old English," *Vetenskaps-Societetens i Lund, Årsbok 1956*, 23–44. The earliest known examples are in the Old Testament, but there, the note of regret is less conspicuous than that of scorn or warning.

# The Seafarer *

Like *The Wanderer*, this poem has been punctuated in accordance with a novel theory of its form, and here it has been neces-

* See Supplement, p. 224, for the editor's retraction of the dialogue theory.

sary to add marginal identifications of the supposed speakers, since the poem is in direct dramatic discourse from beginning to end, lacking entirely the narrative interpolations that identify the speaker or speakers of *The Wanderer* at lines 6 and 111. In this respect *The Seafarer* resembles *The Dream of the Rood, Deor, The Wife's Lament, The Husband's Message, Wulf and Eadwacer,* and most of the Old English riddles; nor has its dramatic character ever been doubted. But ever since 1869, when Max Rieger put forward his theory that the poem is a dialogue between an old man and a youth, there has been disagreement about the number of speakers. Most scholars have preferred to believe that there is only one speaker, since they think the evidence for a second is slight or non-existent; and those who have accepted the idea of a second speaker have not agreed about the limits of his speeches, though they have always supposed, with Rieger, that his first speech begins at line 33b; for it is the sentence that begins there, with its inclusion of the word *self*, that first prompted Rieger to suspect the presence of a second speaker. Indeed this sentence supplies the only grammatical evidence that can be put forward for a change of speakers, and it is my opinion, as it was Kluge's long ago, that there is no other change, at least throughout the fully dramatic part of the poem. But I suspect that the final lines, beginning with the hypermetric verses in line 103, are an epilogue somewhat like that of *The Wanderer*, in which the poet, as master of ceremonies, makes his own comments by way of bringing down the curtain and mediating between the audience and the fully dramatized characters who have spoken hitherto. I take the first speaker to be an experienced seafarer; the second, a younger man who has not yet been to sea and may or may not intend to make an actual voyage; for his philosophic temper and his avowed concern for the joys of the Lord allow us to suppose that he would speak of any great spiritual enterprise under the figure of a voyage.

I have discussed this whole problem at length in the essay

referred to above (p. 80), and must ask those who desire further explanation to consult it. Here I will say only that anyone who prefers to read the poem as a monologue can readily ignore the quotation marks and marginal directions. In my own opinion, much the best of the many interpretations of the poem as a monologue is that of Dorothy Whitelock, "The Interpretation of *The Seafarer*," *Early Cultures of North-West Europe* (H. M. Chadwick Memorial Studies), Cambridge, 1950, pp. 259–272. She believes that the single speaker is a religious man, a *peregrinus pro amore Dei*, who has chosen a life of seafaring and exile abroad as a means of mortifying the flesh and preparing himself for the joys of the life to come. Such characters there were in Anglo-Saxon England, and Professor Whitelock gives ample documentation in support of her theory. She argues very plausibly that such a person would be able to discourse feelingly of life at sea and yet philosophize about ultimate realities in imagery that has nothing to do with seafaring. This may well be so. I have proposed a different theory mainly because I am troubled about the grammatical implications of lines 33b–35, because I am not convinced of the psychological consistency of the discourse when read as a monologue, and still more because I think a poem so remarkably imaginative as this in its individual passages should have a more carefully controlled form than can readily be found in it if everything it contains is attributed to a single speaker. I think the form I have postulated enables one to find a significant progression of themes and contrast of characters; but the evidence for it is by no means incontrovertible.

There is an excellent edition of the poem—which in addition to its formal peculiarities has in some spots a distressingly corrupt text—by Mrs. I. L. Gordon, Methuen's Old English Library, 1960, upon which I have relied heavily in preparing this edition, and to which the reader is referred for bibliography, for a sane and perceptive introduction, and for a very rich and often delightful series of notes.

# Notes

15. *wreċċan lāstum*, "on the paths (or with the steps) of an exile." The theme is relevant, as shown by its proper occurrence at line 57; but the imagery here is confusing, for the notion of frequenting, or remaining on, the sea (*sǣ wunode*) seems essentially static and to that extent inharmonious with the activity of *lāstum* even if one is untroubled by the idea of walking the waves. Since there is one verse too many or too few at this point, I am inclined to cast out *wreċċan lāstum* as a stock phrase that has been carelessly added. Note that the next verse alliterates on *w* and forms an excellent second half-line for 15a. Thus, if we leave out the stock expression the passage becomes flawless in meaning and in meter.

24. *þæt* is a pronoun, object of *beġeall*, referring vaguely perhaps to the scene.

25. *ūriġ-feðra* does not alliterate and is too much like 24a to be right. Mrs. Goldsmith's suggestion, *hyrned-nebba,* applied elsewhere to the eagle, is apt and may be correct, but I am not sure the poet would have imitated so closely the rhythm and grammatical form of 24a. Perhaps *īsiġ-* and *ūriġ-feðra* were really alternate readings of 24a, and something totally different has been lost at 25a.

33b–35. "Truly (or indeed), thoughts are even now beating against my heart, urging that I myself make trial of the high (or deep) seas, the tumult of the salt waves." I accept Mrs. Gordon's suggestion that *heortan* is the object of *cnyssaþ*; but those who take *heortan* as a genitive with *ġeþōhtas*, and *cnyssaþ*, in the sense "urge," as comparable to verbs of saying or commanding, governing the clause only as object, may well be right. The real question is whether *self* does or does not need to imply that the speaker has never been to sea before. Scholars have differed on this point, but it seems to me that the odds are greatly in favor of that implication, and that therefore the speaker at this point is not the man who has been speaking hitherto.

38. *el-þēodiġra eard*. This expression has become a *cause célèbre*. If we take this section of the poem as having to do with ordinary voyaging (and at least on the surface it should), the words in question mean simply "the land of foreigners," those who are foreigners in relation to the speaker. But since this speaker later refers in an obviously metaphorical way to "this dead life on land," scorning not simply the landlubber but the worldling, whether he stays at home or puts to sea, it is possible that *el-þēodiġra eard* will bear a second, metaphorical meaning based on the doctrine that men are exiles on earth and the virtuous among them may hope to return to their proper home in heaven. Thus the phrase would mean "the home-land of those who are strangers on earth," and if so, the speaker is intimating already that heaven is his destination—though I heartily agree with Mrs. Gordon that he is not at the point of death. The notion that *el-þēodiġra eard* means heaven was put forward with a number of pertinent quotations from Old English homilies and their patristic sources by G. V. Smithers, "The Meaning of *The Seafarer* and *The Wanderer*," *Medium Ævum*, XXVI (1957), 137–153 (especially 147–151). I cannot agree that this is the only meaning of the expression, but I think it may be one meaning.

48–49. "The groves burst into bloom, adorn the manors, make beautiful the meadows; the world hastens on." The onset of summer is associated with the onward rush of time, which warns the prospective voyager to set forth before it is too late. The second half of the poem encourages one to extend the meaning to include the thought that the end of the world itself is not far off. J. E. Cross has connected the passage very interestingly with Gregory the Great's interpretation of a saying of Jesus about the figtree and the end of the world. See his note, "On the Allegory in the Seafarer," *Medium Ævum*, XXVIII (1959), 104–106.

53. The mournfulness attributed to the cuckoo may be a Celtic fancy. See Mrs. Gordon's Introduction, p. 17. Whatever its origin, the notion is here made part of the speaker's sense of foreboding.

56. I follow Mrs. Gordon in accepting Grein's emendation, *sēft-ēadiġ*.

58 ff. In this extraordinarily intense and imaginative passage the speaker's soul is likened to a bird that soars out over the waters, sights the far country of its desire, and comes back, a lone flier, ravenous with hunger for what it has seen, to urge the man himself to follow. In the article mentioned above I have suggested that the imagery is appropriate to an eagle.

64b–66. Professor Whitelock showed conclusively, in the article mentioned above, that this is the central statement of the poem, and that if one grasps its significance one cannot dismiss what follows as an interpolation.

68. *þeġna ġehwelcum*. The manuscript reading, *þinga gehwylce*, "in every circumstance," is a familiar formula used elsewhere in Old English poetry and not unintelligible here; but I think it is a careless substitution for the much more pertinent formula with which I have replaced it. The sentence as emended means, "Ever one of three things, for every man, before his last day, becomes a cause of uncertainty: sickness or old age or deadly violence will wrest the life from him who is fated to pass away." The *þeġna* supplies an antecedent for *his* in 69.

69. I follow Mrs. Gordon in accepting Grein's emendation, *tīd-dæġe*.

72 ff. In general my text and interpretation follow Mrs. Gordon, who is responsible for the emendation *biþ* in 72. But I begin a new sentence at 74, making *Þæt* a pronoun, object of *ġewyrċe*, anticipating the explanatory clause at 77. The emendation *fremum* is Kenneth Sisam's.

97 ff. This passage was reconstructed by Kenneth Sisam in the *Review of English Studies*, XXI (1945), 316–317. He noticed in it a general resemblance to Psalm 48 in the Vulgate, 49 in the Authorized Version. Compare the following verses in the latter:

> 6 They that trust in their wealth, and boast themselves in the multitude of their riches;
> 7 None of them can by any means redeem his brother, nor give to God a ransom for him. . . .
> 16 Be not thou afraid when one is made rich, when the glory of his house is increased;
> 17 For when he dieth he shall take nothing away.

Mrs. Gordon slightly modifies Sisam's translation as follows: "Though brother will strew with gold the grave for his brother born, bury [him] beside the dead with various treasures, that (i.e. the gold) will not go with him; nor can gold be a help to the soul that is full of sin in the presence of the terrible power of God, when he hoards it beforehand while he is still alive on earth." For further discussion see Sisam's article and Mrs. Gordon's note.

103. Mrs. Gordon translates this very persuasively: "Great is the terrible power of God, before which the earth will turn aside." She aptly compares *Apocalypsis* 20:11: *a cuius conspectu fugit terra* (Revelation 20:11: "from whose face the earth . . . fled away). The line serves well as the first line of the epilogue, making a solemn pronouncement on a theme glancingly mentioned by the previous speaker.

109–110. Although I accept in general Mrs. Gordon's interpretation, I assume that *mōde*, to which *þæt* refers, is understood as the object modified by the adjectives in 110: "A man must govern a headstrong spirit and keep it steady, and unfailing in its pledges, pure in its ways." Consequently we must not translate *mōde* as "temper."

111–112. I have modified the word-order of Holthausen's emendation, which seems plausible in spite of Mrs. Gordon's objection if we translate somewhat as follows: "Every man should govern with moderation his affection toward one he loves and his malice toward one he hates." What follows is corrupt, but it seems to be a continuation of the same thought: Even though a man should see his friend done to death by an enemy, he must restrain his grief and also be slow to wreak vengeance on the slayer; for men cannot control their destinies nor be held wholly responsible for their actions.

# Deor

This dramatic lyric, spoken by a scop who has had his own misfortune in the world of heroic legend and whose repertory is filled with the sorrows of other famous persons, is as remarkable for its craftsmanship as for its spirit. The unevenly spaced refrain is given gradually increased meaning by the number and variety of illustrations in the first five sections; then, after a delay, it assumes a final, quite unexpected poignancy. The poem has been edited by Kemp Malone, Methuen's Old English Library, 1933; fourth edition, 1966. Since 1933 Professor Malone has made an important discovery about the probable content of the story of Mæþhild and Geat. See his essay, "On *Deor* 14–17," *Modern Philology*, XL (1942), 1–18, reprinted in his *Studies in Heroic Legend and Current Speech*, edited by S. Einarsson and N. E. Eliason, Rosenkilde and Bagger, Copenhagen, 1959, pp. 142–157. His thoughts on the *Þēodrīc* of line 18 are extended in another essay in the same collection, pp. 116–123, "The Theodoric of the Rök Inscription," first published in 1934. M. W. Bloomfield, "The Form of *Deor*," *PMLA*, LXXIX (1964), 534–541, suggests that the refrain owes something to Old English charms. If so, the poet has transformed exorcism into wisdom.

# Notes

1. *Wēland.* The story of Weland the smith, maker of Beowulf's corselet and of many a famous sword, is told at some length in a poem in the Poetic Edda, the *Vǫlundarkviða*, and even more elaborately, but differently, in the Norwegian saga of Dietrich von Bern, the *Þiðrekssaga*. From these two we can piece together an outline that fits the implications in the first two stanzas of *Deor*. Weland, as a young man, came to work for a certain king named Niþhad, who, greedy for his wonderful productions and wanting to prevent his escape, took him by surprise and cut his hamstrings. Weland, in revenge, lured the two sons of Niþhad to his smithy, killed them, and made bowls out of their skulls, gems out of their eyeballs, and brooches out of their teeth. He presented these objects to Niþhad as masterpieces of his art. Later he ravished Niþhad's daughter, Beaduhild. Finally, having made a coat of feathers with the help of his brother Egill, he escaped, perching on the roof of Niþhad's palace long enough to tell him all he had done. Niþhad sickened and died. A son was born to Beaduhild, and within a few years she was reconciled to Weland, with whom she went to live as his wife. Their son, named Widia, was to become a notable adventurer.

1. *be wearnum,* "by hindrances," in allusion to the hamstringing. I have chosen this emendation from among many that have been proposed for the manuscript reading, *be wurman,* because its meaning is plausible and I can offer a conjecture to explain the scribe's mistake. The scribe spelled the smith's name *Welund,* though everywhere else in Old English it is spelled Weland or Welond. This suggests that he may have been copying from an earlier manuscript in which the scribe made his *a*'s with an open top, so that they could only with careful scrutiny be distinguished from *u*'s. Open-top *a*'s of this sort can be seen in the Leningrad MS of Bede and elsewhere. If the scribe mistook *a* for *u* in

*Weland*, he could have misread the next word, *warnum* (the Anglian spelling of *wearnum*) as *wurnum* and, not understanding this, have produced *wurman*, which he may or may not have regarded as a spelling of *wyrmum*, dative plural of *wyrm*, "snake." The spelling *wurm-* for *wyrm-* is common in Late West Saxon manuscripts, but does not appear elsewhere in the Exeter Book. If *be wyrmum* is by chance the right reading, it may, as Kemp Malone has suggested, be a reference to gold snake-rings or to swords with serpentine decoration, either rings or swords being thought of as products of Weland's smithy and a cause of Niþhad's covetousness.

5–6. A witty allusion to the hamstringing, as if the supple sinews, being cut, were equivalent to bonds. [1] The preposition *on* governs the accusative *hine*. The plural *nīeda* is used concretely to mean physical restraints, fetters; though of course these are figurative fetters.

7. Freely, "That (the misfortune just alluded to) has passed over; so may this (whatever is troubling any of us now)." For the curious impersonal construction with genitive, see the glossary, *ofergān*, *magan*, and *þes*.

14–17. This obscure passage, in which *māna* is a normalized form of Malone's emendation, *mōne*, for MS *monge*, may be translated, "We have learned that the lamentations of Mæþhild, the lady of Geat, grew unbounded, so that her sorrowful love deprived her of all sleep." The formulaic *wē . . . ġefrugnon*, "we have learned," frequently encloses part of the statement it in-

---

[1] I am not persuaded by Karl Jost's recent suggestion that the sinew-bonds be taken literally on the assumption that the poet did not know the story of the hamstringing and was thinking of Judges 16:7, where, according to the Vulgate, Samson tells Delilah (falsely) that he can be bound with *septem nerviceis funibus, necdum siccis et adhuc humentibus*, "seven thongs made of sinews, not yet dry and still moist." *Festschrift zum 75. Geburtstag von Theodor Spira*, ed. H. Viebrock and W. Erzgräber (Heidelberg: Carl Winter, 1961), 86–87.

troduces, though nowhere else does it enclose the beginning of a that-clause. Malone, in the article mentioned above, has very persuasively urged that Mæþhild and Geat are the principals in a story told in slightly differing versions in two ballads, one Norwegian, the other Icelandic. In the Norwegian version, Gaute finds his bride Magnhild (Icelandic Gauti and Magnhild) in tears because she foresees that she will drown in a certain river during her wedding journey. In spite of precautions she falls into this river at a bridge, but Gaute, calling for his harp, plays on it so strongly that Magnhild rises up, still seated on her horse, escaping altogether from the power of the water-demon who had tried to capture her. In the Icelandic version, Gauti succeeds in recovering only her dead body. The names correspond pretty well, since Scandinavian *Gaut* is the same as Old English *Ġēat,* and in Old German the name-element *māþ* (OE *mǣþ*), "honor," became confused with *maht,* "power," which corresponds in meaning to Scandinavian *magn.* The OE *Mǣþ-* thus points to Germany rather than Scandinavia as the source of this poet's knowledge of the story.

18. *Þēodrīc* is perhaps the legendary representative of Theodoric, son of Clovis, who ruled the Franks from 511 to 534. Many centuries later, in Germany, a fantastic story had grown up about a hero named Wolfdietrich, who, though his adventures began in the East, is commonly identified with this Theodoric or his son. In the late version of the legend Wolfdietrich spends many years as an exile in a foreign city named Meran, evidently taken to be the well-known city in the Tyrol. Possibly a much earlier form of the legend, otherwise unknown to us, made Theodoric an exile, ruling unhappily over the city of a foreign people called the Mærings. Kemp Malone, who has supported this interpretation, believes that the Mærings of the legend were originally Visigoths, who had held territory in Gaul before they were overcome by Clovis. In that case it might even be supposed that our Þeodric ruled the Mærings as a conqueror and it was they who

were unhappy; but the poet gives us little to go on, and the exile theory is a bit more probable. Other scholars have supposed that Þeodric is the great Ostrogoth, who in legend, as Dietrich von Bern, spent long years in exile among the Huns—but not, so far as we know, in any city connected with a people called Mærings.

21. *Eormanrīc* is the famous Ermanaric of history, king of the Goths for a long period until his death in 375. He was the powerful ruler of a vast empire stretching from the Baltic to the Black Sea, but the stories of his tyrannical behavior—especially his savage treatment of his son, his wife, and several of his nephews, under the influence of a wicked counselor—appear to belong wholly to legend, and to have accumulated gradually until they emerge in Norse saga and Middle High German epic of the twelfth and thirteenth centuries. In the *Þiðrekssaga* Ermanaric has become king of Rome and uncle of Theodoric of Verona (Bern). Added to other crimes against his kin is his responsibility for Theodoric's thirty-year exile among Attila's Huns. The Old Norse *Lay of Hamthir* (*Hamðismál*) in the Edda and the *Vǫlsungasaga* represent older and different traditions, as does *Deor*. The Old English *Widsith*, still older, lays stress on Eormanric's munificence and mentions almost parenthetically his dangerous temper. In *Beowulf* we have one brief allusion to his threatened vengeance against the outlaw Hama, who appears to have stolen from him a necklace of great value and run away from his *heteniðas*. Here in *Deor* his tyranny afflicts everyone in his realm.

26. *ofercumen wǣre*. Observe that *ofercuman* here is used in the same impersonal way as *ofergān* in the refrain. See the glossary.

28. The inverted order here introduces a supposition: "If a man sits full of sorrow."

37. *Dēor*. This character was presumably invented by the poet,

since he is not otherwise known; but he connects himself with persons who figure in a very ancient legend, a version of which in Middle High German, contained in the poem *Kudrun*, comes closer than the Norse versions to explaining the allusion to Heorrenda along with the Hedenings. King Heden laid plans to steal a famous beauty, Hild, from the watchful care of her father, King Hagen. He took with him some helpers, including the giant Wate (still talked of as Wade in Middle English) and a wonderfully talented minstrel named Horant (the Heorrenda of *Deor*). This man so captivated Hild by his singing and harping that she consented to elope with Heden. In the Norse versions, which are older and differently descended, the result is a tragic pursuit and an endless battle between Heden and Hagen, over which Hild, true to her name, presides; but in *Kudrun* we have a more romantic version in which the lovers escape. We may judge that, in the fiction implied here, Heorrenda supplanted Deor in anticipation of his aid in the seduction, or else as a reward for it. In any event Deor was overwhelmed by two forces at once, the sensational artistry of Heorrenda and the spell of Hild.

The main versions of the Hild story, including that which appears in *Kudrun*, are interestingly summarized by R. W. Chambers in *Widsith, A Study in Old English Heroic Legend*, Cambridge, 1912, pp. 100–109.

# Old English Versification

## With Particular Attention to the Seven Poems

The study of versification in any ancient poetry may have several objectives. The most important of these for the lover of poetry is to recapture as nearly as possible the actual sound and movement of the verse as it was uttered by the poets themselves and their most accomplished contemporaries; and concurrently, if the lover is also a critic, to know enough about the prosodical rules to appreciate the poet's skill. But Old English poetry was composed in accordance with a now obsolete tradition. No contemporary has left us an account of its prosody, and the surviving manuscripts, remarkable as they are for their time, fall far short of the accuracy we desire. The first task for modern scholars has been to discover enough about the versification as commonly practiced to guide the editor in lineating his text and clearing it of obvious corruption. Observation of basic rules and classification of syllabic patterns have enabled us to distinguish verses and to determine whether or not a given verse conforms to the usual practice. The metrical rules *consciously* observed by the poets are not fully known. Still less certain are the basic rhythm by which the poets were guided as they composed, and the particular rhythms, or the range of acceptable rhythms, of the spoken verses.

In spite of these uncertainties, the present sketch sets forth, in addition to some more or less incontestable facts about the construction of Old English verses, what I believe is a probable theory of the basic rhythm and a survey of its principal variations, especially as they appear in the seven poems here edited. Elsewhere I have shown the grounds for this theory and exhibited in detail its application to the three thousand odd lines of *Beowulf*.[1] I have also provided readings to illustrate the rhythm

[1] *The Rhythm of Beowulf*, New Haven: Yale University Press, 1942; second, revised edition in paperback, 1966.

on two phonograph records, one for the seven poems and another for *Beowulf*. [2]

The Old English poets inherited from their Germanic ancestors a single verse form. They applied it to all genres, and modified but never abandoned it. Two verses, each· conforming to one of several approved types, are bound together by a carefully controlled system of initial rhyme, loosely called alliteration. The form is often referred to as the alliterative long line, because in modern editions the pair of verses is printed as a single line, usually with a space in the middle to separate the first half-line from the second; but the form was invented before the literary period, and when poems came to be written down, the scribes copied them continuously across the page as if they were prose, marking the metrical form, if at all, merely by points between verses. [3] Hence, although it is convenient to speak of lines and half-lines, the poets themselves would have thought rather of verses and verse-pairs. In what follows the first half-line will sometimes be called the "on-verse"; the second, the "off-verse." [4]

It is necessary to consider as a metrical entity each member of the verse-pair as well as the combination of the two. [5] A single

[2] These records are published by Educational Audio-Visual, Inc., Pleasantville, New York. The seven poems are recorded on both sides of a twelveinch disc containing selections from *The Dream of the Rood* and *The Battle of Maldon* and the other five poems complete except for two and a half corrupt lines near the end of *The Seafarer*. The selections from *Beowulf* are on one side of a ten-inch disc. The other side contains selections from Chaucer, read by the late Helge Kökeritz.

[3] Even Latin poetry at this period was usually written continuously across the page, the verses being marked by punctuation only. See, for example, the treatment of Bede's alphabetic elegiacs in the Moore MS. of his history, f. 86ᵛ. The Leningrad MS., f. 100ᵛ, is exceptional in starting each verse on a new line.

[4] German *Anvers* and *Abvers*. German scholars were the pioneers in analyzing Old Germanic verse, and their terminology has had wide influence. Some writers in English prefer to speak of the "*a*-verse" and the "*b*-verse."

[5] The unpaired verses that occur now and then in the manuscripts usually point to scribal error. There is one poem, however, the lyric *Wulf and Eadwacer* in the Exeter Book, in which the verses are arranged in three unequal groups, each of which is closed in thought and form by an unpaired verse with double alliteration.

verse invariably consists of one or more complete words, and its metrical integrity is usually marked by some degree of syntactical separation from its neighbors and by its conformity to one among several familiar syllabic patterns. The rules governing on-verse and off-verse are basically similar and some verses are interchangeable, but in the on-verse the poets favor certain alliterative and syllabic patterns which they carefully avoid in the off-verse. As a result, the majority of the pairs actually employed are metrically irreversible.

As in modern blank verse and simple couplet forms, patterns that extend beyond the line or verse-pair are irregular and therefore not metrical but syntactical and rhetorical. A tendency toward stanza form has been pointed out in the commentary on Cædmon's Hymn, but it is only a tendency. The refrain in *Deor*, itself a rarity, closes verse groups of markedly unequal length.

In most poems a great deal of the rhythmic interest arises from the varying relation between the syntactical and metrical patterns. The syntactical coherence of the single verse is rarely disturbed, [6] but that of the pair, the long line, is frequently relaxed or negated. Clauses and sentences may run on from verse to verse, now in accordance with the metrical pairing, now in opposition to it. Enjambment of this sort varies in frequency and degree from passage to passage and poem to poem. Cædmon's Hymn, as one would expect from its extreme brevity and its lyrical feeling, is mostly end-stopped; yet even here a syntactical counter-movement is introduced in the middle of the third line. What is more surprising is the prevalence of end-stopped lines in *The Battle of Maldon*. Only now and then—as in Offa's speech in lines 230–243—do we find a succession of heavy medial pauses coupled with a running on at the end of the line.

The verses themselves may be of two main kinds. Much the commoner of these is central to the entire Germanic tradition and is called the "normal" form. The other, being fuller and

---

[6] That is, the boundaries of words and phrases within the verse are usually less conspicuous than those between verses. Among the occasional exceptions is *Wanderer* 64b.

weightier, is called "hypermetric." [7] It may have been no part of
the Germanic heritage but an invention of the Old English poets
prior to the eighth century. If so, they must have passed it along
to the Old Saxons of the continent, for we find it employed with
great frequency in two Old Saxon poems of the ninth century, the
*Heliand* and the fragmentary *Genesis*. Since both forms are rep-
resented in *The Dream of the Rood*, *The Wanderer*, and *The
Seafarer*, both must be described, but much the greater part of
our attention will be devoted to the normal form.

# The Normal Verses

## 1. Alliteration

Some of the finer details of the alliterative technique depend
for their understanding on a thorough acquaintance with the
varying structure of the verses. Nevertheless it is convenient to
begin with alliteration. It is almost the first thing we notice in
Old English poetry, the poets themselves had to pay constant
attention to it, and it serves the modern investigator as a pro-
visional guide to the controlling stresses of the verses. Both nor-
mal and hypermetric forms employ it, and much of what follows
applies to both; but certain generalizations apply with greater
accuracy to the normal form.

The alliteration with which we are here concerned is a strictly
regulated device for linking verses in pairs regardless of their
syntactical relation. As such it is limited to the initial sounds of
stressed syllables, [8] and is more accurately described as a rhyming
of initial consonants, what is called vocalic alliteration being a

[7] Sometimes "expanded" or "swelling" (German *Schwellvers*), but the first
of these two terms is ambiguous because of its application to certain varia-
tions of the normal verses.

[8] Thus, in *Brunanburh* 13—*secga swāte/siþþan sunne upp—siþþan* does
not participate in the conventional alliterative scheme (though of course its
*s* can be heard), because, as a conjunction, it is subordinate to the noun
*sunne* and the adverb *upp*.

special, negative instance rather than an exception. Among
initial consonants the rhyming is usually exact: *b* with *b*, *d* with
*d*, and so forth; but the palatal and the guttural *c*—the one
sounded like *k*, the other like the modern *ch*—were still accepted
as rhymes in spite of the sharp phonetic difference that had
developed between them.[9] The same is true of the palatal and
the guttural *g*, and here the examples are more numerous.[10]
The poet of *Maldon* is exceptional in distinguishing the two
forms.[11] When a syllable begins with two or more consonants, all
may alliterate (as do those beginning with *sw* in *Maldon* 118),
but usually only the first is required to do so. Exceptional are
the combinations *sc*, *sp*, and *st*, each of which normally alliterates
only with itself.[12]

What is called *vocalic* alliteration depends, not on the likeness
of initial vowels, but on the absence of initial consonants. Any

[9] Examples, even in *Beowulf*, are not very common, partly because words of
the substantive class beginning with *c* are not very numerous in the poetry,
and most of those that do appear have the *k*-sound in all dialects. Three
examples in the normalized text of *The Seafarer* depend on *čeald*, "cold,"
which was pronounced *cald* in Anglian, the probable dialect of the poet; and
one in *The Wanderer* involves the doubtfully palatal *c* of the accusative
*ceare*. There are only two persuasive instances in this book: *Seafarer* 5, in-
volving *cēol*, "ship"; and *Maldon* 76, involving the proper name *Cēola*.

[10] E.g., *Brunanburh* 44; *Rood* 7, 16, 18, 39, 77, 146 (with West Saxon
*gealg*, not with Anglian *galg*); *Wanderer* 22, 35, 52, 73; *Seafarer* 40, 62, 83, 92,
101; *Deor* 15.

[11] In *Maldon* the guttural alone alliterates in some twenty lines (13, 32,
etc.); the palatal alone in two (84, 274). In lines 32 and 192 there would be
double alliteration in the off-verse if the two sounds were equated, whereas
both lines alliterate regularly if only the guttural sound is considered.
Evidently the poet wished to observe a distinction. Hence in lines 100 and 265,
where the palatal *g* heads the first stressed syllable of each member of the
pair, the guttural *g* of the second stressed syllable of the on-verse is probably
not to be included in the alliterative scheme.

[12] For example, *sc* alliterates in *Brunanburh* 11, 19, *Rood* 54, and *Maldon*
40, 56, 98, 136; *st* in *Rood* 30, 40, 62, 71 and *Maldon* 19, 25, 122, 127, 249, 301;
*sp* (the rarest) in *Maldon* 34, 137. In *Maldon* 271, *stunde* is probably not
intended to alliterate with *sealde*, for what attracts attention is the end-
rhyme, on which I comment below.

two stressed syllables beginning with vowels are considered sufficiently alike to alliterate with each other, no matter whether the
vowels are the same or different. Indeed, the poets generally avoid
the alliteration of identical vowels, and make no distinction between simple vowels and diphthongs. Typical examples are the
fourth line of Cædmon's Hymn, where *ēce* alliterates with *ōr*, and
the first line of *Brunanburh*, where *Æðelstān* alliterates with
*eorla*. Evidently, then, vocalic alliteration has nothing in common
with assonance. Some theorists believe that it originated at a time
when a stressed syllable beginning with a vowel was preceded by
a glottal stop—the slight coughing sound produced by closure of
the glottis. This is a phenomenon that has been observed locally
among Germanic and other speakers, and it would have provided
a recognizable substitute for an ordinary consonant. It seems
equally possible, however, that the mere directness of attack on
the vowel, the absence of the expected consonant, was apprehended as a likeness; for an initial consonant checks or stops the
breath and produces a distinctive noise as a prelude to the unchecked sonority of the vowel. The unpreluded sonority of a
stressed vowel can be felt, by contrast, as a distinctive feature.

The poets were generally very careful about the number and
position of the alliterating syllables. Most verses have two
syllables that are more strongly stressed than the others. In the
off-verse the first of these two must alliterate and the second must
not. [13] In the on-verse one or both may alliterate, but the choice
is not entirely unrestricted. The first syllable regularly alliterates
unless it is decidedly weaker than the second; [14] and in certain
emphatic variations, where both syllables are heavily stressed,

[13] Exceptions are very rare in the stricter poems, and the few that turn
up in the manuscripts may be the fault of the scribes. Four more or less
plausible exceptions appear in *Maldon* 45b, 75b, and 288b (where the second
stressed syllable alliterates instead of the first), and 29b (where both stressed
syllables alliterate).

[14] So, in Cædmon's Hymn 4a and 8a, *ēce* takes precedence of *Dryhten* because they are both of the substantive class and *ēce* comes first. In line 1a, on
the other hand, the infinitive *herian*, though it comes last, takes precedence
of the adverb *nū*. In *Maldon* 80a, 242a, and 298a the rule is broken, for it
is the second of two grammatically equal words that carries the alliteration.

double alliteration is almost obligatory. Hence, if we consider only the four strongest syllables in the line or verse-pair, and represent those that alliterate by *a*, those that do not by *x* and *y*, the following patterns will represent the usual practice. Each of the three is illustrated by a line of Cædmon's Hymn, with accents to mark the most heavily stressed syllables (whether or not they are *equally* stressed) and bold-face type for the alliteration:

(1) a a : a x   Métodes méahta   and his mód-ġeþánc

(2) a x : a y   éċe Drýhten,   ór astéalde

(3) x a : a y   Nú sculon hérian   héofon-rīċes Wéard

When the principal alliteration is limited to one of the two strongest syllables in the on-verse, as in the second and third patterns above, it is sometimes supplemented by alliteration of a different letter on the syllables designated as *x* and *y*. The second pattern, thus modified, gives what is called "crossed" alliteration; the third, "transverse" alliteration. If we designate the supplementary alliteration by *b*, we have the following patterns:

(4) Crossed alliteration: a b : a b

Nórþ-manna brégu,   níede ġebǽded   (B 33) [15]

lángung-hwíla.   Is mē nū lífes hýht   (R 126)

grýre-léoða súm.   Þā æt gúðe slóg   (M 285)

þe þā wrǽc-lástas   wídost lécgaþ   (S 57)

(5) Transverse alliteration: b a : a b [16]

Swélċe þā ġebróðor   béġen ætsámne   (B 57)

Hwǽðre iċ þǣr lícgende   lánge hwíle   (R 24)

Èode þā ġesíerwed   séċg to þam éorle   (M 159)

Occasionally, even when the on-verse has double alliteration, there is a third syllable with strong secondary stress that alliterates with the second stressed syllable of the off-verse:

[15] Now and hereafter, as in the glossary, the poems are designated as follows: C = Cædmon's Hymn, B = *The Battle of Brunanburh*, R = *The Dream of the Rood*, M = *The Battle of Maldon*, W = *The Wanderer*, S = *The Seafarer*, and D = *Deor*.

[16] The comparative weakness of the first stress in the following examples is indicated by the reversed slope of the accent. In the second example the trisyllabic *licgende* carries the conventionally necessary stresses of the verse.

(6)  a a b : a b

> báðian brím-fùglas,  brǽdan féðra  (W 47)
> héowon héaðu-lìnda  hámora láfum  (B 6)

There is no name for this pattern; and it is even more likely to
be accidental than crossed or transverse alliteration, for in all
three of these variations the basic alliterative requirement is al-
ready satisfied by the syllables designated as *a*. In most instances
of transverse alliteration the *b*-rhyme involves a decidedly weaker
syllable. Yet it is likely enough that the extra alliteration, even
if not deliberately sought, was welcomed when it occurred.

## 2. End-rhyme

End-rhyme was not a regular feature of traditional Germanic
verse. Its consistent use as a means of linking verses appears first
in Latin hymns. Yet it occurs as an embellishment, in *addition* to
alliteration, in *Beowulf* and other relatively early poems. It was
used in this way by Cynewulf on several occasions—most notably
in a personal passage near the end of his *Elene*—and by the
author of the *Rhyming Poem* in the Exeter Book, where the
effort to achieve both rhyme and alliteration throughout leads
to frequent obscurity in the diction. Among the poems in this
book, it is limited to four lines in *The Battle of Maldon*, two of
which (identical except for the names) merely repeat a weakly
stressed though dissyllabic ending:

> Byrhtnōþ maðelode,  bord hafenode  (42)
> Byrhtwold maðelode,  bord hafenode  (309)
> ǣfre ymbe stunde  hē sealde sume wunde  (271)
> Siġebyrhtes brōðor  and swīðe maniġ ōðer  (282)

What is interesting about the last two of these lines is that the
alliteration is unorthodox in one and of secondary interest in the
other, and that the syllabic patterns, though not entirely irregu-
lar, strongly suggest the rhythmic influence of rhymed couplets. [17]

---

[17] Internal rhymes (*bord-ord*, M 110; *weall-steall*, W 88) and rhetorical
repetition (*lǣne*, W 108-109) belong in other categories. The occasional
rhyming of unstressed endings is usually of no interest. In *Seafarer* 48–50a and
95–96 it is a natural consequence of the rhetorical parallelism.

## 3. The Syllabic Patterns

If we were able to trace the evolution of normal verses from primitive Germanic times we might find, as some investigators have surmised, that an Indo-European heritage of regular octosyllabic verses, each consisting of four accentual trochees, had been gradually differentiated as the language changed into the extraordinary variety of verse-patterns we encounter. That variety, however, was already established long before the period with which we are concerned. Not only most of the patterns, but many of the actual verses, since they appear in more than one of our extant poems, must have been inherited from the preliterary period. Indeed, it is the presence of this traditional element that best accounts for the high degree of order we find in the midst of the variety. It is not likely that the poets achieved this order by mastery of a complicated set of rules. Such rules as they had were probably unsystematic, mere rules of thumb. Lettered or un-lettered, they worked with a store of inherited verse-formulas, and fashioned new verses, as we may suppose, more by imitation than by rule. An intuitive sense of a basic rhythm—sharpened, perhaps, by use of the harp as an accompaniment—may often have guided their choice. Nevertheless the order revealed by analysis is sufficiently remarkable.

A fundamental classification of the various syllabic patterns was made by Eduard Sievers, first for the Old English *Beowulf*, then for the whole range of Old Germanic poetry.[18] Other classifications have been devised from time to time, and some of them have merit, but the Sievers classification has been so widely adopted by editors that it is better known than any other. It has

[18] The ground-breaking study, still a model of induction and exposition, is the first part of a continued article, "Zur Rhythmik des germanischen Alliterationsverses: Erster Abschnitt, Die Metrik des Beowulf," *Beiträge zur Geschichte der deutschen Sprache und Literatur*, X (1885), 209–314. The inclusive and standard treatment is his *Altgermanische Metrik*, Halle, 1893. Sievers later changed his mind about the rhythmic implications of his analysis, but his classification of the verses according to the main stress-patterns remains basic.

been, and may well remain, of great service to the textual critic. In itself, it does not tell us by what rhythm the verses are to be read, but no theory of the rhythm has much chance of being correct if it does not take due account of the features to which the Sievers classification calls attention.

As a basis for his analysis, Sievers took the natural word-accent and sentence-stress of Old English and the other Germanic languages as he had come to know them from his grammatical studies. These had to be modified occasionally, but were mainly confirmed by the alliterative patterns and the statistical evidence of the verses themselves, once the most common patterns had been identified. With minor exceptions, Old English shared with the other Germanic languages a fixed word-accent, the first syllable receiving the chief accent except for the prefixes of verbs, a few of the prefixes of substantives (*ġe-*, *be-*, and occasionally *for-*), and the first element in certain compound adverbs, prepositions, and conjunctions (*to-samne*, *on-ġēan*, *on-weġ*, *for-þam*, etc.). Within the phrase or clause, stress fell on the more important words according to a grammatical hierarchy. Nouns, adjectives, infinitives, and participles generally take precedence of finite verbs and adverbs, and these in turn tend to be stronger than personal pronouns, prepositions, conjunctions, and the unemphatic demonstrative or definite article. Both position and specific meaning can, however, change the ordinary rank of a word. A post-positive preposition ranks as a rather emphatic adverb and frequently alliterates. A finite verb, if it denotes a significant action, may rival a noun.

Among stressed syllables, Sievers found it necessary to distinguish two classes, the long and the short. A stressed syllable is long if it contains a long vowel or a long diphthong, or is closed by a consonant; otherwise it is short. One consonant is enough to close a syllable at the end of a word or member of a compound; medially, two consonants are required, because there is no opportunity to pause on a single consonant in that position. Thus *God* qualifies as a long syllable, but the first syllable of *Godes* is short, while the first syllable of *mannes* is long. Since the relatively unstressed syllables can be pronounced less distinctly, and their vowels, if long when stressed, can be shortened, Sievers did not consider their grammatical length, and indeed found no evidence that the poets were consistently attentive to it.

Even for the stressed syllables, Sievers did not believe that there was a fixed ratio, either in ordinary speech or in verse, between long and short. The conventional *length* of a syllable must be distinguished from what is often called its *burden*. Every syllable has a certain burden, a certain number of sounds of a certain degree of difficulty, and burdens vary widely. When words are uttered rhythmically, burden may help to determine the rhythm by helping to regulate the pace of the series or by imposing a peculiar obstacle at a certain spot so as to produce a different configuration of the rhythm. But burden becomes a paramount factor only when we try to utter a series of syllables as fast as possible. This we rarely do in reciting poetry, though we shall find ourselves approaching that limit when we try to pronounce the syllables in some of the more crowded Old English measures. Now it is true that short syllables have very little burden and that long syllables have more—sometimes a great deal more. But the distinction between the two, in languages where it is recognized, has become conventional, and depends on an almost opposite sort of test to that which determines burden. We ask, not how quickly a syllable can be uttered, but whether or not it can be uttered much more *slowly* than usual without losing its character or becoming ridiculous. Sievers brought this out when he recommended the terms *dehnbar* and *undehnbar*, "extensible" and "non-extensible," for the conventional longs and shorts. [19]

For the analysis of the syllabic patterns of the verses, Sievers made use of three key terms: *Hebung*, *Nebenhebung*, and *Senkung*, which are usually translated as "lift," "half-lift," and "drop." A lift consists of a long stressed syllable or its equivalent; that is, usually, a short stressed syllable and its successor, the two together constituting a "resolved" lift; but in some circumstances, a short stressed syllable alone. A half-lift is the same as a lift ex-

[19] *Altgermanische Metrik*, pp. xii and 23.

cept that its stress is secondary in comparison to a neighboring lift. A drop consists of a single syllable or a group of syllables (sometimes as many as four or five) which are relatively unstressed by comparison with neighboring lifts or half-lifts. To represent the syllables of a verse in notation, Sievers designated the lift as $\acute{-}$ (a long stressed syllable), $\acute{\cup}$ (a short stressed syllable), or $\acute{\cup}x$ (a resolved lift, consisting of a short stressed syllable and its successor). He designated the half-lift as $\grave{-}$, $\grave{\cup}$, or $\grave{\cup}x$, and each syllable in a drop as simply x.

Nearly every normal verse in Old English contains at least four syllables, a few contain as many as nine or ten, and the average number in most poems is between five and six. Among the very numerous verses with four syllables, Sievers found five principal stress-patterns, which he designated, in order of frequency, by the first five letters of the alphabet. These are the basis of his five types. By counting resolved lifts and polysyllabic drops as single members, he found that most verses of more than four syllables can be said to have only four members and can be assimilated to the types established by those with four syllables. Some verses, however, have five members so arranged as to seem like verses of type A or type D, rarely type E, with one extra drop. These were classified as A* (expanded A), D* (expanded D), E* (expanded E). The great majority of verses of types A* and D* occur as on-verses with double alliteration. Finally, a few verses otherwise resembling types A, D, or D* have one or two extra unstressed syllables before the first lift. These extra syllables, since they are not needed for the completion of the regular pattern, were treated as "anacrusis" (German *Auftakt*), optional preludes to the verse proper.

An additional feature of the Sievers classification was the assumption that each verse, having two lifts and either four or five members, consisted of two feet, each containing one lift with or without additional members. In my opinion, this feature of the system has been an obstacle to the understanding of the basic rhythm of Old English verse and must be replaced by the rhythmically significant division into measures; but it is retained in the following table.

## THE SIEVERS TYPES [20]

**Type A**: Basic form, *lift, drop, lift, drop.*

A 1: Lifts virtually equal, no weighty syllables in the drops. Alliteration on first lift or (in on-verse) on both lifts. The first drop may have as many as five extra syllables; the second has only one. The minimal form with four syllables is very common:

⊥ x | ⊥ x : ēċe Dryhten (C 4a).

With resolution:

⏑́x x | ⏑́x x : cyning and æðeling (B 58a).

With anacrusis and five syllables in the first drop (a rare maximum): [21]

x | ⊥ x x x x x | ⊥ x : ġebiddaþ him to þissum bēacne (R 83a).

x | ⏑́x x x x x | ⊥ x : ġebæd iċ mē þā to þam bēame (R 122a).

A 2a: A half-lift, consisting of one long stressed syllable or its resolution, replaces the first drop:

⊥ ⊥ | ⊥ x : unrīm herġes (B 31b).

⊥ ⏑̀x | ⊥ x : ferhþ-loca frēoriġ (W 33a).

For the variation with a short second lift, see A 4 below.

A 2b: A half-lift replaces the second drop:

⊥ x | ⊥ ⊥ : fǣġer feorh-bold (R 73a).

⊥ x x | ⊥ ⏑̀x : healde his hord-cofan (W 14a). [22]

20 The subtypes are those distinguished by Sievers, except that subtype A 4 has been added to bring together all verses of type A in which the second lift consists of a single short syllable, and C 1 includes the resolved forms distinguished by Sievers as C 2, so that my C 2 corresponds to his C 3. (I adopted the same changes for the catalogue of rhythmic variations in *The Rhythm of Beowulf.*)

21 Although these two verses have double alliteration, they tend toward the subtype A 3 because the second lift is stronger than the first. The combination *ġebæd iċ* is almost a single word, and *-bæd* should therefore be considered a short syllable.

22 This resolved form is often indistinguishable from subtype D*2, under which I have repeated this verse and listed some other examples of which the classification is equally doubtful. The doubt reflects a weakness of the classification and has nothing to do with the authenticity or the rhythm of the verses concerned. In *The Rhythm of Beowulf,* for convenience of reference, I listed all such verses under D*2.

A 2ab: Half-lifts replace both drops. Not exemplified in these poems. Two good examples from *Beowulf* are:

    ⏁ ⏁ | ⏁ ⏁ : brēost-hord blōd-rēow (1719a) .

    ⏁ ⌣x | ⏁ ⏁ : nȳd-wracu nīþ-grim (193a) .

A 3: The first lift weaker than the second, alliteration on second lift only. An introductory type properly restricted to the on-verse: [23]

    ⏁ x x | ⏁ x : Nū sculon herian (C 1a) . [24]

    ⏁ x x x x x | ⏁ x : Þūhte mē þæt iċ ġesāwe (R 4a) .

This subtype may have a half-lift instead of the final drop, as in A 2b:

    x | ⌣x x x | ⏁ ⏁ : Ġewiton him þā Norþ-menn (B 53a) .

A 4: Here I group variants of the three subtypes above in which the second lift consists of a single short syllable: [25]

    Short A 1 : ⌣x x x | ⌣ x : fæġere ġetrymed (M 22b) . [26]

    Short A 2a: ⏁ ⏁ | ⌣ x : Bord-weall clufon (B 5b) .

           ⌣x ⏁ | ⌣ x : (Hēr) Æðelstān cyning (B 1a) .

    Short A 3 : x | ⏁ x x | ⌣ x : ġesiehþ him beforan (W 46a) .

**Type A\*** (expanded A) : *Lift, half-lift, drop, lift, drop.* The first drop distinguishes this rather rare variant from A 2a:

---

[23] I use a reversed accent to indicate the weakness of the first lift. Occasionally a lift of this sort shares the alliteration, as in subtype A 1, but most of the minor words (conjunctions, prepositions, etc.) lack synonyms and cannot easily be avoided, so that their occasional participation in the alliterative scheme may be accidental. A polysyllabic first drop is usual in this subtype. Some very short and weak exceptions are mentioned below in connection with the use of initial rests.

[24] The ending *-ian* of weak verbs of the *first* class has consonantal *i* (*j*), like the modern English *y* in *year*, and is therefore monosyllabic, whereas in weak verbs of the *second* class, though the ending is spelled the same way, the *i* forms a separate syllable and usually takes secondary accent in the poetry.

[25] The only frequent and obviously approved form in the poetry is short A 2a, of which other examples occur in this book at R 110b, R 117b, W 45b, and S 1b. Short A 1 and A 3 were perhaps tolerated but usually avoided.

[26] The participle normally had only one *m*, but the manuscript, now lost, apparently gave it two, perhaps on the analogy of the infinitive, and it may be that the author pronounced the verse with a long penult.

⏜⏜x | ⏜x : lid-menn to lande (M 99a) .

Byrhtnōþ mid beornum (M 101a) .

⏜ ⏑x x | ⏜x : Lēofsunu ġemǣlde (M 244a) .

earfoða ġemyndiġ (W 6b) . [27]

**Type B**: Basic form, *drop, lift, drop, lift.* Alliteration on the first lift alone or (in the on-verse) on both lifts.[28] The first drop may have as many as five or six syllables; the second is limited as follows:

B 1: The second drop has only one syllable:

x ⏜ | x ⏜ : Hē ǣrest scōp (C 5a) .

þā middan-ġeard (C7a).[29]

x x ⏑x | x ⏜ : and his sunu forlēt (B 42b) .

x x x x x ⏜ | x ⏑x : swā hē ǣr on þam bēame dyde (R 114b) .

Occasionally the second member of a compound occurs in the second drop and may be treated as a half-lift:

x x ⏜ | ⏜ ⏜ : and mīn mund-byrd is (R 130b) .

B 2: The second drop has two syllables: [30]

x ⏜ | x x ⏜ : Mē sendon to þē (M 29a) .

x x x ⏜ | x x ⏜ : and eall þēos mǣre ġesceaft (R 12b) .

x x x x x ⏑x | x x ⏜ : þāra-þe him biþ eġesa to mē (R 86b) .

[27] A doubtful instance, for the second syllable of *earfoða* would probably have been pronounced weakly enough in this position to be felt as part of a drop. The same is probably true of the second syllable of *ǣrende* in M 28a, *ǣrende to þam eorle*, which would otherwise be clumsily overburdened. The examples with proper names are supported by numerous parallels in other poems but the second element of the name may have been so weakly stressed as to cause these verses to be associated with type A 1. The same may be said of R 86a, M 261b, and M 25b.

[28] A form like A 3 with alliteration on the second lift alone is conceivable but the possible instances are extremely rare and can be classified differently.

[29] Sievers recognized that the second lift may be filled by a syllable that would normally be much weaker than the first, but he thought it should be reckoned as a full lift in order to give proper dignity to the second foot.

[30] Examples with three syllables in the second drop are rare and of doubtful authenticity. *Seafarer* 40b, 41a, and 41b are among these examples, but it will be noted that the preposition *to* is unnecessary and is actually not present in the otherwise parallel verse, 40a. If *to* is authentic, we probably have a minor license, a stretching of the measure for the sake of rhetorical emphasis.

The unusually weighty syllables of the second drop in the follow-
ing verses are probably to be spoken with reduced force or re-
tarded tempo: [31]

    x ⊥ | ⊥ x ⊥ : nē Anlāf þȳ mā (B 46b) .

    x x ⊥ | ⊥ x ⊥ : Þā þǣr Byrhtnōþ ongann (M 17a).

              oþ þæt Heorrenda nū (D 39b).

**Type C:** Basic form, *drop, lift, lift, drop.* Alliteration usually on
the first lift alone, occasionally (in the on-verse) on both lifts.
The first drop may have as many as five or six syllables, the
second only one syllable:

  C 1: The second lift consists of one long syllable or its resolu-
tion:

    x ⊥ | ⊥ x : fram cnēo-māgum (B 8a) .

    x x ◡x | ⊥ x : and þæt spere sprengde (M 137a) .

    x x x ◡x | ◡x x : þam-þe þǣr bryne þolodon (R 149b) .

    x x x x x ⊥ | ⊥ x : þonne hit ǣnig mǣþ wǣre (M 195b) .

  C 2: The second lift consists of one short stressed syllable: [32]

    x ⊥ | ◡ x : on camp-stede (B 49a) .

    x x ⊥ | ◡ x : ofer brād brimu (B 71a) .

    x x x x x x ⊥ | ◡ x : Ne þurfon mē ymbe Stūrmere (M 249a) .

The second lift may be much weaker than the first, as when it is
supplied by the dissyllabic ending of a weak verb of the second
class:

    x x x ⊥ | ◡ x : þe wile ealgian (M 52a) .

    x x x x x ⊥ | ◡ x : þæt hē usic geweorðode (S 123a) .

These forms are probably conventionally accepted survivals from
prehistoric times when the endings were *ōjan* and *ōde* respec-
tively.

**Type D:** Basic form, *lift, lift, half-lift, drop,* or *lift, lift, drop,*

---

[31] Sievers was probably right in regarding such verses as variations of type
B rather than ordinary instances of type E preceded by heavy anacrusis,
especially since even light anacrusis before type E was normally avoided.
The context does not favor classification of the last two verses as hypermetric.

[32] Resolution of the first lift is much rarer in C 2 than in C 1. In the
seven poems there are only four examples (M 199a, S 58b, S 104a, and S 118b).

*half-lift.* In both patterns the syntax normally brings the last three members closer to one another than to the first member. When the drop is final it is limited to one syllable. When it comes next to last it may have two syllables. Alliteration, when single, is on the first lift alone. In the on-verse it may be on both lifts.

D 1: The half-lift is in third position and long: [33]

    − | − − x : Frēa ælmihtiġ (C 9b) .

           hrīþ hrēosende (W 102a) .

    ⏑x | − − x : scadu forþ ēode (R 54b) .

    ⏑x | ⏑x − x : lucon lagu-strēamas (M 66a) .

D 2: The half-lift is in third position and short:

    − | − ⏑ x : weorc Wuldor-Fæder (C 3a) . [34]

           self cunnie (S 35b) . [35]

    ⏑x | − ⏑ x : nearu niht-wacu (S 7a) .

    x | − | − ⏑ x : behēold hrēow-ċearig (R 25a) .

    − |⏑x ⏑ x : bord hafenode (M 42b) . [35]

D 3: The second lift is short; the half-lift, in third place, long. A very rare variant, occurring a few times in the older poems and scarcely at all in the later ones. There is but one example in the seven poems:

    − | ⏑ − x : reord-berendum (R 89b) . [36]

D 4: The half-lift comes at the end:

---

[33] Resolution of the half-lift is very rare. It occurs in none of the seven poems and only once, doubtfully, in *Beowulf*: *milts unġyfeðe*, 2921b, where the stress on *un-* is optional and may better be subordinated to that of the root syllable. The verse would then be classified as A 1.

[34] At the date of Cædmon's Hymn, *Wuldor* could be pronounced as either one syllable, *Wuldr*, or two syllables, *Wuldor*, the vowel having been supplied to ease pronunciation after the loss of the earlier ending. Here it should probably be treated as a monosyllable.

[35] This subtype, as an off-verse, is the favorite resting-place for weak verbs of the second class, though they also appear occasionally in the on-verse and in other types.

[36] The indicated stress-pattern is almost impossible to produce unless the penult is held longer than necessary so as to produce an effect of syncopation. I think most speakers in the historic period would have said *réord-bérendùm*. The burden of the medial syllable, even if it were unstressed, would have added needed weight to the verse.

　　́ | ́ x ́ : hār hilde-rinc　(B 39a) .
　　　　bord ord onfēng　(M 110b) .
　　　　hrīm hrūsan band　(S 32a) .
　　⌣x | ́ x ́ : cyning ūt ġewāt　(B 35b) .
　　́ | ́ x ⌣x : Bærst bordes læriġ　(M 284a) .[37]

**Type D\*** (expanded D) . Like D in its various forms, with the addition of a drop of one or two syllables (rarely more) after the first lift. Expanded D 3 does not occur, either here or in *Beowulf*.[38] The expanded type occurs almost exclusively in the on-verse, where it regularly has double alliteration.

D\*1:

　　́ x | ́ ́ x : sellan sǣ-mannum　(M 38a) .
　　⌣x x | ́ ́ x : eaforan Ēadweardes　(B 7a) .
　　́ x | ⌣x ́ x : hēowon here-flīeman　(B 23a) .
　　x | ́ x | ́ ⌣x x : behangen hrīm-ġicelum　(S 17a) .
　　́ x x | ́ ́ x : Wōdon þā wæl-wulfas　(M 96a) .[39]
　　́ ́ x | ́ ́ x : Anwealda ælmihtiġ　(R 153a) .[40]

D\*2:

　　́ x | ́ ⌣x : beorna bēag-ġiefa　(B 2a) .
　　　　　ġielleþ ān-floga　(S 62b) .[41]
　　́ ́ ⌣x ⌣ x : Byrhtnōþ maðelode　(M 42a; cf. M 309a) .[42]

The following verses could perhaps be classified as A 2b with resolution because of the even balance; but uncertainty of classi-

---

[37] Resolution of the half-lift is very rare. It occurs only twice in *Beowulf* and once, in the verse here cited, in the seven poems.

[38] A possible instance in *Beowulf*, *Wuldur-cyninge*, 2795a, can be read with monosyllabic *Wuldr-* or classified as A 1 in spite of the long penult.

[39] Note the very rare triple alliteration. A somewhat comparable instance occurs in *Beowulf* in a verse of type E, *syn-snǣdum swealh*, 743a. Both instances, though perhaps accidental, come at moments of heightened emotion.

[40] A sort of double D, highly exceptional but rhythmically sound and appropriate as an honorific.

[41] The only off-verse of this subtype in the seven poems.

[42] This formula, with other compound names, occurs twenty-five times in *Beowulf*. It is more logical to classify it as D\*2 than as A 2ab, because there is a variation with a monosyllabic noun, *Weard maðelode* (*Beowulf* 286a), and also because the inflectional ending is descended from \*-ōde. Note the D 2 off-verse that follows in *Maldon*, *bord hafenode*.

fication does not entail doubt of authenticity or any difference of rhythm:

 ´x x | ´ ∪ x : healde  his  hord-cofan   (W 14a).
         Ieldu him on fareþ  (S 91a).
 ´x x x | ´ ∪ x : Offa þone sǣ-lidan   (M 286a).
         Wōriaþ  þā  wīn-salu   (W 78a). [43]
 x | ∪x x | ´ ∪ x : Onġietan sceal glēaw hæle   (W 73a).
D*4:
 ´ x | ´ x ´ : wēriġ, wīġes sǣd  (B 20a).
         wǣpen upp ahōf  (M 130b). [44]
         hungor innan slāt  (S 11b). [44]
 ´ x | ∪x x ´ : drēoriġ daroða lāf  (B 54a).
         cwīðdon Cyninges fiell  (R 56a).
 ´ x | ´ x ∪x : Bearwas blōstmum nimaþ  (S 48a).
 x | ´ x | ´ x x ´ : onwendeþ  wyrda ġesceaft  (W 107a).
 x | ´ x | ´ x x ∪x : alīefan landes tō fela   (M 90a).


**Type E:** Basic form, *lift, half-lift, drop, lift*. The first two members are usually more closely related to each other than to the fourth member. The drop may be either enclitic or proclitic. It may have two syllables, one enclitic, the other proclitic; rarely are both enclitic. The alliteration may be on the first lift alone, or (in the on-verse) on both lifts. [45]

 ´ ´ x | ´ : andlangne dæġ  (B 21a)
         mann-cynnes Weard  (C 7b)
         æsc-holt ascōc  (M 230b)
 ∪x ´ x | ´ : heofon-rīċes Weard  (C 1b).
 ´ ∪x x | ´ : Ælfwine þā cwæþ  (M 211a).
 ´ ´ x | ∪x : Norþ-manna bregu  (B 33a).
 ´ ´ x x | ´ : wæl-reste ġeċēas  (M 113b).
 ∪x ´ x x | ´ : fela ealra ġebād  (R 125b).

---

[43] The penult of the verb here has certainly lost the secondary accent it usually receives in the poetry.

[44] These are the only off-verses of subtype D*4 in the seven poems. In the older poetry *wǣpen* and *hungor* could be treated as monosyllables, so that such verses as these would have had the pattern of unexpanded D 4.

[45] Highly irregular is *scield-burg tobrocen* (M 242a), in which *b* alliterates.

Very rarely the half-lift consists of a single short syllable:

$\perp \smallsmile x \mid \perp$ : earfoðu drēag (D 2b) .

earfoða dǣl (D 30b) .

**Type E\*** (expanded E). Sievers placed in this class some verses of a very uncommon pattern which could be likened to type E with an extra drop after the first lift.[46] There are three such verses in the seven poems, all off-verses with single alliteration on the first lift:

$\perp x \perp x \mid \perp$ : Wyrd biþ full arǣd (W 5b) .

Swimmaþ eft on-weġ (W 53b) .

ēċan līfes blǣd (S 79b) .

In spite of the alliteration, which suggests D\*4, one might place here the following on-verse—

$\perp x \perp x \, x \mid \perp$ : hrūsan heolstre bewrāh (W 23a)

—because the first two words go together; but if so the half-lift should be elevated to the rank of the full lifts, and the pattern is one for which Sievers did not expressly provide. The verse just quoted from *The Seafarer* is syntactically similar and calls for the same treatment in spite of having only single alliteration. See below, p. 123.

Such, then, are the Sievers types of the normal verses. A few verses that appear in company with normal verses yet do not precisely fit any of the types are listed and discussed below, pp. 127 ff.

## 4. The Basic Rhythm and its Variations

The classification made by Sievers does not tell us all we need to know to achieve a satisfactory recitation of the poetry. It is even misleading in certain details, such as the division into feet of seemingly divergent, even contrary forms, and occasional ex-

---

[46]There are at least three such verses in *Beowulf*. See *The Rhythm of Beowulf*, pp. 318 and 371. See also *Brunanburh* 3b as it was probably pronounced in its own day (p. 135 below); but in the older poetry, such as *Beowulf*, *ealdor* would have been treated as a monosyllable, *ealdr*, giving a verse of the ordinary type E.

aggeration of natural stresses to meet the requirements of these falsely imagined feet. Verse rhythm does require us to modify natural stresses in partial recognition of metrically established expectations, but if we misconceive the meter we modify them wrongly. On the whole, however, Sievers put the stresses in the right place, and the distinction he made between lifts and drops, though exaggerated, is essentially true to the nature of the language. The Sievers types help us to generalize what is at first a bewildering variety of syllabic sequences. Taken together with the obviously careful use of alliteration, the types bespeak a fundamental orderliness such as we expect in a well-developed art. The types have helped us to recognize and compare various patterns, to describe them concisely, to know which patterns were preferred, and to detect irregularities. But this orderliness in the midst of variety suggests that there ought to be a basic rhythmic order to contain all the variations. We need, on the one hand, a higher generalization than the types provide, and on the other, a greater particularity. We must be able to deal sensitively with all the syllables, those in the drops as well as those in the lifts.

It is my belief, founded on experimental readings, that the rhythmic basis of every normal verse, whether on-verse or off-verse, is a pair of dipodies, or four-beat measures, of the form | í 1 ì 1 | í 1 ì 1 |, where the figure 1 represents the unitary beat governing a time interval equal to the usual quantity of a short stressed syllable, while the accents mark the primary beat at the beginning of the measure and the secondary beat in the middle of it. If we substitute musical notation for numbers and designate the unitary beat by an eighth-note, we shall have two measures of 4/8 time. As with musical rhythms, the basic rhythm can be greatly varied by combining and subdividing beats, by substituting rests (measured silences), and now and then replacing two beats by three of proportionately reduced quantity (1 1 by $\frac{2}{3}$ $\frac{2}{3}$ $\frac{2}{3}$). The normal verses of *Beowulf* can be spoken in accordance with this rhythm, as I have tried to show in *The Rhythm of Beowulf*, and so can all other normal verses, including those in the seven poems. Before entering into detail, however, I must explain my use of a few technical terms and notational devices.

Rhythm as here considered is an ordering, in time, of the

dynamic pulses of speech. [47] The relative intensity of these pulses and the relative intervals of time between them are the physical sources of the rhythm, though they are only an approximation, sometimes a crude one, of the order perceived by the mind. Every clearly articulated syllable has a crest of intensity, usually at the onset of the vowel, that serves as a point of measurement for the ear. In a rhythmic sequence of syllables, the interval between the dynamic crest of a syllable and that of its successor, as compared with neighboring intervals, is the *quantity* of the syllable in that particular sequence. [48] Some crests are stronger than others and these are distinguished as accents. They mark the regularly recurrent intervals we designate as measures or parts of measures. The rhythm we are considering calls for primary accents on every fourth beat to mark the measures and secondary accents half way between to mark half-measures. Comparatively weak syllables can receive rhythmic accents without distortion of meaning if they are spoken at the time when an accent is expected. For instance, if we utter the first line of Cædmon's Hymn according to the following rhythm,

Nú scùlon hériàn    héofon-rìċes Wéard

| 2   1  1 | 2  1 ∧ | 1  1   1 1 | 2    ∧ |

(where a caret marks a rest equivalent to one beat, or the multiple of one indicated by the subscript number) , we need not exert a great deal of force in uttering the first syllable of *sculon* and the second syllable of *herian* (pronounced as two syllables with consonantal *i*) in order to feel that they have received

[47] William Thomson defines it more generally as "an ordering of blows." See *The Rhythm of Speech* (Glasgow: Maclehose, Jackson and Co., 1923), p. 28. This is a work to which I am much indebted. It is full of eccentricities and hard to use, but Thomson had trained himself to hear speech rhythms with remarkable sensitivity and to record them accurately.

[48] Thus the rhythmic "syllable" is not the same as the grammatical one. In the verse *ēċe Dryhten*, for example, the boundaries of the rhythmic syllables are approximately indicated by the following slashes: *ēċ/e Dr/yht/en*. The second "syllable," extending from the crest of *e* to that of *y*, includes not only the two consonants of the third grammatical syllable, but whatever period of silence there may be between the two words.

secondary accent. Merely uttering them at the right time helps to convey the impression. They should naturally have less intensity than the first syllable of *rīces*, which may be said to have *stress*. Similarly, *Nū*, though it deserves a modicum of stress, is inferior in that respect to the first syllables of *herian* and *heofon*, and to *Weard*. Yet *Nū* has the primary accent of the first measure by virtue of its relation, in time as well as intensity, to *sculon*.

Verse rhythm usually requires us to modify in this way the contrasts between syllables that deserve relatively heavy stress in their own right and those that do not. A reader of the line under discussion will automatically adjust the dynamic force of the accents if he pays equal attention to the rhythm and the meaning. But for analytical purposes I find it useful to distinguish between accents that are bestowed largely for the sake of the rhythm and those that are demanded by the meaning as well. The latter are properly stronger than the others and are therefore marked with double accents, ″ for primary, ˄ for secondary. In general, those that receive double accents are those that are distinguished as lifts or half-lifts by Sievers, including those that regularly bear alliteration. I exclude, however, the relatively weak syllables that Sievers designates as lifts primarily for the sake of the meter. Accordingly I mark the first line of Cædmon's Hymn as follows:

Nú scùlon hériàn  héofon-rīces Wéard.

| 2   1 1  | 2  1 ∧ | 1  1   1 1   | 2      ⅍  |

The distinction is only in part a matter of auditory perception. No one need be disturbed if his ear refuses to distinguish all the grades of intensity that the notation might seem to imply. The chief service of the double accents is to bring out the interplay of the perfectly regular (because empty) basic rhythm we imagine and the variously weighted words and phrases that give it partial expression without sacrifice of their individual character.

My treatment of syllabic quantity results from an effort to reconcile the natural demands of the individual syllable with those of the basic rhythm. I take 1 as the normal quantity of a short stressed syllable, 2 as the normal quantity of a long stressed syllable. Both long and short stressed syllables in crowded measures can be compressed to half their usual length, the short to $\frac{1}{2}$ , the long to 1—even, in very rare instances, to $\frac{2}{3}$ , the quantity of one beat in a triplet, though this theoretical shortening may be offset by compensatory retardation of the tempo. The short syllables cannot, in my opinion, be extended beyond their normal quantity, 1, but the long can sometimes be extended to 3 or 4, the quantity of a full measure, by intoning the long vowel, lingering on one or more of the consonants (including sometimes a consonant that belongs to the next grammatical syllable) , or filling out the time with a rest. Unstressed syllables (including some that take secondary accent in virtue of their position) generally *require* no more than the quantity 1 and are sometimes reduced to $\frac{1}{2}$ , but proclitics and enclitics must be distinguished. A proclitic syllable, whether or not it is a separate word, tends to be followed quickly by the stressed syllable it introduces, so that its dynamic crest is at least as close to the one that follows as to the one that precedes. Practically, this means that its quantity is limited to 1 unless it is an independent monosyllable preceded by an initial rest, as I explain below. Enclitics, on the other hand, can often be extended, either by lingering on a closing consonant or filling out the time with a rest, or else by deliberate utterance of the opening consonant of the next grammatical syllable. In the line quoted above, the second syllable of *herian* requires no more than the quantity 1, but we can supplement it with a rest of the same quantity, or linger on the *n* enough to justify assigning it the quantity 2. The effect is then what might be called a *legato* reading, which is desirable when the sense runs on closely. Some enclitics, when thus supplemented, can have the quantity 3, but it must be understood that they are always uttered completely enough for recognition within the time of the quantity 1.

It is relatively easy to utter the verses of types A, D, E, and their expanded variants in conformity to the basic rhythm. More than half of the verses in most Old English poems are of type A, so that the rhythm we assign to them will be especially influential. The following table shows my reading of the principal subtypes of A and of A*:

A 1: ḗċè Drýhtèn      (C 4a)

|2 2   |2 1   ∧ |

hórd and hāmas      (B 10a)

| 2 ∧ 1   |2 1   ∧ |

glá̈d òfer grúndàs      (B 15a)

|2 1 1   |2 1 ∧ |

flṓtenà and Scóttà      (B 32a)

|1 1 1 1      |2 1 ∧ |

fǣ́ġe tò ġefḗohtè      (B 28a)

|$\frac{4}{3}$ $\frac{2}{3}$ 1 1 | 2 1 ∧ |

Ġebǣ́d iċ mē þà̀ to þam bḗamè      (R 122a) [49]

1 | $\frac{2}{3}$ $\frac{2}{3}$ $\frac{2}{3}$ 1 $\frac{1}{3}$ $\frac{2}{3}$   | 2 1 ∧ |

A 2a: mǎnn-cỳnn sḗċàn      (R 104b)

|2   2   |2 1   ∧ |

fḗrhþ-lòca frḗorìġ      (W 33a)

|2 1 1   | 2 1 ∧ |

A 2b: Sḗldlíċ wæ̀s se síġe-bḛ̄am      (R 13a)

| 1 1   $\frac{4}{3}$ $\frac{2}{3}$ | 1 1 2   |

A 3: Swélċe þæ̀r ḛ̀ac se frṓdà      (B 37a) [50]

| 1 $\frac{1}{3}$ $\frac{2}{3}$   $\frac{4}{3}$ $\frac{2}{3}$ | 2 1 ∧ |

Ġewíton hìm þā Nṓrþ-mènn      (B 53a)

1 |1 1 1   1   | 2   2   |

A 4 (short A 2a) : Bórd-wḛ̀all clúfon      (B 5b)

| 2   2   | 1 1 𝄢 |

A 4 (short A 1) : fǣ́ġerè ġetrýmed      (M 22b)

|1 1 1   1 | 1 1   𝄢 |

A 4 (short A 3) : ġesíehþ hìm befṓran      (W 46a)

1| 2   $\frac{4}{3}$   $\frac{2}{3}$ | 1 1   𝄢 |

[49] The grammatically almost parallel verse, ġebíddaþ hìm to þissum bḗacnè (R 83a), seems to me to require the indicated accents and to be essentially unreadable without a breach of rhythm or a drastic change of tempo. Such awkward verses are exceedingly rare.

[50] The *essential* pattern of the first measure requires the utterance of three syllables in the first half and two in the second. If the reader manages this he will approximate the specified rhythm, which readers of music will recognize as a variation of a measure consisting of two triplets.

A*:    lȳd-mĕnn to lắndè        (M 99a)
       | 2    $\frac{4}{3}$    $\frac{2}{3}$ | 2  1  ∧ |

       Lēofsŭnu ġemǽldè       (M 244a)
       | 2  $\frac{2}{3}$ $\frac{2}{3}$ $\frac{2}{3}$ | 2  1  ∧ |

When we turn from type A to the other four types, we find
that they have one characteristic in common: they are particu-
larly suited to the reception of the three-member[51] compounds
or combinations of words in which the language, especially the
poetic language, abounds. Type A 2 and A* can accomodate a
compound such as *ferhþ-loca* with short penult, but more often
even this form is found in types C 2, D 2, and D*2. Compounds
such as *wræc-lāstas* and simple trisyllables such as *hrēosende*, with
the first two syllables long, are found in types C 1, D 1, D*1, and
E. Compounds such as *hilde-rinc* and combinations such as
*wīġes sæd, mǣre ġesceaft, wundra ġehwæs* are found in types B,
D 4, and D*4.[52] In types D and E the three-member words or
groups are offset by a single lift; in D* by a lift and a drop; in
B and C by an introductory drop.

Type E, in which the isolated lift is at the end, is readily ad-
justed to the basic rhythm by prolonging this lift or adding a
rest:

       mănn-cȳnnes Wĕard        (C 7b)
       | 2    1    1    | 2    𝄐 |

       Nŏrþ-mănna brĕgu        (B 33a)
       | 2    1    1  | 1  1  𝄐 |

       wǽl-rĕste ġecĕas      (M 113b)
       | 2  1  $\frac{1}{2}$  $\frac{1}{2}$ | 2    𝄐 |

The rare E* crowds the first measure but can be spoken with-
out much difficulty:

       Wȳrd biþ fŭll arǽd       (W 5b)
       | $\frac{4}{3}$    $\frac{2}{3}$    $\frac{4}{3}$    $\frac{2}{3}$ | 2    𝄐 |

[51] I use this expression instead of trisyllabic in order to include extra
syllables resulting from resolution or dissyllabic drops between lifts.

[52] It must not be supposed that three-member words and combinations of
words are the only ones that can appear in any of these types. Verses of type
B, in particular, often have a different syntactical structure.

éċan lífes blǽd    (S 79b) [53]

|1  1  1 1   | 2  Å |

Type D is a little harder because the isolated lift comes first; and in order to adjust it to the rhythm as well as to emphasize its partial separation from the three-member group that follows, the reader must either prolong it or supplement it with a rest: [54]

D 1:    Frḗa ǽlmìhtiġ        (C 9b)

| 2 Å | 2   1   1 |

D 2:    néaru níht-wàcu        (S 7a)

|1   1 Å | 2   1   1 |

D 3:    réord-bérendùm        (R 89b)

| 4   |1 1   1   ∧|

D 4:    hár hílde-rìnc        (B 39a)

|2  Å | 4/3  2/3   2   |

D*1:    séllàn sǽ-mànnum        (M 38a)

|2  2    |2   1   1    |

The rhythms of the other varieties of D* can readily be inferred since they differ from those of the unexpanded type only in the first measure, which is filled out like that of the simpler forms of type A.

The three types of verses that have now been considered, A, D, and E, all begin with a lift (except for the few in which the lift is preceded by a syllable or two of anacrusis), and the feet marked by Sievers correspond to the measures of my interpretation, though the implications are different, for Sievers did not think the feet of his analysis were isochronous. Up to this point, moreover, my interpretation of the rhythm is substantially the same as that of Andreas Heusler, whose influence in Germany

[53] I have marked what is usually a half-lift with double primary accent because I think we are dealing with a variation that the Sievers scheme does not allow for, though it is a natural one. In effect, the compound measure has been replaced by two simple ones, but we keep the expected compound in mind. See *The Rhythm of Beowulf*, revised edition, pp. xx–xxiii.

[54] For a fuller treatment of this problem, see *The Rhythm of Beowulf*, revised edition, pp. xvii–xx.

has rivaled that of Sievers.[55] Types B and C, which remain to be considered, begin with a drop of one or more syllables, and like Heusler I find it necessary to postulate measures that do not correspond to Sievers' feet; but the rhythms I recommend for these verses are not for the most part at all the same as Heusler's.

The Sievers patterns for types B and C can be generalized as follows by using dots to indicate the possibility of extra syllables in the drops and remembering that the long syllable of any lift may be resolved:

B:  x . . . . . $\stackrel{\angle}{}$ | x . $\stackrel{\angle}{}$

C:  x . . . . . $\stackrel{\angle}{}$ | $\stackrel{\smile}{}$ x

We notice at once that the feet designated by Sievers cannot well be the same as measures. Rhythmic measures, if they are complete, begin with primary accent, for it is the interval from one such accent to the next that we can hear as a measure. Since the first lift in verses of these types is always at least as strong as the second, usually stronger, and bears the alliteration when it is single, the accent of this lift must certainly mark the beginning of a measure. To replace the Sievers feet by measures we must therefore place one bar before the first lift:

B:  x . . . . . | $\stackrel{\angle}{}$ x . $\stackrel{\angle}{}$

C:  x . . . . . | $\stackrel{\angle}{}$ $\stackrel{\smile}{}$ x

The position of the other bar may vary.

In *The Rhythm of Beowulf* I have shown that the frequent resemblance of the last three members of types B and C to the last three of various forms of type D entitles us to treat the second lift designated by Sievers as a half-lift and include all three members in one measure. If we do this we must assume that this measure is preceded by one that is incomplete or lightly filled. If it is incomplete it must begin with a rest. If it is lightly filled it must begin, like the first measure of type A 3, with a weak primary accent. Thus we have such readings as the following:

---

[55] See his *Deutsche Versgeschichte* (H. Paul's *Grundriss der germanischen Philologie*, VIII), Berlin and Leipzig: Walter de Gruyter, 1925–1929, vol. I, part II, "Der altgermanische Vers," pp. 86–314. The introductory part, pp. 1–85, lays down general principles somewhat like those of William Thomson.

B 1:        Hè ǽrest scŏp        (C 5a)
    | ♏ 2 | 1  1       2 |

            ànd his sŭnu forlĕt        (B 42b) [56]
    | ♏ 1       1  | 2/3  2/3  2/3  2 |

B 2:    þára þe hìm biþ ĕgesa to mĕ        (R 86b)
    | 1 1/2  1/2  1       1 | 1/2  1/2  1/2  1/2       2 |

C 1:        fràm cnĕo-mă̆gum        (B 8a)
    | ♏ 2       | 2   1 1       |

            ànd þæt spĕre sprĕnġde        (M 137a) [57]
    | ♏ 1       1  | 1 1       1   1 |

        þŏnne hit ă̆niġ mǽþ wă̆re        (M 195b)
    | 1  1/2  1/2  1 1   | 2       1 1   |

C 2:        òfer brá̆d brìmu        (B 71a) [58]
    | ♏ 1 1       | 2       1   1  |

        Ne þúrfon mè ymbe Stŭrmĕre        (M 249a)
        1  | 1  1       1 1/2  1/2 | 2       1 1   |

The rhythms just described represent the majority of the verses
in types B and C, and among them those calling for initial rests
are much the most numerous. [59] These rests are the chief means
by which my theory of the rhythm escapes difficulties that beset

---

[56] The same rhythm will serve for the unusual verse, *oþ-þæt Heorrenda nū*
(D 39b), but with retarded tempo to allow for the weight of the trisyllabic
name with its two long syllables.

[57] A reader may choose to give extra time to the first syllable of the verb.
If he does, the irregularity will probably seem expressive and therefore
pleasing.

[58] In these crowded measures there is no *rhythmic* difference between C 1
and C 2, but the difference in *burden* is noticeable, because in C 2 the short
penult has its normal and maximum quantity, whereas in C 1 the long
penult is compressed to half its usual quantity. This may sometimes lead
to a slight irregularity, as suggested in the previous note. In the alternative
readings of types B and C discussed below, the rhythms of C 1 and C 2 are
noticeably different.

[59] Unusually light verses of type A 3 may also be read with initial rests;
e.g. R 109a, *on þissum lǣnè* ( | ∧ 1 ì 1 | 2̄ ì ∧ | ), and R 111a, *for þàm wŏrdè*
( | ∧ 1 2̇ | 2̄ ì ∧ | ).

other theories, notably Heusler's, for whom the syllables of the first drop in the B and C verses are an unmeasured prelude to the verse proper. Initial rests are conspicuous, since they replace syllables marking the expected primary beat of the first measure of a verse, and their frequency in my reading of the poetry makes them a distinctive feature that requires comment. In most poems the rests seem both natural and expressive, because they come at moments when the phrasing permits or demands a pause, so that they help to punctuate a sequence of verses without interrupting the rhythmic flow. I am strongly inclined to believe that they were first introduced in prehistoric times as a natural development from the practice of accompanying the verses with the harp. Precisely how the harp was used is not known, but it might well have served partly to mark the main beats of the verses, and so led performers, when introducing clauses or adding half-separable phrases, to begin with some rather weak syllables after the first beat had sounded, a practice familiar to us in operatic recitative but not in poetry. Once the habit had become established, the harp would not have been needed. [60]

A number of verses of types B and C, however—mainly to be found among those that begin with a monosyllabic drop—cannot well be treated in the manner I have described. The clearest instances are furnished by the comparatively rare verses in which the monosyllable is a mere prefix. Consider the following lines, in which the off-verses belong to type C:

fólcès ġefﬞellèd beﬞóran þíssùm    (B 67)

$|2 \quad \frac{4}{3} \quad \frac{2}{3}\ |2 \quad \frac{4}{3} \quad \frac{2}{3}|1\ 3\ \ |2\ \ 1\ \ \wedge\ |$

þe hé hìm to dúguðè gedón hﬞæfdè    (M 197)

$1\ \ |2 \quad \frac{4}{3} \quad \frac{2}{3}\ |1\ 1\ 1\ \ \ 1|\ 4\ \ |2\ \ 1\ \wedge\ |$

bítrè bréost-ćèare ġebíden hﬞæbbè    (S 4)

$|2\ \ 2\ \ \ |2 \quad \ 1\ \frac{1}{2}\ \ \ \frac{1}{2}|\ 1\ 3\ \ \ |\ 2\ \ 1\ \wedge\ |$

---

[60] See *The Rhythm of Beowulf*, pp. 88–95. How frequently the harp was still used during the historical period is uncertain. Bede's story of Cædmon supplies the most positive bit of evidence for its use as an accompaniment. Its continued popularity as an instrument is unquestioned. The little harp found at Sutton Hoo and the references to harps in the poetry have encouraged speculation.

The rhythms here indicated can scarcely be doubted, for the pre-
fixes are too weak to fill the second half of a measure, there is no
reason to pause between verses, and the balanced treatment of the
lifts in the off-verses is satisfactory in itself. Hardly less clear is the
following verse where, although the monosyllable is independent
enough to be lengthened, if necessary, after an initial rest, the
sense is too continuous to justify such treatment:

þæt gé mid ùrum scéattùm   to scípe gángèn      (M 56)

$$1 \ \left| \ \tfrac{4}{3} \ \ \tfrac{2}{3} \ \ 1 \ \ 1 \ \ \right| \ 2 \ \ \tfrac{4}{3} \quad \tfrac{2}{3} \ \left| \ 1 \ 1 \ \diamondsuit \right| 2 \ \ 1 \ \wedge \ \right|$$

Or consider the following sequence, where the on-verse is of type
B and a direct running on, with balanced treatment of the two
lifts, seems easier and more expressive than the alternative:

cýning ùt ġewãt      (B 35b–36a)

$$\left| 1 \ \ 3 \ \right| \ \tfrac{4}{3} \ \ \tfrac{2}{3} \ \ \tfrac{4}{3}$$

on féalonè flôd

$$\tfrac{2}{3} \ \left| \ 1 \ 1 \ 2 \ \right| 2 \ \diamondsuit \ \right|$$

It appears, then, that a few verses of types B and C must be
treated in the manner just described, and that several others may
be so treated, the decision resting on the reader's feeling for the
movement of the passage. I find myself reading some of these
ambivalent verses differently on successive occasions. [61]

Before concluding this survey of the rhythm of the normal
verses I must say something of an unclassified remainder. Even
in *Beowulf*, our chief model for Old English versification, there
are a few verses that occur in a context of normal verses but do
not fit any of the Sievers types, some appearing to be slightly
deficient, some excessive. Several of these are manifestly corrupt,
but others may well be authentic. *The Dream of the Rood* has
two such verses, *The Wanderer* two, *The Seafarer* three (to men-
tion only verses that make good sense), and *The Battle of
Maldon* at least five.

[61] This problem is more fully treated in *The Rhythm of Beowulf*, pp.
57–64, where certain verses with two syllables in the first drop are included.
I regard the following line, with its combination of types C 2 and B 1, as
a quite exceptional fusion of two verses into an undivided whole, the on-verse
filling only a little more than a measure and the off-verse filling the better
part of three measures:

ġewéorðôde  ófer èall wífà cýnn      (R 94)

$$1 \ \left| \ 2 \ \ 1 \ 1 \ \right| 1 \ 1 \ 2 \quad \left| \ 2 \ 2 \ \right| 2 \ \ \diamondsuit \ \right|$$

Several of these verses might be considered hypermetric, since the last four syllables resemble type A 1 and these are preceded by two, three, or five minor syllables at the beginning—in every case too much for ordinary anacrusis. Those who judge by syllabic patterns alone, or who do not recognize a rhythmic distinction between normal and hypermetric, would label them hypermetric without further ado. But, as I explain below, I use the term "hypermetric" to describe verses that are to be read in accordance with a different basic rhythm. The verses here in question appear among normal verses and can easily be adjusted to the same basic rhythm as their neighbors. Hence I am inclined to treat them as minor deviations from, or a combination of, types B and C:

x x | ⌣́x ⌣̀x :        mìd his míclan mèahte        (R 102a)

    | 𝄞  1     1  |  1   1      1      1 |

and similarly,        þæt þǣr mōdiġlíce        (M 200a)

               swā nū missenlíce        (W 75a)

perhaps also,        and his brōðru mid him        (M 191a)

x x x | ⌣́x ⌣̀x :        nē ỳmbe áwiht èlles        (S 46a)

    | ⋀  1   1     1 |  1 1      1     1 |

x x x x x | ⌣́x ⌣̀x :   Ne scúlon mè on þǣre þèode   (M 220a)

    1  | 1 1      $\frac{4}{3}$ $\frac{2}{3}$  | 1  1    1    1 |

Another, somewhat similar verse has perhaps a slightly different stress-pattern:

x x | ⌣́ ⌣̀ x x :        ànd on drýhtlícestum        (S 85a)

    | 𝄞 1        1      | 2 $\frac{2}{3}$ $\frac{2}{3}$   $\frac{2}{3}$  |

Still another is usually considered hypermetric and is certainly very full, but I prefer to read it in accordance with the normal rhythm, as if it were D*1 with a remarkably heavy opening:

⌣́x ⌣̀x | ⌣x ⌣́x :   wíntra dǣl on wèorold-ríce   (W 65a)

   | $\frac{4}{3}$   $\frac{2}{3}$   $\frac{4}{3}$   $\frac{2}{3}$  | 1  1     1 1 |

Finally, there are four verses that resemble type A 3 in that a number of minor syllables lead up to an alliterating lift, but there is no final drop, the ending being abrupt like that of type E:

⌣́ x x x | ⌣́ :        wǣron mìne fét        (S 9a)

    | 1  1      1  1 | 2  𝄞 |

$\stackrel{\_}{\smile}$ x x x x | $\stackrel{\_}{\smile}$ :　　Hwǽðre iċ þùrh þæt góld　　(R 18a)

$$| \; 1 \; \frac{1}{3} \; \frac{2}{3} \; 1 \quad 1 \; | \; 2 \quad \text{Ⓐ} \; |$$

þá hē hǽfde þæt fólc　　(M 22a)

$$| \; 1 \quad 1 \quad 1 \quad \frac{1}{3} \; \frac{2}{3} \; | \; 2 \quad \text{Ⓐ} \; |$$

$\stackrel{\_}{\smile}$ x x x x x | $\stackrel{\_}{\smile}$ :　　þá on-èfen hira frḗan　　(M 184a)

$$| \; \frac{4}{3} \; \frac{2}{3} \; \frac{1}{2} \frac{1}{2} \quad \frac{1}{2} \frac{1}{2} \; | \; 2 \quad \text{Ⓐ} \; |$$

The first of these verses has the same number of syllables and the same rhythm as *þenden hē wið wulf* (*Beowulf* 3027a), and I think all four are authentic. [62]

# The Hypermetric Verses

In *The Dream of the Rood*, *The Wanderer*, and *The Seafarer*, as in several other Old English poems, we encounter clusters of verses that appear to exceed the normal metrical limit by several rather weighty syllables. Sometimes these are syllables that can be treated as all or part of a drop, sometimes they include an alliterating lift. Most of the verses resemble normal varieties of type A to which several syllables have been prefixed. A few end like this or that other type, and have similar prefixes. I find it convenient to classify them as HA, HB, etc. if the prefixed syllables include an alliterating lift, and as hA, hB, etc. if they do not. In the following examples, taken from the three poems in this book, the alliteration is distinguished by boldface type, and in the notations, the bar marks the point after which the pattern of a normal verse, or the part of a normal verse that starts with its first lift, may be observed: [63]

HA 1:　　$\stackrel{\_}{\smile}$ x | $\stackrel{\_}{\smile}$ x $\stackrel{\_}{\smile}$ x :　**e**fstan **e**lne miċle　(R 34a)

　　　　$\stackrel{\_}{\smile}$ x x | $\stackrel{\_}{\smile}$ x x $\stackrel{\_}{\smile}$ x :　**b**eorn of his **b**rēostum acȳðan

　　　　　　　　　　　　　　　　　　　　(W 113a)

HA 2a:　$\stackrel{\_}{\smile}$ x x | $\stackrel{\_}{\smile}$ $\smile$ x $\stackrel{\_}{\smile}$ x :　**S**tormas þǣr **s**tān-clifu bēoton

　　　　　　　　　　　　　　　　　　　　(S 23a)

---

[62] See *The Rhythm of Beowulf*, revised edition, pp. xxx and 321.

[63] Thus, where the comparison is to type B or type C, the bar does not mark the place where the corresponding normal verse would begin.

HA 4:    ´ x x x x | ´ ´ ∪ x :  Ēadiġ biþ sē-þe ēaþ-mōd
                                                    leofaþ    (S 107a)

hA 1:    x x x x | ´ x x ´ x :  Eall ic wæs mid sorgum
                                                    ġedrēfed    (R 20b)

hA 2a:   x x x x x | ´ ´ ´ x :  Ongunnon him þā mold-ærn
                                                    wyrċan    (R 65b)

hA 4:    x x x x x | ´ ´ ∪ x :  Ongunnon him þā sorg-lēoþ
                                                    galan    (R 67b)

HB 1:    ∪ x x x | ´ x ´ :  fæġere þurh forþ-ġesceaft    (R 10a)

hB 1:    x x x | ´ x ∪ x :  sōhton him wuldres Cyning
                                                    (R 133b)

HC 1:    x ∪ x x x | ∪ x ´ x :  begoten of þæs Guman sīdan
                                                    (R 49a)

HC 2:    x ∪ x x x x x | ´ ∪ x :  Onġierede hine þā
                                                    ġeong Hæleþ    (R 39a)

HD 1:    x ´ x x x | ´ ´ ´ x :  Aleġdon hīe þær lim-wēriġne
                                                    (R 63a)

hD 1:    x x x x | ´ ´ ´ x :  Ġeseah iċ þā Frēan mann-cynnes
                                                    (R 33b)

hD 2:    x x x x | ´ ´ ∪ x :  þā hīe woldon eft sīðian    (R 68b)

hE:      x x x x x | ´ ´ x x ´ :  Ġenāmon hīe þær ælmihtiġne
                                                    God    (R 60b)

hE*:     x x x x | ´ x ´ x ∪ x :  Behēoldon þær enġel-dryhta
                                                    fela    (R 9b as emended)

Almost invariably the strong openings marked *H* are in the on-verse and have double alliteration, which occurs on the lift of the opening and the first lift of the normal close. The weak openings marked *h* are characteristic of the off-verse, and in that position have single alliteration on the first lift of the normal close. On the rare occasions (not exemplified in this book) when weak openings occur in the on-verse, they tend to have double alliteration on the two lifts of the normal close. The following off-verse is exceptional:

HA 1:  x ´ x x | ´ x ´ x :  ġestāg hē on ġealgan hēanne    (R 40b).
The opening of this verse would pass for weak if the alliteration

were on *g*, as might be expected; but it is actually on *st*, and the opening must therefore be considered strong. In general, hypermetric verses alliterate with great regularity at the points indicated. Supplementary alliteration of a different letter occurs now and then on rather prominent syllables, but quite unpredictably.

The rare instances of hypermetric verses that close like type B or type C are troublesome because ambiguous. They are often not clearly distinguishable from normal verses of the same types or, if they have strong openings, from normal verses of type D*. The four *ubi sunt* verses in *The Wanderer* (lines 92–93) have this sort of ambiguity. They conform to the normal types B and C but are heavy enough to be treated as hB and hC. Since they stand by themselves and are not decisively hypermetric in form I prefer to regard them as normal verses, but to read them—the opening verse especially—at a retarded tempo.

It would be a great mistake to suppose that the poets, in composing hypermetric verses, simply took normal verses and added preludes to them. They are constructed as whole verses of another order; yet the resemblance of the close to a normal verse is, I think, a clue to their basic rhythm. By a rather complicated series of inferences (of which I have given some idea in *The Rhythm of Beowulf*) I have come to believe that this rhythm resembles the normal in structure but is twice as long. We have two measures of quadruple time for each verse, but the unitary beat is 2 instead of 1. If we use musical notation and call the normal time 4/8, the hypermetric time is 4/4. Thus the second measure of a hypermetric verse is equal in duration to both measures of a normal verse. Each half of this slower measure is equivalent to one normal measure and can assert a quasi-independence. [64]

The verses already quoted can be adjusted to the basic rhythm as follows:

HA 1:        ĕfstàn    ĕlne mĭcle      (R 34a)
            | 4   2   ♠ | 2  2     2   1   ∧ |

---

[64] The absence of consistent emphasis at the mid-point of the first measure is one of the reasons for thinking of two double measures rather than four of the normal sort. Another is the position of the alliteration. For full discussion of this problem, see *The Rhythm of Beowulf*, pp. 121 ff.

bēorn of his brēostum acȳðan　(W 113a)

| 4 ⚮ 1 1 | 2 1 1 2 1 ∧ |

HA 4:　Ēadiġ biþ sē-þe ēaþ-mōd lēofaþ　(S 107a)

| 2 2 2 1 1 | 2 2 1 1 ⚮ |

hA 2a:　Ongùnnon him þā mōld-ærn wȳrċan　(R 65b)

| ⚮ 1 1 1 1 1 | 2 2 2 1 ∧ |

HB 1:　fǣgere þurh fōrþ-ġescēaft　(R 10a)

| 1 1 1 ⚮ 2 | 3 1 2 ⚮ |

hB 1:　sòhton him wŭldres Cȳning　(R 133b)

| ⚮ 2 1 1 | 2 2 1 1 ⚮ |

HC 1:　begōten of þæs Gŭman sĭdan　(R 49a) [65]

1 | 1 3 ⚮ 1 1 | 1 3 2 1 ∧ |

HC 2:　Ongī́erede hìne þā ġēong Hǣleþ　(R 39a) [66]

1 | 1 1 2 1 1 2 | 2 ⚮ 1 1

HD 1:　Alēġdon hìe þǣr līm-wēriġne　(R 63a)

1 | 2 2 2 2 | 4 2 1 1 |

hE:　Ġenāmon hīe þǣr ǣlmihtiġne Gŏd　(R 60b)

| ⚮ 1 1 1 1 1 | 2 1 ½ ½ 2 ⚮ |

Hypermetric verses appear in many different contexts and can produce various effects. The extra long quantities that characterize a good many of the strong openings require a half-chanting delivery and can create an effect of deliberation or of measured solemnity. In contrast, the polysyllabic weak openings can seem almost garrulous. In *The Dream of the Rood* they may suggest impulsive outpourings of the speaker's feelings, alternating with the slow openings that arrest movement and bring out the depth of his emotion. At the end of *The Wanderer* and *The Seafarer* the hypermetric verses are associated by their content with gnomic wisdom and may seem somewhat aloof and oracular. In *The Seafarer* they have, in addition, a rather grim intensity. No verse form, however, can be said to have a meaning of its own.

[65] Better, perhaps, with a "semi-strong" opening: | ⚮ 1 1 1 1 1 | 1 3 2 1 ∧ | .

[66] I avail myself of the last part of the second measure to start the next verse, thus coverting the latter to a normal verse with anacrusis so that it matches the completely normal sequel, line 40a.

Certain forms seem appropriate to certain ranges of emotion, but it is the chief function of any verse form to enhance the specific meanings that are carried by the words, partly by conferring on them the added solemnity of a basic order, partly by admitting the little rhythmic variations that their individuality requires.

## Illustrative Notations of Consecutive Passages

In the foregoing account attention has been focused on individual verses. The beginning and end of such analysis, however, is the consecutively composed poem. We must begin with the verse as it occurs in its context, and must test the value of our results by the extent to which they accord with and deepen our understanding of whole passages. As an aid to this kind of testing I have supplied consecutive rhythmic notations for three passages chosen from the first three poems in the book. Much more extensive notations, making use of the traditional musical symbols, will be found in *The Rhythm of Beowulf*. My own way of reading all these poems is illustrated fully on the phonograph record to which I have referred at the beginning of this account.

The student should be encouraged to acquire for himself the art of reading these poems aloud with due attention not merely to rhythm but to the full expression of their meaning. There is no substitute for this kind of poetic understanding, and it is worth striving for even though, with our limited knowledge, it cannot be fully achieved. A step in the right direction can be taken long before the student has mastered the details of Old English versification. The application of a rhythmic notation, with due attention to quantity, requires careful study and long practice, whereas a respectably rhythmic reading of most verses can be accomplished much more simply. If the student will learn to pick out the governing accents, time them with reasonable accuracy, supply rests where accents are missing, and observe a distinction between long and short syllables, he need not work out the quantitative details. They will take care of themselves.

It is good practice to beat time to the measures, bringing the hand down for the primary beat at the beginning of the measure, up for the secondary beat in the middle of it. The effect will be too mechanical but it is a proper beginning. The subtle modulations of an expressive recitation will follow in due course when the basic order is mastered.

## Cædmon's Hymn

Nú scùlon hériàn    héofon-rìċes Wéard,
| 2  1 1 | 2 2 | 1 1  1 1 | 2  𝄐 |

Métodès méahtà    ànd his mód-ġeþànc,
| 1 1 2 | 2  1 ∧ | 𝄐 1   1 | $\frac{4}{3}$ $\frac{2}{3}$ 2 |

wéorc Wúldor-Fǣder,    swà hē wúndra ġehwǣs,
| 2  𝄐 | 2    1 1 | 𝄐  1  1 | 1  $\frac{1}{2}$ $\frac{1}{2}$ 1 ∧ |

éċè Drýhtèn,    ór astéaldè.
| 2 2 | 2 1 ∧ | 3 1 | 2 1 ∧ |

Hè ǽrest scòp    íeldà béarnùm
| 𝄐 2 | 1 1    2 | 2 2 | 2 1 ∧ |

héofon to hrófè,    hǽliġ Sċíeppeǹd;
| 1  2   1 | 2 1 ∧ | 2 2 | 2  2 |

þà míddan-ġeàrd    mánn-cýnnes Wéard,
| 𝄐 2 | 1 1 2 | 2  1 1 | 2  𝄐 |

éċè Drýhtèn,    ǽftèr téodè—
| 2 2 | 2 1 ∧ | 2 2 | 2 1 ∧ |

fírùm fóldàn    Frḗa ǽlmìhtiġ.
| 2 2 | 2  1 ∧ | 2 𝄐 | 2  1 1 |

# The Battle of Brunanburh

## Lines 1–20a

Ǽðelstằn cẏning,    éorlà drẏhtèn,

| 1  1  2 | 1  1  𝄐 | 2  2 | 2  1  ∧ |

béornà béag-ġìèfa,    ànd his brốðor ēằc,

| 2  2 | 2  1  1 | 𝄐 1    1  | 1  1    1  ∧ |

Éadmuǹd ǽðelìng,    éaldor-lằngne tĩr

| 2    2 | 1  1  1    ∧ | $\frac{4}{3}$  $\frac{2}{.3}$  $\frac{4}{3}$  $\frac{2}{3}$ | 2  ∧

ġeslốgoǹ æt sǽċċè    swéordà écgùm

| 1 | 2  1  1 | 2  1 ∧ | 2  2 | 2  2 |

ẏmbe Brũnanbừrh.    Bốrd-weằll clúfon,

| 𝄐 1    1  | 1  1    1    ∧ | 2    2 | 1  1  𝄐 |

héowòn héaðu-lĩnda    hằmorà lắfùm

| 2  2 | 1  1  1  1 | 1  1  2 | 2  1  ∧ |

éaforàn Éadweằrdes,    swā him ġe-ǽðele wằs

| 1  1  2 | 2    1    1 | ∧    1    $\frac{4}{3}$  $\frac{2}{3}$ | $\frac{2}{3}\frac{2}{3}$  2 |

fràm cnéo-mằgum    þæt hĩe æt cắmpe ồft

| 𝄐  2 | 2  1  1 | ∧  1  1  1 | $\frac{4}{3}$  $\frac{2}{3}$  2 |

wìþ lắðra ġehwồne    lắnd eắlgồden,

| 𝄐  2 | 1  $\frac{1}{2}$  $\frac{1}{2}$  1  1 | 2 𝄐| 2  1  1 |

hốrd and hằmàs.    Héttènd crũngon,

| 2   ∧  1 | 2  1 ∧ | 2  2 | 2  1  ∧ |

Scốttà léodè    and scĩp-flốtan,

| 2  2 | 2  1    1 | 2 𝄐| 1  1  𝄐 |

fắġè féollòn.    Féld dénnồde

| 2  2 | 2  1    ∧ | 2  𝄐| 2  1  1

sécgà swắtè    sìþþan sũnne ừpp

| 2  2 | 2  1 ∧| 𝄐  1  1 | $\frac{4}{3}$  $\frac{2}{3}$  1    ∧|

òn mốrgen-tĩd,    mǽrè tũngồl,

| 𝄐  2 | 1  1  2 | 2  2 | 2  1  ∧ |

glǽd òfer grúndàs,     Gódes càndel béorht,

| 2   1   1 | 2   1 ∧ | 1   1   1   1 | 2     ♌ |

ḗċès Drýhtnès,     òþ sēo ǽðele ġescèaft

| 2  2     | 2    2 | ♌  1ʼ    1 | $\frac{1}{2}$ $\frac{1}{2}$$\frac{1}{2}$ $\frac{1}{2}$  2     |

sǽg to sétlè.     Þ̀ær læġ sḗcg màniġ

| 3    1 | 2  1∧ | ♌   1     1 | 2     1  1 |

gǽrum aġ́ietèd,     gúma Nórðèrna

| 2ʼ  1    1 | 2  1     ∧ | 1   1  ♌ | 2  1   1 |

òfer scíeld scòten,     swèlċe Scýttisc èàc,

| ♌ 1  1     | 2     1  1 | ♌   1   1    1 | 1  1    1    ∧ |

wḗrìġ, wíges sǽd.

| 2  1∧ | 1  1    2     |

# The Dream of the Rood

## Lines 1–23

Hwæ̀t, iċ swḗfna cỳst     sḗcgàn wíllè,

| ♌    $\frac{4}{3}$  $\frac{2}{3}$    | $\frac{4}{3}$ $\frac{2}{3}$  2     | 2  2     | 2  1 ∧ |

hwæ̀t mè̀ ġemǽttè     to mídrè níhtè,

| 2     1  1 | 2  1     1 | 2  2     | 2  1 ∧ |

sìþþan rḗord-bèrend     rḗstè wúnodòn.

| ♌ 1  1     | 2     1  1     | 2  2    | 1  1  2     |

Þúhte mḕ þæt iċ ġesáwè     sḗldlìcre trḗo

| 1  $\frac{1}{3}$    $\frac{2}{3}$  $\frac{2}{3}$  $\frac{2}{3}$  $\frac{2}{3}$ | 2  1 ∧ | 2  1   1     | 2 ∧ |

on lýft lǽdàn     lḗohtè bewúndèn,

| 1     | 2  ♌ | 2  1 ∧ | 2   1   1 | 2  1    ∧ |

bḗamà bḗorhtòst.     Èall þæt bḗacen wǽs

| 2   2 | 2     2     | ♌  1     1     | 1  1     $\frac{4}{3}$ |

begóten mid góldè;     gímmàs stódòn

| $\frac{2}{3}$  | 1  2     1     | 2  1 ∧ | 2    2    | 2  2     |

fǽgere æt fóldan scèatum,     swèlċe þær fífe wæ̀ron

| 1  1  1 ♌ 2  | 2   2        2  2     | ♌     1   1  2 | 2 2     2  2     |

úppe on þam éaxl-ġespànne.     Behèoldon þǽr

|2  2⚹1  1   1  |2  1  1   2  1 ∧| ⚹ 1  1  1   2

ǽnġel-dryhta féla,

| $\frac{4}{3}$ $\frac{2}{3}$  1  1  1  1 ⚹|

fǽġere  þurh fórþ-ġesceàft;     ne wæs þǽr hùru

|1  1  1⚹ 2    | 3   1  2   ⚹ | ∧ 1   1   1   2  2

frácuðes ġeàlga,

|1  1  2   2  1

ac híne þǽr behéoldòn     hálġè gástàs,

1  |1  1  $\frac{4}{3}$   $\frac{2}{3}$| 2  2     |2  2 |2  1  ∧ |

ménn òfer móldàn    and èall þēos mǽre ġesceàft.

|2   1  1   |2  2  |∧ 1   1   1    |1  $\frac{1}{2}$  $\frac{1}{2}$  2   |

Séldlīc wæs se síġe-bèam,    and ìc sýnnum fàg,

|1  1   $\frac{4}{3}$  $\frac{2}{3}$ |1  1  2    |∧ 1  2  |1  1   $\frac{4}{3}$

forwúndòd mid wámmùm.     Ġesèah iċ wúldres trèo

$\frac{2}{3}$ |2  1   1   |2  2   |∧ 1  1  1   |1  1   2  |

wǽdùm ġewéorðòd     wýnnùm scīnàn,

|2  $\frac{4}{3}$   $\frac{2}{3}$ |2  1  ∧  |2   2   |2  $\frac{4}{3}$

ġegíered mid góldè;    ġímmàs hǽfdòn

$\frac{2}{3}$| 1  2   1   |2  1  ∧ |2   2   |2   $\frac{4}{3}$

bewríġen  wéorþlìċe   Wéaldèndes trèo.

$\frac{2}{3}$ |1  1  ⚹ |2  1  1    | 2   1  1   |2 ⚹ |

Hwǽðre iċ þùrh þæt góld    onġíetan méahtè

|1  $\frac{1}{3}$ $\frac{2}{3}$  1    1   |2  ∧ 1  |1  3   |2  1 ∧ |

eármrà ǽr-ġewìnn,    þæt hit ǽrest ongànn

|2    2 | $\frac{4}{3}$ $\frac{2}{3}$  2   |⚹ 1   1 | $\frac{2}{3}$ $\frac{2}{3}$ $\frac{2}{3}$  2   |

swǽtan on þā swìðran hèalfe.    Èall iċ wæs

|2  2⚹1  1    |2  2   2  1 ∧| ⚹ 1  1  1

mid sórgum ġedrǽfed;

1  |2  1  1  21  ∧ |

fórht iċ wæs for þǽre fǽġeran ġesìhþe.   Ġesèah

|3   1   1  1   1 1 |1  1  $\frac{4}{3}$   $\frac{2}{3}$2   1  ∧ |⚹ 1  2

iċ þæt fúse bèacen

1  1  |2  2  2  2  |

wéndan   wǽdum and blēoum:    hwílum hit wæs

| 2   2  Ⓐ | 2   1   1     2   1 ∧     | 2   1   1   2

mid wǽtan bestīemed,

2  | 2   1     1   2   $\frac{4}{3}$

beswíled   mid swǽtes gánge,    hwílum mid

$\frac{2}{3}$  | 1  1  Ⓐ   2   | 2  2   2   1 ∧ | Ⓐ   2   1     1

sínce geġīerwed.

| 2   1   1   2   1 ∧ |

# GLOSSARY

The order is alphabetical. The ligature *æ* is treated as *ae*, falling between *ad* and *af*. The voiceless spirant *þ*, interchanging medially with voiced *ð*, follows *t* as a separate letter. Words beginning with the prefix *ġe-* are listed according to their stems; for example, *ġe-beorg* follows *beorg*.

The treatment of compounds is unusual. All words separated into two elements by hyphens in the text of the poems (unless the first element is merely an unstressed prefix, as with *ġe-* when the stem begins with a vowel, or *oþ-* when the stem begins with *þ*) are registered according to their separate elements and also as compounds. Thus *brim-fuglas, Wanderer* 47, is listed according to its elements, *brim* and *fugol*; but also, under the first element, *brim*, the whole compound is listed and defined, and under *fugol* there is a cross-reference to the compound. The student is advised to learn the simple elements rather than the compounds, for the poets use a comparatively limited group of elements to produce a great variety of compounds, most of which can be interpreted successfully by anyone who knows the meaning of the elements. At the same time there are often several possible meanings in an element, and now and then subtleties in the combinations that require careful interpretation. It is therefore safer to define the compound as well as its elements, making sure that the definition fits the immediate context. Most of the compounds are nominal or adjectival, but even such minor combinations as *for-þon, on-weġ, sē-þe*, and *þā-ġiet* are treated in the same way for the sake of consistency.

Hyphenation has not been extended in the text to mere prefixes and suffixes, and therefore such words as *anforht* and *fǣrlīce* are treated like simple words even though it is easy to separate their elements. In the glossary itself hyphenation has been extended to prefixes for the sake of clarity, and cross-references are employed to connect prefixed with unprefixed forms.

Prefixes are ordinarily left undefined, since full definitions would fill a great deal of space. Most of them appear also as separate words and are likewise familiar in modern English. Exception is made on behalf of the very common prefixes *ge-* and *a-*, because they do not appear independently and their meanings, though sometimes important, are elusive. Those who desire further guidance should consult the Bosworth-Toller *Anglo-Saxon Dictionary* and *Supplement*, and the *Oxford English Dictionary*.

Verbs are cross-referenced with particular care, in order to enable the student to keep track of, and compare, the simple verb and its prefixed variations. The unprefixed form is used as a guide, by cross-reference, to the prefixed forms. Hence it is always entered even if it does not actually occur in the poems.

As a further aid to the student, class-numbers are assigned to the verbs, and the principal parts of all the strong and preterite-present verbs are spelled out, along with those of a few particularly troublesome weak verbs. The principal parts will be found under the unprefixed verb if it actually occurs in the poems; otherwise under one or more of the prefixed forms.

Nouns that do not belong to the main declensions (masculine and neuter *a*-stems, feminine *ō*-stems) are classified either as weak (wk.) or by stems: *ja*-stem, *i*-stem, *u*-stem, etc. This will not always be of practical assistance to the student, but often it will guide him (by way of his reference grammar) to the reason for an unusual ending or the presence of *i*-mutation in the stem-vowel. Adjectives are similarly treated, though the useful distinctions are fewer. The *ja-/jō*-stems are marked simply "ja-stem"; the *wa-/wō*-stems simply "wa-stem". All others follow the regular *a-/ō*-declension, except for *cwic(u)*, which is marked "u-stem".

Familiarity with *i*-mutation and the vowel-gradation exhibited most obviously in the strong verbs enables one to associate a number of words that would otherwise appear to be unrelated. For this reason attention has been called to a good many of the unmutated base-words on which weak verbs of the first class (characterized by the prehistoric ending *-jan with its regular mutating power) are formed, and to a few of the more conspicuous and helpful gradational correspondences.

# Abbreviations

The poems are cited according to the order of the texts, by initial and line-number: C (Cædmon's Hymn); B (Brunanburh); R (Rood); M (Maldon); W (Wanderer); S (Seafarer); D (Deor). Immediately following the boldface entry of a word is a grammatical notation. Nouns are classified by gender (*m.*, *f.*, or *n.*) and also, as mentioned above, page 142, by the prehistoric stem-endings indicating their declension if they are not the regular *a*- or *ō*-stems. The weak declension (*n*-stems) is marked *wk.* before the specification of gender.

Verbs are classified as follows:

*v.1* to *v.7* = strong verb, class 1 to class 7 (Arabic numbers).
*wk.v.I* to *wk.v.III* = weak verb, class I to class III (Roman).
*pret.-pres.v.* = preterite-present verb.
*anom.v.* = anomalous verb.          *contr.v.* = contract verb.

The other parts of speech are designated by easily recognized abbreviations: *pron., adj., adv., prep., conj., interj.; poss.* for possessive, *rel.* for relative, *num.* for numeral; *comp.* for comparative, *superl.* for superlative. On the designation of stem-endings for certain adjectives, see above, page 142.

Declensional forms of nouns are described by case (*n., v., g., d., a., i.* for nominative, vocative, genitive, dative, accusative, instrumental) and number (*s., p.,* for singular, plural) in that order (*ns., gs.,* for nominative singular, genitive singular, etc., with period after the second letter only). Adjectives have a third letter for the gender: *nsm.* for nominative singular masculine, etc., but this is omitted for the genitive and dative plural, where there is never any distinction of gender in the endings. When there is need to give case alone or number alone, fuller abbreviations are used (*nom., gen., dat., acc., instr.; sg., pl.;* and *part. gen.* for partitive genitive). The combinations *dis.* and *dip.* mean dative or instrumental, singular and plural respectively. This formula is used for nouns with dative case-endings when they stand alone (without prepositions) in an apparently instrumental function. Nouns with such endings following prepositions are said to be dative unless there is clear evidence (from an adjective or article) that they are instrumental.

Verb-forms are marked *inf.* (infinitive), *pres. part.* (present participle), *pp.* (past participle), or according to tense (*pres.* or *pret.*), person and number (*1s.* for first person singular, *1p.* for first person plural, etc.). The mood is not specified if it is indicative. Imperatives are marked *imper.* (*s.* or *p.*), and subjunctives, *subj.* Occasionally there is reason to indicate whether a verb is transitive (*trans.*) or intransitive (*intrans.*), or that it is used absolutely (*absol.*).

After the main entry, its classification, and a definition, the particular forms occurring in the texts are cited. If the form is the same as the main entry, it is not repeated. If it differs by simple addition of an ending, a dash for the uninflected entry is followed by the letters to be added; if the change is partly internal, the whole form is given. For example, under *burg, f. cons.-stem,* the notation *as. M 291* means, accusative singular *burg,* Maldon 291; *dp.—um* means, dative plural *burgum;* but for *ap.* (accusative plural) the internally altered form *byriġ* is given entire.

Occasionally, when a form already indicated is repeated, only its initial is given. Thus, following citation of the form *abrēoðe, a. his anġinn* stands for *abrēoðe his anġinn.*

Among other, commonly received abbreviations are *OE* for Old English, *Gmc.* for Germanic, *cf.* for *confer* (compare), *q.v.*

for *quod vide* (which see). In certain grammatical descriptions, *w.* stands for with.

# Dictionaries and Grammars

For full definition with illustrative quotations from prose and poetry, the student must consult Joseph Bosworth, *An Anglo-Saxon Dictionary*, edited and enlarged by T. Northcote Toller, 1882–1898, and the *Supplement* by Toller, 1908–1921, both volumes published at Oxford by the Clarendon Press, reprinted 1929 and 1954 and still available; often called "Bosworth-Toller" for short. Both volumes must be consulted for a given word. Since a number of Old English texts have been edited since the completion of Toller's *Supplement* and others are still unedited, no dictionary is complete. The most up-to-date for its list of words and the handiest for quick reference is *A Concise Anglo-Saxon Dictionary* by J. R. Clark Hall, 4th ed. with a Supplement by Herbert D. Meritt, Cambridge University Press, 1960. Of great value as a partial concordance to the poetry is C. W. M. Grein's *Sprachschatz der angelsächsischen Dichter*, newly edited by F. Holthausen and J. J. Köhler, Heidelberg: Carl Winter, 1912–1914. A complete concordance, based on the texts of the Krapp-Dobbie *Anglo-Saxon Poetic Records*, is in preparation by J. B. Bessinger, Jr. Useful for etymology is F. Holthausen, *Altenglisches etymologisches Wörterbuch*, Heidelberg: Carl Winter, 1934; 2nd ed. with bibliographical supplement, 1963. For all words that have survived in the language after 1100, the thirteen-volume *Oxford English Dictionary* is often of great value. Middle English forms of these words, if not the latest on record, are sometimes entered for cross-reference, but the main entry is under the *latest* spelling.

The fullest and most authoritative grammars are A. Campbell, *Old English Grammar*, Oxford: The Clarendon Press, 1959, and Karl Brunner, *Altenglische Grammatik, nach der angelsächsischen Grammatik von Eduard Sievers*, 3rd ed., Tübingen: Max Niemeyer, 1965 (usually called "Sievers-Brunner").

# A

ā, adv. *always, ever;* M 315; S 42, 47.

a- (or ā-). unstressed verbal prefix of various origin (Æ-, OR-, AN-, etc.) and various meaning *(up, on, from, away,* etc.), but often modifying only slightly the meaning of the unprefixed verb.

a-bēodan, v.2. *announce, deliver (a message);* imper. s. abēod, M 49 (absol. use); pret. 3s. abēad, M 27. [Cf. bēodan.]

a-brēoðan, v.2. *fail, come to naught;* pres. 3s. subj. abrēoðe, M 242 (a. his anginn, *may his conduct have an evil end*—Gordon). [BRĒOÐAN, BRĒAÞ, BRUÐON, BROÐEN, without the usual grammatical change, ð to *d.*]

ac, conj. *but;* R 11, 43, 115, 119, 132; M 82, 193, 247, 252, 269, 318; S 47.

a-cweċċan, wk.v.I. *shake, brandish,* pret. 3s. acweahte, M 255, 310. [CWEĊĊAN (Gmc. *CWACJAN), CWEAHTE, CWEAHT; cf. CWACIAN, wk.v.II, *quake.*]

a-cweðan, v.5, trans. *speak, utter;* pres. 3s. acwiþ, W 91. [Cf. cweðan.]

a-cȳðan, wk.v.I. *make known, manifest;* inf. W 113. [Cf. ġe-cȳðan.]

ādl, f. *disease, sickness;* ns. S 70.

æfen(n), n. ja-stem (also m.). *evening.* æfen-tīd, f. i-stem. *evening hour;* as.—e, R 68. (Possibly ap., *in the evening hours,* but tid sometimes has as. —e like the ō-stems.)

æfre, adv. *ever;* B 66; D 11; æfre ymbe stunde, *ever and anon, repeatedly,* M 271 [see ymbe].

æftan, adv. *from behind;* B 63.

æfter, prep. *after.* (a) w. dat. (temporal), R 65; M 65. (b) w. acc. (marking object of affection), *with longing for,* W 50.

æfter, adv. *after(wards);* C 8: S 77 (i.e., *after death).* æfter-cweðende, pres. part., pl., as noun, *those speaking afterwards (speaking of a man after his death);* gp. —cweðendra, S 72.

æġhwelċ, pron. and adj. *each, every (one).* — as pron. w. part. gen., nsm. M 234 (w. ūre, *of us);* asm. —ne, R 86 (w. gp. ānra, *each one).* —as adj., nsf. R 120. [ā, *ever,* plus ġe-hwelċ, q.v.]

æġðer, pron. *each (of two), either;* nsm. M 133. —conj. æġðer . . . and, *both . . . and,* M 224. [Shortened from ǣĠHWÆÐER, ā plus ġe-hwæðer, *each of two*].

ælmihtiġ, adj. *almighty;* nsm. C 9; R 39, 93, 98, 106, 153, 156; asm. —ne, R 60. [ǢL-, combining form of eall, *all,* plus mihtiġ, *mighty.*]

æniġ, pron. and adj. *anyone, any.* — pron., nsm. R 110, 117; M 70; dsm. —um, R 47. — adj., nsf. M 195; gsm. ǣnġes, S 116.

ǣr, adv. *before, formerly, already;* R 118, 137, 145; M 60; W 43, 113; S 102; D 41; — giving pluperf. value to past tense, R 114, 154; M 158, 198, 290. ǣr-ġewinn, n.

*former struggle, agony;* as. R 19. [See **ǽror, ǽrest.**]

**ǽr,** prep. w. dat. *before,* S 69. **ǽr-þon,** conj. *before,* R 88.

**ǽr,** conj. w. subj. *before;* M 61 (correl. w. **ǽr,** adv.) , 279, 300; W 64, 69; S 74.

**ǽrende,** n. ja-stem. *message;* as. M 28.

**ǽrest,** adv. superl. *earliest, first;* C 5; M 124, 186; R 19 (þæt hit ǽrest ongann, *in that it had straightway begun*[?]);—þā . . . ǽrest, *when first, as soon as,* M 5.

**ærn,** n. *dwelling, house.* See **mold-ærn.**

**ærnan,** wk. v.I. *cause (a horse) to run; gallop;* pret. 3p. **ærndon,** M 191. [Gmc. *RANNJAN, causative based on RANN, second gradation of RINNAN, v.3, *run;* in OE the *r* in these forms was frequently metathesized.]

**ǽror,** adv. comp. *earlier,* R 108.

**ǽr-þon,** see **ǽr,** prep.

**ǽs,** n. *food, carrion;* gs. —es, B 63; M 107.

**æsc,** m. *ash (-wood).* —(a) *spear (of ash);* as. M 43, 310; gp. —a, W 99. **æsc-holt,** n. *(ash-wood) spear;* as. M 230. — (b) *ship (of ash):* **æsc-here,** m. i-stem, *army coming in ships; viking army;* ns. M 69. (The cognate Old Norse ASKR was applied to the typical viking warship.)

**æt,** prep. w. dat. *at, in, by;* B 4, 8, 42, 44; R 8, 63; M 10, 39 (æt ūs, *at our hands, from us*), etc. (16 times); W 111; S 7.

**ǽterne,** see **ǽtren.**

**æt-foran,** prep. w. dat. *before, in front of,* M 16. [Cf. **be-foran.**]

**æt-gædere,** adv. *together, in unison.* **bū-tū æ.,** *both together,* R 48; **samod æ.,** *in joint action together,*

*both together,* W 39. [Cf. **to-gædere,** usually with sense of interaction or interrelation or meeting rather than mere association or simultaneity.]

**ǽtren, ǽterne,** adj. *poisoned, deadly;* nsm. **ǽterne,** M 146; asm. **ǽtrenne,** M 47. [Properly **ǽtren,** later **ǼTTREN,** from **ĀTER,** poison. The odd form **ǽterne** was perhaps influenced by **norðerne, sūðerne,** etc., or by some old poetic use of a weak form, **ǼTRENA,** metathesized as **ǼTERNA.**]

**æt-samne,** adv. *together;* **bēgen æ.,** *both together,* B 57.

**æt-wītan,** v.I, w. dat. *reproach;* inf., M 220, 250. [Cf. **ġe-wītan.**]

**æðele,** adj. *noble;* nsm. M 280; nsf. wk. B 16; asm. wk. **æðelan,** M 151.

**ġe-æðele,** adj. *befitting noble descent;* nsn. B 7.

**æðeling,** m. *nobleman, prince;* (as title) *member of the royal family, prince;* ns. B 3, 58; *Prince,* ds. —e, R 58; (broadly) gp. —a, S 93.

**æðelu,** n. ja-stem, pl. *descent, (noble) origin;* ap. M 216.

**æwisc,** adj. *ashamed.* **æwisc-mōd,** adj. *ashamed in spirit;* npm. —e, B 56.

**a-feallan,** v.7. *fall, be laid low (in death);* pp. **afeallen,** nsm. M 202. [Cf. **feallan.**]

**a-flieman,** wk.v.I. *put to flight;* pret. 3s. **afliemde,** M 243. [Cf. **ġe-flieman.**]

**a-fȳsan,** wk.v.I. (a) *urge forward, impel;* pp. **afȳsed,** nsm. R 125; (b) *drive away;* inf. M 3. [Cf. **fȳsan.**]

**āgan,** pret.-pres. v. *have, possess;* inf. M 87; pres. ls. **āg,** M 175; 3s. **āg,** R 107; S 27 (as aux. w. pp.); 3s. subj. **āge,** W 64; lp. subj. **āgen,** S 117; pret. ls. **āhte,** D 38; 3s **āhte,** M 189; D 18, 22. — neg. **nāgan,**

*have not;* pres. 1s. **nāg,** R 131.
[ĀGAN, ĀG, ĀGON, ĀHTE.]

**a-ġiefan,** v.5. *give, render;* pret. 3s.
**aġeaf,** M 44; pp. **aġiefen,** nsn. M
116. [ĊIEFAN, ĊEAF, ĊĒAFON,
ĊIEFEN.]

**a-ġietan,** wk.v.I. *destroy (by shedding
blood);* pp. **aġieted,** nsm. B 18.
[Base-word ĊEAT, as in pret. s. of
ġēotan, q.v.]

**a-hafen,** see **a-hebban.**

**a-hēawan,** v.7. *cut down;* pp.
**a-hēawen,** nsm. R 29 [Cf. hēawan.]

**a-hebban,** v.6. *raise, lift up;* pret. 1s.
**ahōf,** R 44; 3s. M 130, 244; 3p.
**ahōfon,** R 61; fig. (with ref. to
lifting up the voice) , *utter loudly;*
pret. 1p. **ahōfon,** M 213; pp.
**ahafen,** nsm. M 106. [Cf. hebban.]

**āhte,** see **āgan.**

**a-lecgan,** wk.v.I, *lay;* pret. 3p.
**aleġdon,** R 63. [Cf. lecgan.]

**a-līefan,** wk.v.I. *allow;* inf. M 90.
[Base-word **lēaf,** f. *permission;* cf.
ge-līefan.]

**amen,** Lat. (from Hebrew, *verily*) ;
(as closing formula) *may it be so!*
S 124.

**a-mierran,** wk.v.I. *cripple, wound;*
pret. 3s. **amierde,** M 165. [Base-
word *MEARR;* cf. ĠE-MEARR, n.
*hindrance.*]

**ān,** pron. and adj. *one;* — as pron.,
asm. —ne, M 117; gp. —ra, w.
ǣghwelċ, ġehwelċ, *each one, every-
one.* R 86, 108; — as adj., asm. —
ne, M 226. **ān-floga,** wk. m. *solitary
flier;* ns. S 62. **ān-haga,** wk. m. *one
who dwells alone; a solitary; a
friendless man;* ns. W 1; as. —n,
W 40. [For the element -HAG- see
haga.]

**āna,** adv. *alone,* R 123, 128; M 94;
W 8. [Often used adjectively
after noun or pron. as if nsm. wk.

of **ān,** but extended to other cases
and genders.]

**and,** conj. *and;* C 2, and frequently
in the other poems. [Spelled *and*
or *ond* when written out in the
MSS., but usually abbreviated as
7.]

**anda,** wk. m. *enmity, spite;* ds. —n,
W 105.

**and-lang,** adj. *entire* (with reference
to a period of time or a spatial
dimension); asm. —ne, B 21.
[and-, *against, corresponding,*
plus lang, *long;* here the prefix is
stressed; the same word with stress
on lang gave modern "along."]

**and-swaru,** f. *answer;* as. —sware,
M 44. [and-, *against, counter,* plus
SWARU, *asseveration;* cf. SWERIAN,
v.6, *swear.*]

**an-forht,** adj. *(very) frightened, terri-
fied:* nsm. R 117. [an-, stressed form
of on, here intensive. MS. has
variant spelling *un-,* which ob-
scures contrast with negative **un-,**
R 110. Cf. **forht, unforht.**]

**an-ġinn,** n. *beginning; action, con-
duct;* as. M 242. [Cf. **on-ġinnan.**]

**an-hyġdiġ,** adj. *strong-minded;* nsm.
D 2. [Probably intensive an-
rather than **ān-,** *single.*]

**an-mēdla,** wk. m. *pomp, glory;* np.
—n, S 81. [Base-word mōd, q.v.]

**an-rǣd,** adj. *resolute;* nsm. M 44,
132. [Uncertain whether first
syllable is intensive prefix an- or
**ān,** one, indicating singleness of
purpose.]

**an-sīen,** f. i-stem. *appearance, face;*
ns. S 91. [Cf. **wǣfer-sīen,** ġe-sīene,
and ġe-sēon.]

**an-wealda,** wk. m. *ruler, Lord;* ns.
R 153. [Cf. wealdan.]

**ār,** m. *messenger;* ns. M 26.

**ār,** f. *grace, favor, mercy;* ns. S 107;

as. —e, W 1, 114; *honor, glory*, as. —e, D 33. **ār-hwæt**, adj. *abounding in glory, glorious;* npm. —e, B 73. (See note in Campbell's ed. of B, p. 121.)

**a-rǣd**, adj. *determined, inexorable* (?); nsf. W 5. [The word is not very well attested. In poetry only here. Perhaps a shortened form of A-RǢDED; cf. **rǣdan**.]

**a-rǣran**, wk.v.I. *rear, erect;* pp. arǣred, nsm, R 44.

**a-rīsan**, v.1. *arise;* pret. 3s. arās, R 101. [RĪSAN, RĀS, RISON, RISEN.]

**a-sǣġde**, see a-secgan.

**a-scacan**, v.6. *shake;* pret. 3s. ascōc, M 230. [SCACAN, SCŌC, SCŌCON, SCACEN.]

**ġe-āscian**, wk.v.II. *learn (by asking);* pret. 1p. —āscodon, D 21.

**a-secgan**, wk.v.III. *say, speak out, tell;* inf. W 11; pret. 3s. asǣġde, M 198. [Cf. secgan.]

**a-settan**, wk.v.I. *set, set up, place;* pres. 3s. subj. asette, R 142; pret. 3p. asetton, R 32. [Cf. ġe-settan.]

**a-stāg**, see a-stīgan.

**a-stellan**, wk.v.I. *establish;* pret. 3s. astealde, C 4. [STELLAN, STEALDE, STEALD; cf. on-stellan.]

**a-stīgan**, v.1. *ascend;* pret. 3s. astāg, R 103. [Cf. ġe-stīgan.]

**a-styrian**, wk.v.I. *remove;* pp. astyred, nsm. R 30. [STYRIAN, STYREDE, STYRED, *stir, move;* from *STURJAN, related to **storm**, m. *storm.*]

**a-swebban**, wk.v.I. *put to sleep (kill);* pp. aswefed, npm. B 30. [SWEBBAN, SWEFEDE, SWEFED; from *SWǢFJAN; cf. SWǢF, pret. of SWEFAN, v.5, *sleep.*]

**atol**, adj. *terrible;* asn. S 6.

**āwa**, adv. *always,* S 79.

**ā-wiht**, n. i-stem. *anything, aught;* as. S 46.

## B

**ġe-bād**, see ġe-bīdan.

**bæc**, n. *back;* as. in ofer bæc, *to the rear, back,* M 276.

**bæd, bǣdon**, see biddan.

**ġe-bǣdan**, wk.v.I. *constrain;* pp. ġebǣded, nsm. B 33.

**bǣl**, n. *fire;* esp. *funeral fire, pyre;* ds. —e, S 114.

**bǣren, bǣron**, see beran.

**bærnan**, wk.v.I, trans. *burn.* See for-bærnan.

**bærst**, see berstan.

**bana**, wk. m. *slayer* (whether a person or a thing: "*bane*"); ns. M 299; gs. —n, R 66 (referring to the Rood, apparently; Cook emended to BANENA, gp., referring generally to those who crucified the Lord).

**band**, see bindan.

**baðian**, wk.v.II. *bathe;* inf. W 47.

**be**, stressed form bī, prep. w. dat. *by.* — (a) *by, beside, near;* M 319; W 80; S 8, 98; be healfe, *by the side (of),* M 152, 318; bī (postpositive), M 182. — (b) *about, concerning;* S 1; D 35. — (c) *by, from* (marking agency or source), D 1; be þām, *by that (this),* M 9.

**bēacen**, n. *sign, portent;* ns. R 6; as. R 21; ds. bēacne, R 83; gp. bēacna, R 118.

**beadu**, f. wō-stem. *battle;* ds. beadwe, M 185. **beadu-rǣs**, m. *rush of battle;* ns. M 111. **beadu-weorc**, n. *deed of war;* gp. —a, B 48 [The nominative of beadu is not recorded as an independent word.]

**bēag**, m. *ring, crown, necklace* (any ornament of precious metal bent or looped together; as a plural, in formulas, virtually equivalent to *money* or *wealth*); ap. —as, M 31, 160. [Cf. būgan.] **bēag-ġiefa**, wk. m.

*ring-giver* (typifying the generous patron); ns. B 2; d. or as. —n, M 290.

**bealdlíce,** adv. *boldly;* M 311; superl. **bealdlícost,** M 78.

**bealu,** n. wa-stem. *evil; malice; pain, hardship;* as. S 112 (*malice*). **bealu-síþ,** m. *grievous journey* or *bitter experience;* gp. —a, S 28. **bealu-ware,** m. pl. *dwellers in iniquity, evil-doers;* gp. —wara, R 79 (perhaps an error for BEALUWA or BEALWA, gp. of bealu).

**béam,** m. *tree, wooden beam;* spec., *rood-tree, cross;* ns. R 97; ds. —e, R 114, 122; gp. —a, R 6. [Cf. **síge-béam.**]

**bearn,** n. *child, son;* ns. R 83; M 92, 155, 186, 209, 238, 267, 300, 320; ap. S 93; — *ielda bearn, children of men (the human race, people);* np. S 77; dp. —um, C 5 (var. eorðan b., *children of earth*).

**bearu,** m. wa-stem. *grove;* np. **bearwas,** S 48.

**béatan,** v.7. *beat;* pret. 3p. **béoton,** S 23. [BÉATAN, BÉOT, BÉOTON, BÉATEN.]

**béc,** see **bóc.**

**be-cuman,** v.4. *come;* pret. 2p. **be-cómon,** M 58; 3p., B 70. [The prefix indicates arrival but is not usually to be translated. [Cf. **cuman.**]

**be-dǽlan,** wk.v.I, w. dat. or instr. *separate (from), deprive (of);* pp. **bedǽled,** nsm. W 20; D 28. [Cf. **dǽlan.**]

**be-delfan,** v.3. *bury;* pret. 3s. **bedealf,** R 75. [DELFAN, DEALF, DULFON, DOLFEN, *dig.*]

**be-drífan,** v.1. *cover over, envelop;* pp. **bedrifen,** asm. —ne, R 62. [DRÍFAN, DRÁF, DRIFON, DRIFEN.]

**be-droren,** adj. w. dat. or instr.

*deprived, bereft (of);* nsm. S 16; npm. —e, W 79. [pp. of *BE-DRÉOSAN; cf. dréosan.]

**be-foran,** prep. w. dat. *before;* B 67 (*earlier than*); W 46 (*in front of*). [Cf. **æt-foran.**]

**be-ġeall,** see **be-ġiellan.**

**be-ġeat, be-ġeaton,** see **be-ġietan.**

**béġen,** m. dual (bá, f., bú, n.). *both;* nom. B 57; M 182, 183 (by mistake?), 191, 291, 305. [Cf. **bú-tú.**]

**be-ġéotan,** v.2. *cover* (as with liquid); pp. **begoten,** nsn. R 7; *suffuse, drench;* same form, nsm. R 49. [Cf. **ġéotan.**]

**be-ġiellan,** v.3. *scream round about* (?); pret. 3s. **beġeall,** S 24 (w. acc. þæt, referring perhaps to the cliffs collectively or the scene as a whole). [Recorded here only; cf. **ġiellan.**]

**be-ġietan,** v.5. *get possession of, conquer;* pret. 3p. **beġéaton,** B 73; *keep, hold,* pret. 3s. **beġeat,** S 6. [ĠIETAN, ĠEAT, ĠÉATON, ĠIETEN; cf. **on-ġietan.**]

**be-hangen,** see **be-hón.**

**be-healdan,** v.7. *behold, gaze at, keep watch over;* pret. 1s. **be-héold,** R 25, 58; 3p. **behéoldon,** R 9, 11, 64. [Cf. **healdan.**]

**be-hindan,** prep. w. dat. *behind,* B 60 (postpos.). [Cf. **hindan.**]

**be-hón,** contr.v.7, w. dat. -instr. *hang around (with)*; pp. **be-hangen,** nsm. S 17. [HÓN (from *HANHAN), HÉNG, HÉNGON, HANGEN.]

**be-hroren,** adj. w. instr. *fallen upon (by), covered (with).* npm. —e, W 77. [pp. of BE-HRÉOSAN, the active verb recorded only as intrans., *fall;* see **hréosan.**]

**be-nam,** see **be-niman.**

**benċ,** f. i-stem. *bench;* ds. —e, M 213.

bend, f. jō-stem. *bond;* see sinu-bend.

be-niman, v.4, w. acc. of person, instr. of thing. *deprive (of);* pret. 3s. benam, D 16. [Cf. niman.]

benn, f. jō-stem. *wound;* np. —a, W 49.

bēodan, v.2. *announce, forebode;* pres. 3s. bēodeþ, S 54. [BĒODAN, BĒAD, BUDON, BODEN; cf. a-bēodan.]

bēon-wesan, anom. v. *be;* inf. bēon, M 185; wesan, R 110, 117.

(1) ordinary present forms: 1s. eom, M 179, 317; 2s. eart, M 36; 3s. is, R 80, etc. (8 times); M 31, etc. (4 times); W 106; S 86, 88, 121; 3p. sindon, R 46; W 93; sind, S 64, 80, 86; 3s. subj. sīe, R 112 (see note), 144; M 215; S 122; D 30.

(2) present forms of bēon, used in general statements or with future sense: 3s. biþ, R 86; W 5, etc. (12 times); S 44, 72 (MS. þæt), etc. (7 times); 3p. bēoþ, W 49.

(3) preterite forms of wesan: 1s. wæs, R 20, etc. (9 times); M 217; D 36; 3s. wæs, B 7, 40; R 6, etc. (12 times); M 23, etc. (18 times); D 8, 11, 19, 23, 37; 3p. wǣron, R 8; M 110; S 9, 83; 3s. subj. wǣre, M 195, 240; W 96; D 26.

(4) negative forms: pres. 3s. nis, *is not,* W 9; S 39; 3p. nearon, *are not,* S 82 (MS. *næron*); pret. 3s. næs, *was not,* M 325.

beorg, m. *hill, mountain;* as. R 32; ds. —e, R 50.

ġe-beorg, n. *defense, protection;* ds. —e, M 31, 131, 245.

beorgan, v.3, w. dat. *protect, save;* pret. 3p. burgon, M 194. [BEORGAN, BEARG, BURGON, BORGEN.]

beorht, adj. *bright;* nsf. B 15; W 94; dsm. wk. —an, R 66; superl.

beorhtost, asm. (uninflected) R 6.

beorn, m. *warrior, man;* ns. B 45; R 42; W 70, 113; S 55; as. M 270; gs. —es, M 131, 160; ds. —e, M 154, 245; np. —as, R 32, 66; M 92, 111, 182; ap. —as, M 17, 62, 277, 305, 311; gp. —a, B 2; M 257; dp. —um, M 101.

bēot, n. *vow* (typically made before battle; hence) *boast; threat;* as. M 15, 27 (on bēot, *threateningly*), 213; W 70. [From *BĪ-HĀT; cf. ġe-hātan, and see Gordon's note on M 27.]

bēotian, wk.v.II. *vow, boast;* pret. 3s. bēotode, M 290.

bēoton, see bēatan.

bēoþ, see bēon-wesan.

beran, v.4. *bear, carry;* inf. M 12, 62; pres. 3s. bereþ, R 118; pret. 3p. bǣron, R 32; M 99; 3p. subj. bǣren, M 67. [BERAN, BÆR, BǢRON, BOREN; cf. oþ-beran and ġe-boren.]

-berend, m. nd-stem. *bearer;* see gār-, reord-berend.

berstan, v.3. *burst;* inf. R 36; pret. 3s. bærst, M 284. [BERSTAN, BÆRST, BURSTON, BORSTEN; orig. BRESTAN, etc. Cf. to-berstan.]

be-slēan, contr.v.6, w. gen. *bereave of (by slaughter);* pp. beslæġen, nsm. B 42. [Cf. slēan.]

be-standan, v.6. *stand around, surround;* pret. 3p. bestōdon, M 68. [Cf. standan.]

be-stīeman, wk.v.I. *make moist, suffuse;* pp. bestīemed, nsm. R 48; nsn. R 22. [Base-word stēam, m. *hot vapor, moisture, blood.*]

be-swīcan, v.1. *betray;* pp. beswicen, apm. —e, M 238. [SWĪCAN, SWĀC, SWICON, SWICEN.]

be-swillan, wk.v.I. *drench;* pp. be-swiled, nsn. R 23. (MS. *beswyled* is best interpreted so, with

Dickins and Ross; earlier editors proposed a poorly supported BE-SYLED, *defiled*.)

betera, adj. comp. *better* (declined wk.); nsm. M 276 (as noun); nsn. betere, M 31; npm. beteran, B 48.

betst, adj. superl. *best;* nsn. S 73 (as noun w. part. gen.).

be-wāwan, v.7. *blow against;* pp. bewāwen, npm. bewāwne, W 76 (winde b., *beaten by the wind*). [WĀWAN, \*WĒOW, \*WĒOWON, WĀWEN — only pres. stem and pp. on record.]

be-windan, v.3. *wind (about), encircle, enwrap;* pp. bewunden, asn. R 5. [Cf. windan.]

be-wrēon, contr.v.1. *put a covering around; cover;* pret. 1s. bewrāh, W 23; pp. bewriġen, uninfl., R 17, 53. [WRĒON (from \*WRĪHAN), WRĀH, WRIGON, WRIGEN; cf. on-wrēon.]

bī, see be.

bidan, v.1. *remain;* inf. S 30. [BĪDAN, BĀD, BIDON, BIDEN.]

ġe-bīdan, v.1. (a) intrans., *wait;* inf. W 70; (b) trans., *obtain by waiting, live to see; experience, endure;* pres. 3s. ġebīdeþ, W 1; pret. 1s. ġebād, R 125; M 174; pp. ġebiden, uninfl. R 50, 79; S 4, 28.

biddan, v.5. *bid, urge, exhort, ask, pray;* pret. 3s. bæd, M 20, 128, 170, 257 (*urged, bade*); pret. 3p. bǣdon, M 87 (*asked*), 262 (*prayed, besought*), 306 (*exhorted*). [Construed w. clause or (M 170) inf., and sometimes acc. of person (M 170, 262). BIDDAN, BÆD, B.ĒDON, BEDEN.]

ġe-biddan, v.5, w. refl. pron. dat. and prep. to, *pray to;* pres. 3p. ġebiddaþ, R 83; pret. 1s. ġebæd, R 122.

bieldan, wk.v.I. *embolden, encour-*

*age;* bielde, pret. 3s. M 169, 209 (b. forþ, *incited to advance*), 320; pres. 3s. subj., M 234. [Base-word BEALD, bold.]

biergan, wk.v.I. *taste;* pret. 3s. bieriġde, R 101. [Cf. on-biergan.]

bifian, wk.v.II. *tremble;* inf. R 36; pret. 1s. bifode, R 42.

bill, n. *sword;* as. M 162; dp. —um, M 114. bill-ġeslieht, m. or n. (*sword-*) *slaughter;* gs. —es, B 45.

ġe-bind, n. *fastening, band; aggregation;* as. in waðuma ġebind, W 24, 57 (*congregated waters? confinement of the waves? waves' embrace?*) [No other occurrences in poetry; cf. bindan.]

bindan, v.3. *bind;* pres. 3s. bindeþ, W 102; 3p. bindaþ, W 18; 3s. subj. binde, W 13; pret. 3s. band, S 32. [BINDAN, BAND, BUNDON, BUNDEN.]

ġe-bindan, v.3. *bind, hold captive;* pres. 3p. ġebindaþ, W 40; pp. ġebunden, uninfl. (for npm. ĠE-BUNDNE) S 9; nsm. D 24.

bisġu, f. in-stem. *toil, trouble;* as. S 88.

bisiġ, adj. *busy, at work;* npm. —e, M 110.

bismerian, wk.v.II. *mock, revile;* pret. 3p. bismerodon, R 48.

biter, adj. *bitter; painful, grievous;* gsm. biteres, R 114; asf. bitre, S 4, 55 (MS. *bitter*) ; *grim, fierce,* nsm. M 111; apm. bitere, M 85. [Orig. \*BITR; hence the variation between bitr- and biter-, which is allowed to stand for possible rhythmic value, though it is probably scribal.]

biþ, see bēon-wesan.

blācian, wk.v.II. *grow pale;* pres. 3s. blācaþ, S 91.

blǣd, m.(*vital spirit;*) *joy, glory;* ns.

W 33 (foldan b., *earth's glory* — perhaps also *fruitful abundance;* blǣd, f. *blossom, fruit, growth*); S 79, 88; as. D 34; dp. —um, R 149. [blǣd, m. is related to BLĀWAN, v.7, *blow,* blǣd, f., to BLŌWAN, v.7, *bloom.* The first is more frequent in poetry.]

ġe-bland, n. *mixture.* See ēar-ġebland.

blanden, pp. adj. *mixed.* [blandan, v.7.] blanden-feax, adj. *grizzle-haired;* nsm. B 45.

blēo, n. ja-stem. *color;* dip. blēoum, R 22.

bliss, f. *bliss;* ns. R 139, 141; ds. —e, R 149, 153. [From *BLĪþ-s; cf. next word.]

blīðe, adj. ja-stem. *glad, joyful;* isn. R 122; comp. blīðra, nsm. M 146 (*better pleased*).

blōd, n. *blood;* ds. —e, R 48.

blōdiġ, adj. *bloody;* asm. —ne, M 154.

blōstma, wk.m. *blossom;* dip. —um, S 48.

bōc, f. cons.-stem. *book;* np. bēċ, B 68.

boda, wk.m. *messenger;* vs. M 49. [Cf. bēodan.]

boga, wk.m. *bow;* np. —n, M 110. [Cf. būgan.]

bold, n. *dwelling.* See feorh-bold.

bord, n. *shield;* ns. M 110; as. M 15, 42, 62 (or pl.), 131, 245, 270, 283, 309; gs. —es, M 284; gp. —a, M 295; dp. —um, M 101. bord-weall, m. *shield-wall;* as. B 5; M 277.

ġe-boren, adj. (pp., see beran) as noun, *one born in the same family; brother;* dsm. —um, S 98. [Cf. beran.]

bōsm, m. *bosom;* ds. —e, B 27.

bōt, f. *remedy;* as. —e, W 113.

brād, adj. *broad;* asn. M 15, 163; apn. B 71.

brǣc, see brecan.

ġe-brǣc, n. *clash;* ns. M 295. [Cf. brecan.]

brǣdan, wk.v.I. *spread;* inf. W 47. [Base-word brād.]

brǣġd, see breġdan.

brēac, see brūcan.

breahtm, m. *noise, clamor;* gp. —a, W 86.

brecan, v.4. *break;* pret. 3s. brǣc, M 277 (*broke through*—see Gordon's note) ; pp. brocen, ns. M 1 (the noun modified is missing) . [BRECAN, BRÆC, BRÆCON, BROCEN; cf. to-brecan.]

breġdan, v.3. *move quickly; draw, pluck out;* pret. 3s. brǣġd, M 154, 162. [BREĠDAN, BRÆĠD, BRUGDON, BROGDEN.]

bregu, m. u-stem. *sovereign, chief;* ns. B 33.

brēost, n. *breast* (usually pl. where mod. English has sing.) ; dp. —um, R 118; M 144; W 113. brēost-cearu, f. *breast-care, sorrow of heart;* as. —ċeare, S 4. brēost-cofa, wk.m. *the recesses of the breast;* ds. —n, W 18. brēost-hord, n. (*what is treasured in the breast*); *inmost feelings;* as. S 55.

brēoðan. v.2. *waste away.* See a-brēoðan.

brim, n. *sea* (*-surge*); ap. —u, B 71. brim-fugol, m. *seabird;* ap. —fuglas, W 47. brim-lād, f. *sea-passage, voyage;* ds. —e, S 30. brim-līðend, m. nd-stem. *seafarer;* gp. —ra, M 27 (*vikings*). brim-mann, m. cons.-stem. *seaman;* np. —menn, M 295; gp. —manna, M 49 (*vikings*).

bringan, wk.v.1 (pres., strong 3) . *bring;* pres. 3s bringeþ, W 54. [BRINGAN, BRŌHTE, BRŌHT.]

ġe-bringan, wk.v.I. *bring;* pres. 3s. subj. ġebringe, R 139.

brocen, see brecan.

brōðor, m. r-stem. *brother;* ns. B 2; M 282; S 98; np. brōðru, M 191; gp. brōðra, D 8.

ġe-brōðor, m.pl. *brothers* (considered together as children of the same parent); nom. B 57; M 305 (alt. form —brōðru).

brūcan, v.2, w. gen. *enjoy, partake of, use;* inf. B 63; R 144; pres. 3p. brūcaþ, S 88 (b. þurh bisġu, gen. HIRE understood: *gain the use of it by toil*); pret. 3s. brēac, W 44. [BRŪCAN, BRĒAC, BRUCON, BROCEN.]

brūn, adj. *brown;* (of metals) *gleaming.* brūn-ecg, adj. *with gleaming blade;* asn. M 163.

brycg, f. jō-stem. *bridge; ford, causeway;* as. —e, M 74, 78. brycg-weard, m. *guard of the causeway;* ap. —as, M 85.

bryne, m. i-stem. *fire;* as. R 149.

brytta, wk.m. *dispenser, giver* (typically w. gen. of a word for treasure, characterizing a generous lord); sinces bryttan, as. W 25 (or gs. if sele-drēoriġ is taken as two separate words).

bryttian, wk.v.II. *divide, distribute;* (hence) *dispose of, enjoy;* inf. B 60.

būgan, v.2. *bow, bend down;* inf. R 36, 42; *turn, retreat;* inf. M 276; pret. 3p. bugon, M 185. [BŪGAN, BĒAG, BUGON, BOGEN: cf. bēag, boga: also for-būgan.]

ġe-bunden, see ġe-bindan.

bune, wk. f. *cup, beaker;* ns. W 94 (as symbol of drinking in the hall).

būr, n. *bower, bedchamber.* būr-þeġn, m. *servant of the bower; chamberlain;* ds. —e, M 121.

burg, f. cons.-stem. *stronghold, stockaded dwelling or manor; walled town, city;* as. M 291 (probably Byrhtnoþ's manorhouse; see Gordon's note); D 19; dp. —um, S 28; ap. byriġ, S 48 (less probably np.). burg-ware, m.pl. *keepers of the stronghold, citizens;* gp. —wara, W 86. [Cf. scield-burg.]

burgon, see beorgan.

būtan, conj. (w. subj.) *unless,* M 71; (after negative) *but, except,* S 18.

bū-tū, n. dual. *both;* acc. R 48. [See bēġen and twēġen.]

-byrd, f. i-stem. *what one bears* (cf. ġe-byrd, *birth*) — in compounds, sometimes a social or legal responsibility that one bears. See mund-byrd. [Cf. beran.]

byre, m. i-stem. *opportunity;* as. M 121. [Cf. beran.]

byrġan, wk.v.I. *bury;* inf. S 98. [Cf. beorgan.]

byriġ, see burg.

byrne, wk.f. *corselet, coat of mail;* ns. M 144, 284; as. byrnan, M 163. byrn-wiga, wk. m. *(mailed) warrior;* ns. W 94.

## C

cāf, adj. *quick, vigorous, valiant;* asm. —ne, M 76 (c. mid his cynne, *valiant as was his kindred, come of a valiant stock*—Gordon).

cāflīċe, adv. *valiantly;* M 153.

camp, m. *battle;* ds. —e, B 8. camp-stede, m. i-stem. *battlefield;* ds. B 29, 49.

ġe-camp, m. *battle;* ds. —e, M 153.

candel, f. *candle;* ns. B 15. [From Lat. CANDĒLA, applied to large candles used in churches; hence the application to heaven's candle, the sun.]

cāsere, m. ja-stem (adapt. of Lat. CAESAR). *emperor;* np. cāseras, S 82.

ċeald, n. *(the) cold;* dis. —e, S 8.

ċeald, adj. *cold;* asn. M 91; dip. —um, S 10; superl. ċealdost, nsn. w. part. gen. S 33. [Cf. hrīm-, īs-, winter-ċeald.]

ċeallian, wk.v.II. *call, shout;* inf. M 91.

ċeariġ, adj. *troubled, sad, sorrowful.* See earm-, hrēow-, mōd-, sorg-, winter-ċearig.

cearu, f. *care; sorrow, grief, anxiety;* ns. W 55; as. ċeare, W 9; np. ceara, S 10. cear-seld, n. *abode of care;* gp. —a, S 5. [Alt. form caru, whence mod. "care"; association with Lat. *cura* had already begun in OE. On the diphthong of nom. cearu, which probably did not have palatal c (ċ), see Campbell, *OE Gram.* 208. Cf. brēost-cearu.]

ġe-ċēas, see ġe-ċēosan.

cellod, adj. meaning unknown; asn. M 283, describing a shield.

cempa, wk.m. *warrior;* ns. M 119. [Cf. camp.]

cēne, adj. ja-stem. *keen, bold, warlike;* nsm. M 215; npm. M 283 (or adv. *boldly*); comp. cēnre, nsf. M 312. [*CŌNJA-.]

ċēol, m. *ship;* ds. —e, S 5.

ċeorfan, v.3. *carve, hew out;* pret. 3p. curfon, R 66. [ĊEORFAN, ĊEARF, CURFON, CORFEN.]

ċeorl, m. *freeman of the lowest rank, yeoman, churl* (but less derogatory than at a later period); ns. M 256; ds. —e, M 132 (a common viking in contrast to the English earl: *"the earl to the churl"*).

ġe-ċēosan, v.2. *choose;* pret. 3s. ġeċēas, M 113. [ĊEOSAN, ĊEAS, CURON, COREN.]

ċierm, m. i-stem. *cry, clamor, uproar;* ns. M 107.

ċierran, wk.v.I. *turn.* See on-ċierran.

clǣne, adj. ja-stem. *clean, pure;* asn. S 110.

clamm, m. *grip, fetter;* dip. —um, S 10.

clēofan, v.2. *cleave, split;* pret. 3p. clufon, B 5; M 283. [CLĒOFAN, CLĒAF, CLUFON, CLOFEN.]

clif, n. *cliff;* dp. —um, S 8. [Cf. stān-clif.]

clipian, wk.v.II. *call out;* pret. 3s. clipode, M 25, 256.

clufon, see clēofan.

clyppan, wk.v.I. *embrace;* pres. 3s. subj. clyppe, W 42. [Cf. ymb-clyppan.]

cnāwan, v.7. *know.* See on-cnāwan.

cnearr, m. *ship;* ns. B 35. [Probably borrowed from, certainly alluding to, Old Norse KNǪRR as a specific term for a viking ship; cf. næġled-cnearr.]

cnēo, n. wa-stem. *knee;* ds. W 42 (contraction of *CNĒOWE); —fig., *a step in genealogy:* cnēo-mǣġ, m. *a kinsman in one's genealogical line; ancestor;* dp. —māgum, B 8.

cniht, m. *young man, youth;* ns. M 9, 153.

cnossian, wk.v.II. *toss, pitch, drive?* pres. 3s. cnossaþ, S 8. [Recorded only here. The base-word *CNOSS is the same as for cnyssan and implies beating or striking; cf. ĠE-CNOSS, *collision;* but perhaps striking waves rather than rocks.]

cnyssan, wk.v.I. *beat against;* pres. 3p. cnyssaþ, W 101; —fig., *urge insistently, importune,* S 33. [Base-word *CNOSS; see cnossian.]

cofa, wk.m. *coffer, recess, room.* See brēost- and hord-cofa.

cōlian, wk.v.II. *cool;* pret. 3s. cōlode, R 72.

collen-, adj. combining-form, pp. of a lost verb *CWELLAN, *swell, spring* *up, grow big*—which has cognates in other languages. **collen-ferhþ,** adj. *stout-hearted, proud, brave;* nsm. W 71.

**cōm, cōmon,** see **cuman.**

**corn,** n. *kernel, grain;* gp. —a, S 33.

**cræftiġ,** adj. *skilled.* See **lēoþ-cræftiġ.**

**crēad,** see **crūdan.**

**cringan,** v.3. *fall in battle, perish;* inf. M 292; pret. 3p. **crungon,** B 10; M 302. [CRINGAN, CRANG, CRUNGON, CRUNGEN.]

**ġe-cringan,** v.3. *fall, perish;* pret. 3s. **ġecrang,** M 250, 324; W 79.

**Crist,** m. *Christ;* ns. R 56; ds. —e, R 116.

**crūdan,** v.2. *(crowd,) press on;* pret. 3s. **crēad,** B 35. [Only pres. subj. and pret. 3s. recorded.]

**crungon,** see **cringan.**

**cuman,** v.4. *come;* pres. 3s. **cymeþ,** W 103; S 61, 106, 107; 1p. subj. **cumen,** S 118 *(make our way);* pret. 3s. **cōm,** B 37 *(made his way);* R 151, 155; M 65; 3p. **cōmon,** R 57; pp. **cumen,** nsm. R 80; nsf. M 104; —hwǣr **cōm,** pret. 3s. *what has become of, where is,* W 92 (three times), 93. [CUMAN, CŌM, CŌMON, CUMEN; cf. **be-, ofer-cuman.**]

**cumbol,** n. *banner.* **cumbol-ġehnāst,** n. *collision of banners* (in battle) ; gs. —es, B 49.

**cunnan,** pret.-pres. v. *(can,) know, know how;* pres. 3s. subj. **cunne:** w.inf., *know how to,* W 113; w. **gear(w)e,** *know for certain,* W 69 (used absolutely, w. same implication as next), 71 (w. ind. quest.). [CUNNAN, CANN, CUNNON, CŪÐE.]

**cunnian,** wk.v.II. *test, find out (by trial); make trial of, experience;* inf. M 215 (**mæġ cunnian,** *one can find out;* see **magan**); pres. 3s.

**cunnaþ,** W 29; 1s. subj. **cunnie,** S 35; pret. 3s. **cunnode,** D 1 (w. gen.).

**ġe-cunnian,** wk.v.II. *explore, make trial of, come to know;* pp. **ġe-cunnod,** uninfl., S 5.

**curfon,** see **ċeorfan.**

**cūþ,** adj. *known, familiar;* nsn. D 19; gp. —ra, W 55. [Cf. **cunnan.**]

**cwæþ,** see **cweðan.**

**cweċċan,** wk.v.I. *shake.* See **a-cweċċan.**

**cweðan,** v.5. *say, speak;* inf. R 116; pres. 3s. **cwiþ,** R 111 (future sense); pret. 3s. **cwæþ,** M 211, 255; W 6, 111. [CWEÐAN, CWÆÞ, CWÆDON, CWEDEN; cf. **a-, on-cweðan,** and **æfter-cweðende.**]

**ġe-cweðan,** v.5. *speak;* pret. 3s. **ġe-cwæþ,** M 168.

**cwic(u),** adj. u-stem. *alive;* pl. as noun, *the living;* gp. **cwicra,** W 9.

**cwide,** m. i-stem. *speech, discourse.* **cwide-ġiedd,** n. ja-stem. *saying, utterance;* gp. —a, W 55 (**cūðra c.,** *familiar utterances*—almost, *familiar accents?*). [Cf. **lār-cwide.**]

**cwiþ,** see **cweðan.**

**cwiðan,** wk.v.I. *bewail, lament;* inf. W 9; pret. 3p. **cwīðdon,** R 56.

**cymeþ,** see **cumán.**

**cyne-,** adjectival combining-form. *royal.* **cyne-rīċe,** n. ja-stem. *kingdom;* gs. —s, D 26. [From *CUNI-, related to **cyning** and **cynn.**]

**cyning,** m. *king;* ns. B 1, 35, 58; D 23; gs. —es, R 56 *(King);* as. R 44, 133 *(King);* np. —as, B 29; S 82.

**cynn,** n. ja-stem. *kind, race, family, kindred;* as. R 94 (**wīfa c.,** *womankind*); gs. —es, M 217, 266; ds. —e, M 76. [Cf. **mann-cynn.**]

**cyssan,** wk.v.I. *kiss;* pres. 3s. subj. **cysse,** W 42. [COSS, m. *kiss, embrace.*]

cyst, f. i-stem. (a) *the best, choicest;* as. R 1. [Cf. ċēosan.] — (b) *(picked) band;* see ēorod-cyst. [But perhaps the word in this second context is unrelated to ċēosan and should be normalized as ċiest, an i-stem from *CÆSTI-, meaning simply *band, troop, crowd.* Cf. Old Norse KOSTR, *pile, heap.*]

ġe-cȳðan, wk.v.I. *make known, declare;* inf. M 216. [Base-word cūþ, q.v.; cf. a-cȳðan.]

cȳþþ, f. iþō-stem. *known region or people, home;* as. —e, B 38, 58. [Base-word cūþ; cf. *"kith* and *kin."*]

## D

dǣd, f. i-stem. *deed;* dp. —um, S 41; dip. —um, S 76.

dæġ, m. *day;* as. B 21; M 198 (or endingless locative: on dæġ, *upon a [certain] day, one day*); np. dagas, S 80; gp. daga, R 136.

dæġ-weorc, n. *day's work;* gs. —es, M 148. [Cf. dōm-, tīd-dæġ; ġēar-, ġe-swinċ-dagas.]

dǣl, m. i-stem. w. gen. *share, portion (of);* ns. D 30; *a good share, a deal (of), many,* as. W 65; D 34.

dǣlan, wk.v.I. *deal out or share;* pres. 1p. subj. dǣlen, M 33 (hilde d., *should join battle*). [Base-word DĀL, n. *division, portion;* cf. be-dǣlan.]

ġe-dǣlan, wk.v.I. *divide, share;* deaðe ġedǣlde, pret. 3s. *shared with Death,* W 83.

dagas, see dæġ.

daroþ, m. *spear;* as. M 149, 255; gp. —a, B 54.

dēad, adj. *dead;* nsn.wk. —e, S 65 (fig.); dp. —um, as noun, *the dead,* S 98.

dēag, see dugan.

dēaþ, m. *death;* ns. S 106; D 8; as. R 101; gs. —es, R 113; ds. —e, W 83 (personified).

delfan, v.3. *dig.* See be-delfan.

dēman, wk.v.I., w. dat., *pass judgment on, judge;* inf. R 107. [Base-word dōm, q.v.]

dennian, wk.v.II. *become wet, flow?* pret. 3s. dennode, B 12. [The only occurrence; meaning doubtful. Holthausen, *Altenglisches etym. Wörterbuch,* cites Sanskrit DHANVATI, *flows,* as a possible relative.]

dēofol, m. and n. *(the) devil;* ds. dēofle, S 76.

dēop, adj. *deep;* asn. B 55; dsm.wk. —an, R 75.

dēope, adv. *deeply,* W 89.

dēor, n. *animal;* as. B 64.

dēor, adj. *brave, valiant;* nsm. S 41; dip. —um, S 76.

deorc, adj. *dark* (with various emotional overtones); asn.wk. —e, W 89 (*mysterious and cheerless?*); dp. —um, R 46 (*iron-colored and sinister?*). [For possible influence of the Irish cognate, meaning *red, bloody,* at R 46, see note in Dickins and Ross.]

derian, wk.v.I, w. dat. *injure, harm;* inf. M 70.

dīere, adj. ja-stem. *dear;* nsm. D 37 (w. dat., *dear to*).

dōgor, n. (or m.) *day;* gp. dōgra, W 63.

dol, adj. *foolish;* nsm. S 106.

dolg, n. *wound;* np. R 46.

dōm, m. (a) *doom, judgment;* gs.

—es, R 107; (b) *stipulation, choice;* as. M 38; (c) *favorable judgment, praise, glory, renown;* as. M 129; ds. —e, S 85. dōm-dæġ, m. *day of judgment;* ds. —e, R 105. dōm-ġeorn, adj. *eager for praise;* npm. —e, W 17 (as noun: *men of repute, aspirants to honor*). [Cf. dēman.]

dōn, anom. v. *do;* pret. dyde, (a) as substitute for a verb previously used: *did,* 3s. R 114; (b) *did, acted* (in a specified manner), 3s. M 280; (c) w. acc. object and to, *made to serve as, took for,* 1s. S 20.

ġe-dōn, anom. v., trans. (a) *do, perform;* pp. ġedōn, M 197; (b) w. to, *bring into a condition,* or *put to a purpose;* inf. S 43 (to hwon hine dryhten ġedōn wille, [*as to*] *what the Lord will bring him to* —so Mrs. Gordon, following Miss Whitelock).

dorste, see durran.

-drǣdan, v.7. *dread;* only w. prefixes; see on-drǣdan.

drēag, see drēogan.

drēam, m. *joy, delight, festivity; music, musical entertainment;* ns. R 140; S 80; gs. —es, R 144; dis. —e, W 79; np. —as, S 65, 86; dp. —um, R 133. [Mod. "dream" is a sense not recorded in OE. Cf. sele-drēam.]

ġe-drēfan, wk.v.I. *trouble, afflict;* pp. ġedrēfed, nsm. R 20, 59. [Baseword DRŌF, adj. *turbid, troubled.*]

dreng, m. *(viking) warrior;* gp. —a, M 149. [The vikings' own term for their warriors; see Gordon's note.]

drēogan, v.2. *undergo, endure;* pres. 3p. drēogaþ, S 56; pret. 3s. drēag,

D 2. [DRĒOGAN, DRĒAG, DRUGON, DROGEN.]

drēoriġ, adj. *(bloody;) sad, dejected;* nsf. B 54 *(dejected—and bloody?*); asm. —ne, W 17 (modifying hyġe understood). drēoriġ-hlēor, adj. *sad-faced;* nsm. W 83. [Cf. sele-drēoriġ.]

drēosan, v.2. *fall, droop, fail;* pres. 3s. drēoseþ, W 63. [DRĒOSAN, DRĒAS, DRURON, DROREN; cf. be-droren.]

ġe-drēosan, v.2. *fail, come to an end;* pret. 3s. ġedrēas, W 36; pp. ġedroren, *fallen;* nsf. S 86.

drīfan, v.1. *drive.* See be-, þurh-drifan.

drinc, m. *drink;* see medu-drinc.

ġe-droren, see ġe-drēosan.

dryht, f. i-stem. *army, host.* See en-ġel-dryht.

dryhten, m. (a) *lord (leader of a dryht);* ns. B 1; S 41; ds. dryhtne, D 37; —(b) *the Lord* (used attributively or as a proper name); ns. C 4, 8; R 101, 105, 144; M 148; S 43, 124; D 32; as. R 64; S 106; gs. dryhtnes, B 16; R 9 (MS. — emended to -dryhta), 35, 75, 113, 136, 140; S 65, 121. [Cf. mann-, wine-dryhten, sense (a).]

dryhtlīcest, adj. superl. *most lordly;* dsm. —um, S 85.

dugan, pret.-pres. v. *avail;* pres. 3s. dēag, M 48 (future sense). [DUGAN, DĒAG, DUGON, DOHTE.]

duguþ, f. (a) *that which avails, benefit, advantage;* ds. —e, M 197 (him to d., *for their benefit*). —(b) *seasoned retainers;* (less specifically) *military band, company of noble warriors, host;* ds. —e, W 97; *(heavenly) host,* dp. — um, S 80. [Cf. dugan.]

durran, pret.-pres. v. *dare;* pres. subj.

1s. **durre**, W 10; pret. 1s. **dorste**, R 35, 42, 45, 47. [DURRAN, DEARR, DURRON, DORSTE.]

**dyde**, see **dōn**.

# E

**ēa**, f. cons.-stem. *river.* **ēa-stæþ**, n. *river-bank;* ds. **-e**, M 63.

**ēa**, interj. *O!* **ēa-lā**, interj. *O, lo; alas!* W 94 (twice), 95.

**ēac**, adv. *also,* B 2; R 92; S 119. **swelċe . . . ēac**, *and likewise, also;* B 19, 30, 37.

**ēac**, prep. w dat. *in addition to,* M 11.

**ēacen**, adj. *increased, great; pregnant;* nsf. D 11. [Pp. of obsolescent ĒACAN, v.7, *increase.*]

**ēadiġ**, adj. *blessed;* nsm. S 107; *prosperous, fortunate;* see **sēft-ēadiġ**.

**ēadiġness**, f. jō-stem. *beatitude, happiness;* as. **-e**, S 120.

**eafora**, wk.m. *son, heir, descendant;* np. **-n**, B 7; ap. **-n**, B 52.

**eald**, adj. *old;* nsm. B 46; M 310; wk. **-a**, M 218 (e. **fæder**, *grandfather*); npn. **eald**, W 87; apn. **-e** (the generalized form, or asn. wk.), M 47; npm. **-e**, B 69. **ealdġewyrht**, f. i-stem (or n.). *deed of old, former action;* dp. **-um**, R 100.

**ealdian**, wk.v.II. *grow old;* pres. 3s. **ealdaþ**, S 89.

**ealdor**, m. *lord;* ns. M 202, 222, 314; gs. **ealdres**, M 53; ds. **ealdre**, M 11; **-w.** limiting gen., *the Lord:* **wuldres ealdor**, ns. R 90; S 123. **ealdor-mann**, m. *nobleman of the highest rank, "ealdorman";* ns. M 219.

**ealdor**, n. *life; age, eternity;* ds. **ealdre**, S 79 (**āwa to ealdre**, *ever*

*for life, for ever and ever*). **ealdorlang**, adj. *age-long, eternal;* asm. **-ne**, B 3.

**ealgian**, wk.v.II. *defend;* inf. M 52 (MS. *gealgean;* see Gordon's note); pret. 3p. subj. **ealgoden**, B 9.

**eall**, adj. *all;* nsm. W 74; nsn. R 6 (or adv.) ; W 106, 110; nsf. R 12, 55, 82; W 36, 79, 115; S 86; asn. R 58, 94; W 60; asf. **-e**, M 304; S 124; ism. **-e**, D 16; npm. **-e**, R 9 (MS. **-em**. to **fela**), 128; M 63, 203, 207; S 81; np.(n.?) **-e**, S 50 (**ealle þā**, indef. antecedent); apm. **-e**, R 37, 74, 93; M 231, 238, 320; apf. **-e**, M 196; gp. **ealra**, R 125; M 174; W 63; dp. **eallum**, R 154; M 233. **−** as pron., asn. M 256 (**ofer eall**, see **ofer**); dp. **eallum**, *to all men,* M 216. [Cf. **ælmihtiġ**.]

**eall**, adv. *entirely;* R 6 (or adj., nsn.), 20, 48, 62; M 314.

**ēar**, m. *sea.* **ēar-ġebland**, n. *concourse of waters, sea-surge;* as. B 26.

**eard**, m. *land, homeland, country;* as. B 73; M 53, 58, 222; S 38. **eard-ġeard**, m. *(enclosed) plot of ground, dwelling-place, region;* as. W 85. **eard-stapa**, wk.m. *land-treader, wanderer;* ns. W 6.

**earfoðe**, n. ja-stem (also **earfeðe**). *hardship, tribulation, trouble;* ap. **-u**, D 2 (MS. **-a**); gp. **-a**, W 6; D 30. **earfoþ-hwil**, f. *time of hardship;* as. **-e**, S 3.

**earfoþlīċ**, adj. *full of trouble, distressful;* nsn. W 106.

**earg**, adj. *slack, cowardly;* nsn. M 238. [Cf. **un-earg**, **iergþu**.]

**earm**, m. *arm;* as. M 165.

**earm**, adj. *poor, destitute, wretched, miserable;* asm. **-ne**, W 40; npm. **-e**, R 68; gp. **-ra**, R 19 (as noun). **earm-ċeariġ**, adj. *wretched*

*and sorrowful, miserably sad;* nsm.
W 20; S 14.

earn, m. *eagle;* ns. M 107; S 24; as.
B 63.

ġe-earnian, wk.v.II. *earn, deserve;*
pres. 3s. ġe-earnaþ, R 109.

ġe-earnung, f. *act deserving gratitude
(or other recompense); favor;* ap.
—a, M 196.

eart, see bēon-wesan.

ēastan, adv. *from the east;* B 69.

ēaþ-, combining-form of ēaðe, adj.
and adv. *easy, easily; gentle, gen-
tly.* ēaþ-mōd, adj. *humble, meek,
submissive;* nsm. R 60; S 107.

eaxl, f. *shoulder;* dp. —um, R 32.

eaxl-ġespann, n. *shoulder-beam or
shoulder-joint, intersection;* ds. —
e, R 9.

ebba, wk.m. *ebb-tide;* ds. —n, M 65.

ēċe, adj. ja-stem. *eternal;* nsm. C 4,
8; S 124; gsm. —s, B 16; gsn.wk.
ēċan, S 79; asf.wk. ēċan, S 120.
[From *ōCJA-.]

ēċe, adv. *eternally, for ever;* S 67.

ecg, f. jō-stem. *edge, (sword-) blade;*
ns. M 60; dip. —um, B 4, 68. ecg-
hete, m. i-stem. *sword-hate, deadly
violence;* ns. S 70. [Cf. brūn-ecg.]

efstan, wk.v.I. *hasten;* inf. R 34;
pret. 3p. efston, M 206. [Base-
word OFOST, f. *haste;* cf. ofostlíċe.]

eft, adv. *again, back, afterwards;* B
56; R 68, 101, 103; M 201; W 45,
53 (MS. *oft*); S 61; eft ongēan,
*back again, in reply,* M 49, 156.

eġesa, wk. m. *awe, terror; awful
power;* ns. R 86; S 103; ds. —n,
S 101.

eġesliċ, adj. *fearful, dreadful;* nsf.
R 74.

el-, combining-form (from prehist.
*ALJA-, *ALI-), *other, alien, for-
eign.* [Cf. elles.] el-þēodiġ, adj. *of
a foreign country;* gp. —ra, S 38

(as noun: *of foreigners, strangers
—possibly, strangers on earth,* PER-
EGRINI).

ellen, n. (rarely m.), *courage, valor,
zeal, fortitude;* as. on ellen, *val-
iantly,* M 211; ds. mid elne, *val-
iantly,* W 114; is. elne miċle, *with
great zeal,* R 34, 60, 123.

elles, adv. *of another sort; else;* S
46. [gs. of unrecorded adj. *ELL
(from *ALJA-), *other, alien;* cf.
el-.]

ende, m. ja-stem. *end, outermost
part;* ds. R 29 (*edge*). ende-lēas,
adj. *endless;* nsm. D 30.

enġel, m. *angel;* np. englas, R 106;
gp. engla, M 178; dp. englum, R
153; S 78. [Lat. ANGELUS, vulg. AN-
GILUS; pronunciation of g in ob-
lique cases uncertain.] enġel-dryht,
f. *host of angels;* gp. —a, R 9 (emen-
dation; an unrecorded compound;
MS. *engel dryhtnes*).

ent, m. *giant;* gp. —a, W 87 (enta
ġeweorc, *work(s) of giants*—a re-
current poetic expression for an-
cient ruins, presumably occasioned
by wonder at the remains of Ro-
man building in Britain).

ēode, ēoden, ēodon, see gān.

eodor, m. *enclosure, dwelling;* np.
—as, W 77.

eoh, m. *war-horse, charger;* as. M
189.

eom, see bēon-wesan.

eorl, m. (a) *nobleman, man (of rank),
leader;* ns. M 51 (partly sense b);
W 84, 114; D 2; ds. —e, W 12;
D 33; ap. —as, W 99; gp. —a,
B 1; W 60; S 72; D 41. (b) *earl*
(a title corresponding to Old
Norse JARL and used in late Old
English times as equivalent to the
native title ealdormann; in M it is
applied exclusively to Byrhtnoþ);

ns. M 6, 51 (partly sense a), 89, 132, 146, 203, 233; gs. —es, M 165; ds. —e, M 28, 159;—referring to Norse JARLS, np. —as, B 31.

**eornoste**, adv. *resolutely,* M 281.

**ēorod**, n. *troop* (orig. *of horsemen:* eoh, *horse,* plus RĀD, *group of riders.*) **ēorod-cyst**, f. i-stem. *picked company,* or -ċiest, f. i-stem. *band of horsemen;* dip. —um, B 21. [See cyst.]

**eorðe**, wk.f. *earth, the earth;* eorðan, gs. C 5 (var.); R 37; W 106, 110; S 61, 81, 89, 105; ds. R 42, 74, 137, 145; M 107, 126, 157, 233, 286, 303; S 32 (or as.), 93; as. S 39. **eorþ-scræf**, n. *earth-pit, grave;* ds. —e, W 84. **eorþ-weġ**, m. *earthly way;* ds. —e, R 120. **eorþ-wela**, wk. m. *earthly wealth;* in pl., *earthly riches, worldly goods;* np. —n, S 67.

**ēow**, see ġē.

**ēðel**, m. *home, native land;* ns. R 156; as. M 52; S 60 (fig., hwæles e.) dis. ēðle, W 20. [*ōðIL·.]


## F

**fæder**, m. r-stem. *father;* ds. W 115 (*Father*); ealda fæder, *grandfather,* ns. M 218. [Cf. hēah-, wuldor-fæder.]

**fǣġe**, adj. ja-stem. *fated to die (fey);* nsm. M 119; npm. B 12, 28; M 105; gsm. —s, M 297 (as noun); dsm. fǣġum, S 71 (as noun); dsm.wk. fǣġan, M 125.

**fæġen**, adj. *glad, cheerful;* nsm. W 68.

**fæġer** or **fǣġer**, adj. *beautiful, fair;* nsn. fǣġer, R 73; dsf.wk. fæġeran, R 21; fæġere, npm. R 8, npf. R 10.

**fæġere**, adv. *fairly, well;* M 22.

**fæġrian**, wk.v.II. *make beautiful, adorn;* pres. 3p. fæġriaþ, S 48. (Less probably, *become beautiful;* see Mrs. Gordon's note.)

**fæġrost**, adv. superl. *most pleasantly,* S 13.

**fǣhþ(u)**, f. iþō-stem. *hostility, feud;* gs. or as. fǣhþe, M 225. [Base-word FĀH, adj. *hostile.*]

**fǣr**, m. *sudden attack.* **fǣr-scaða**, wk. m. *sudden raider* (viking); ds. —n, M 142.

**fǣrlíċe**, adv. *suddenly, with terrible swiftness;* W 61.

**fæst**, adj. *firm, fixed.* See sigor-, stede-, þrymm-fæst.

**fæste**, adv. *firmly, fast;* (a) *so as not to be moved or shaken,* w. standan, R 38, 43; M 171, 301; (b) *so as not to be overcome: securely,* M 103; (c) *with firm grasp or restraint,* M 21; W 13, 18.

**fæsten**, n. ja-stem. *fastness, place of safety;* as. M 194.

**fæstlíċe**, adv. *stoutly, resolutely;* M 82, 254.

**fæstnian**, wk.v.II. *make fast, confirm;* inf. M 35.

**ġe-fæstnian**, wk.v.II. *fasten;* pret. 3p. ġefæstnodon, R 33.

**fæstnung**, f. *firmness, stability, permanence;* ns. W 115.

**-fæt**, m. uncertain meaning, perhaps related to fōt; not the same as FÆT, n. *container, vat;* appears only as second element of sīþ-fæt, q.v.

**fāg**, adj. *colored, stained* (hence *guilty*) ; *decorated;* nsm. R 13 (*stained*); W 98 (*decorated*). [In both instances there may be overtones of FĀH, adj. *hostile, proscribed:* the MSS. spell both words alike, either *fag* or *fah.*]

**faran,** v.6. *go, pass;* inf. M 88, 156; w. **on,** adv., and dat. of person, *advance* (relatively to someone), *gain upon, overtake:* pres. 3s. him on fareþ, *overtakes him,* S 91. [FARAN, FŌR, FŌRON, FAREN.]

**faru,** f. *expedition, passage.* See **hægl-faru.**

**fēa,** adv. (apn. of **fēawe,** adj. npm. *few*), *(few things), little, but little;* R 115. **fēa-sceaftig,** adj. *wretched, desolate;* asn. S 26. (The usual adj. is FĒA-SCEAFT, *having few things, destitute;* perhaps it is here modified for figurative application to spiritual poverty.)

**feaht,** see **feohtan.**

**feallan,** v.7. *fall;* inf. R 43; M 54, 105; pres. 3s. fealleþ, W 63; pret. 3s. fēoll, M 119, 126, 166, 286, 303; S 32; 3p. fēollon, B 12; M 111. [FEALLAN, FĒOLL, FĒOLLON, FEALLEN; cf. a-feallan.]

**fealu,** adj. wa-stem. *fallow; yellow;* (a) characterizing the appearance of the sea or its waves: the color-notion is uncertain, perhaps merely *dusky;* asm. fealone, B 36; apm. fealwe, W 46. (b) **fealu-hilte,** adj. ja-stem. *having a yellow (golden) hilt;* nsn. M 166.

**feax,** n. *hair (of the head);* as adjectival suffix, *haired.* See **blanden-, gamol-feax.**

**ġe-feċċan** (earlier -fetian), wk.v.II (orig. III). *carry off, take, fetch;* inf. M 160 (MS. *gefecgan*) ; pres. 3s. subj. ġefeċċe, R 138 (MS. *gefetige*) .

**fela,** n., indecl. pron. *much, many* (w. part. gen.); nom. R 9 (em. for MS. **ealle**); M 73; acc. R 50, 125, 131; M 90; W 54; S 5; (indicating extent of time) D 38.

**ġe-fēlan,** wk.v.I. *feel;* inf. S 95. [From *FŌLJAN.]

**feld,** m. u-stem. *field;* ns. B 12; ds. —a, M 241. [Cf. **wæl-feld.**]

**fēng,** see **fōn.**

**feoh,** n. *property; money; wealth;* ns. W 108; as. M 39. **feoh-ġifre,** adj. *greedy for wealth;* nsm. W 68.

**ġe-feoht,** n. *fight;* ds. —e, B 28; M 12.

**feohtan,** v.3. *fight;* inf. M 16, 261; pret. 3s. feaht, M 254, 277, 281, 298. [FEOHTAN, FEAHT, FUHTON, FOHTEN; cf. **un-befohten.**]

**ġe-feohtan,** v.3, trans. *acquire by fighting, win;* inf. M 129.

**feohte,** wk.f. *battle;* ns. M 103.

**fēol,** f. *file.* **fēol-heard,** adj. *hard as a file;* apn. —e (generalized form), M 108. ("The file was used to test the temper of the blade."—Gordon.)

**fēoll, fēollon,** see **feallan.**

**fēond,** m. nd-stem. *enemy;* np. —as, R 30, 33; ap. —as, R 38; gp. —a, S 75 (either secular enemies or devils); dp. —um, M 103, 264; ap. **fiend,** M 82. [**fiend** is standard West Saxon for nap. but **fēondas** occurs in poetical texts, esp. those from Anglian sources.]

**feorh,** n. (rarely m.) *life, soul, spirit;* ns. S 94; as. B 36; M 125, 142, 184; S 71; gs. feores, M 260, 317; ds. feore, M 194, 259. **feorh-bold,** n. *dwelling of the soul, body;* ns. R 73. **feorh-hūs,** n. *house of the soul, body;* as. M 297. [Cf. **fīras.**]

**feorr,** adv. *far, afar, far away;* M 3, 57; W 26; S 37, 52 ; w. dat., *far from,* W 21; *at a distance in time, long ago,* W 90.

**feorran,** adv. *from afar,* R 57.

**ġe-fēra,** wk.m. *companion, comrade; member of a lord's comitatus, re-*

*tainer;* ns. M 280; ap. —n, M 170, 229; in figurative use, ds. —n, W 30. [Base-word **fōr**, f. *journey;* cf. **faran** and **fēran**.]

**fēran**, wk.v.I. *go, journey;* inf. M 41, 221; S 37. [Base-word **fōr**, f., corresponding to pret. 1s. of **faran**; see preceding word.]

**ferhþ**, m. or n. *spirit, soul, heart;* ns. W 54; as. S 26 (here neuter), 37; ds. —e, W 90. **ferhþ-loca**, wk. m. *enclosure of the spirit, breast; thoughts; feelings* (conceived as locked in the breast); ns. W 33; as. —n, W 13. [Cf. **collen-ferhþ**.]

**ferian**, wk.v.I. *carry, transport;* pret. 3s. **ferede**, W 81; rare meaning , *go;* inf. M 179 (mistake for **fēran**?) [Base-word **fǣr**, n. *a going, passage.*]

**fēt**, see **fōt**.

**feter**, f. *fetter;* dip. —um, W 21.

**fēða**, wk.m. *troop (on foot);* as. —n, M 88. [Not related to **fōt**.]

**feðer**, f. *feather;* ap. **feðra**, W 47.

**-feðra**, wk.m. *feathered one* (formed from adjectival **-feðer**). See **isiġ-**, **ūriġ-feðra**. [These compounds have the same form as wk. adjectives but their position in the verse suggests that they are nouns.]

**fiell**, m. i-stem. *fall, death;* as. R 56; M 71, 264.

**fiellan**, wk.v.I. *fell, cut down;* inf. R 73. [Cf. **feallan**.]

**ġe-fiellan**, wk.v.I. (a) *fell, kill;* inf. R 38; pp. **ġefielled**, nsn. B 67; (b) *deprive of (by killing),* w. gen., pp. **ġefielled**, nsm. B 41 (perhaps a mistake for **befielled**, since *be-* normally gives this sense with verbs of killing).

**fiend**, see **fēond**.

**fierd**, f. i-stem. *army* (on the march); spec., the local levy organized for the defense of the realm; ds. —e, M 221. **fierd-rinc**, m. *warrior* (of the English levy); ns. M 140.

**fif**, num. adj. *five;* npm. **fife**, B 28; R 8.

**findan**, v.3. *find;* inf. W 26; pret. 3p. **fundon**, M 85. [FINDAN, FAND or FUNDE, FUNDON, FUNDEN; cf. **onfindan**.]

**firas**, m.pl. *men, human beings;* dp. **firum**, C 9. [Related to **feorh**, q.v.]

**flǣsc**, n. i-stem. *flesh.* **flǣsc-hama**, wk.m. *fleshly covering, body;* ns. S 94.

**flān**, m. *arrow, dart;* as. M 269 (generic); gs. —es, M 71.

**flēag**, see **flēogan**.

**flēam**, m. *flight* (of a fugitive); as. M 81, 254; ds. —e, B 37; M 186.

**flēogan**, v.2. (a) *fly;* inf. M 7, 109, 150; pret. 3s. **flēag**, S 17; (b) *flee;* inf. M 275 (instead of **flēon**,—perhaps for extra syllable). [FLĒOGAN, FLĒAG, FLUGON, FLOGEN.]

**flēon**, contr.v.2. *flee;* inf. M 247; pret. 3p. **flugon**, M 194. [FLĒON (from *FLĒOHAN), FLĒAH, FLUGON, FLOGEN.]

**flēotan**, v.2. *float; fleet;* pres. part. **flēotende**, as noun, *floating or fleeting one;* gp. **flēotendra**, W 54. (Both senses may be operative if the actual seabirds are confused with the visionary companions.) [FLĒOTAN, FLĒAT, FLUTON, FLOTEN.]

**flett**, n. ja-stem. *floor* (typically of a hall; hence metaphorical for the life of a noble retainer and also for life on the floor of this earth); as. W 61.

**fliema**, wk.m. *fugitive.* See **herefliema**.

**ġe-flieman**, wk.v.I, *put to flight;* pp.

ġefliemed, nsm. B 32. [Cf. fléam and a-flíeman.]

flōd, m. or n. *flood;* (a) *current, stream, sea;* as. (m.) B 36; (b) *flood-tide;* ns. M 65, 72 (m.). flōd-weġ, m. *sea-way;* ap. —as, S 52 *(paths of ocean).* [Cf. mere-flōd.]

-floga, wk.m. *flier.* See ān-floga.

flot, n. *water?* (occurs only in prep. phrases, to flote, on flot, *afloat;* might mean the act or state of floating, or water deep enough to float a ship); as. in on flot, B 35, M 41. [Cf. flēotan.]

flota, wk.m. *floater: sailor, viking;* as. —n, M 227; np. —n, M 72; gp. flotena, B 32. [Cf. scip-flota.]

flōwan, v.7. *flow;* pres. part. flōwende, nsm. M 65. [FLŌWAN, FLĒOW, FLĒOWON, FLŌWEN.]

flugon *(fled),* see flēon.

flyht, m. i-stem. *flight;* as. M 71.

folc, n. (a) *people;* ns. R 140; M 45; as. M 54; D 22; gs. —es, B 67; M 202; (b) *army, host;* ns. M 241; as. M 22; ds. —e, M 227, 259 (on folce, *on an [enemy] host?),* 323. folc-stede, m. i-stem, *place of assembly, battlefield;* ds. B 41.

folde, wk.f. *earth, ground, land;* foldan, gs. R 8, 43; W 33; ds. R 132; M 166, 227; S 13, 75; as. C 9; M 54.

folgoþ, m. *(position of) service; office;* as. D 38.

folme, wk.f. *hand;* ds. folman, M 150; dp. folmum, M 21, 108. [FOLM, f., is the commoner form, but M 150, confirmed as ds. by handa, 149, points to wk. folme.]

fōn, contr.v.7. *take, seize;* pret. 3s. fēng, M 10 (to wǣpnum t., *took up arms).* [FŌN, (from *FANHAN), FĒNG, FĒNGON, FANGEN; cf. on-fōn.]

for, prep. w. dat., instr., or acc. *for;* —(a) w. dat. or instr., *in the presence of, before,* R 112; S 101, 103 (for þon, *before which,* or *because of which); because of,* R 21, 111 (unforht for, *unafraid of);* M 64, 89; *for the sake of,* R 113; *in expiation of,* R 99, 146; *for (fear or dislike of),* M 96; *for (fear of losing),* M 259. —(b) w. acc., *for the sake of,* R 93 (see note). for-þon, adv. and conj. (a) adv. *therefore, wherefore,* R 84; M 241; W 17, 64; *indeed,* W 37, 58; S 27, 33 *(as for that? but yet?),* 39 *(for indeed?),* 58, 72.—(b) conj. *for, because,* S 64, 108. [In S 103, þon is probably a relative pronoun: see above, for (a). The interpretation of for-þon, in S and elsewhere, has been much disputed. The suggestions above are offered without conviction.] for-hwon, interr. adv. and conj. *for what reason, why, wherefore;* as conj., W 59.

fōr, f. *journey.* See sǣ-fōr.

for-bærnan, wk.v.I. *burn up, consume* (in fire); pp. forbærned, asm. —ne, S 114.

for-būgan, v.2, w. acc. *turn away from, flee from;* pret. 3s. forbēag, M 325. [Cf. būgan.]

for-cūþ, adj. *infamous;* see un-forcūþ, and cf. fracuþ, with stress on first syllable.

ford, m. u-stem. *ford;* as. M 88; ds. —a, M 81.

fore, prep. *for, in place of;* w. acc., S 21; w.dat., S 22. (Possibly we should read hleahtre, dat., for hleahtor, acc. in S 21.)

for-ġiefan, v.5. *give (away), grant;* pret. 3s. forġeaf, R 147; M 139,

148; pp. forġiefen, ap. (m. or n.)
—e, S 93 (given up, consigned).
[Cf. a-ġiefan.]

for-ġieldan, v.3, w. acc. buy off;
pres. 2p. subj. forġielden, M 32.
[GIELDAN, ĠEALD, GULDON, GOLDEN,
yield, give, pay.]

for-grindan, v.3. grind to pieces,
destroy; pp. for-grunden, asm.
uninfl. B 43. [Cf. ġe-grindan.]

for-heard, adj. very hard; asm. —ne,
M 156 (gār understood; stressed
on first syllable).

for-hēawan, v.7. hew down, cut
down; pp. forhēawen, nsm. M 115,
223, 288, 314. [Cf. hēawan.]

for-hogode, see for-hycgan.

forht, adj. afraid, fearful; nsm. R 21;
W 68. [Cf. an-, un-forht.]

forhtian, wk.v.II. be afraid; pres. 3p.
forhtiaþ, R 115 (future sense);
pret. 3p. subj. forhtoden, M 21.

for-hwon, see for.

for-hycgan, wk.v.III (and II). des-
pise, scorn; pret. 3s. forhogode,
M 254. [Cf. hycgan.]

for-lǣtan, v.7. (a) leave, abandon;
inf. M 2, 208; pret. 3s. forlēt,
B 42; M 187; 3p. forlēton, R 61; (b)
w. inf., let, cause to; pret. 3s.
forlēt, M 149, 156, 321. [Cf. lǣtan.]

forma, wk.adj. earliest, first; asm.
—n, M 77.

for-maniġ, adj. very many; nsm. M
239 (stressed on second syllable).

for-niman, v.4. carry off, destroy;
pret. 3s. fornam, W 80; 3p. for-
nāmon, W 99. [Cf. niman.]

forst, m. frost; dis. —e, S 9.

for-swelgan, v.3. swallow (up); inf.
S 95. [SWELGAN, SWEALG, SWULGON,
SWOLGEN.]

forþ, adv. forth, away, onward; B
20; R 54, 132; M 3, 12, 170, 205,
209, 225, 229, 260, 269, 297; —

tō forþ, too successfully, too
deeply, M 150. forþ-ġeorn, adj.
eager to advance; nsm. M 281.
forþ-ġesceaft, f. pre-ordained con-
dition; as. R 10 (see note). forþ-
weġ, m. the way forth (into the
hereafter); as. R 125 (MS. ds.
—e,); W 81 (MS. ds. —e).

ġe-forþian, wk.v.II. carry out, ac-
complish; pp. ġeforðod, uninfl.
M 289.

for-þolian, wk.v.II. endure the ab-
sence of, do without, forgo; inf.
W 38. [Cf. þolian.]

for-þon, see for.

for-wegan, v.5. carry off, destroy,
kill; pp. for-weġen, nsm. M 228.
[Cf. wegan.]

for-wundian, wk.v.II. wound (sorely);
pp. forwundod, nsm. R 14, 62. [Cf.
ġe-wundian.]

fōt, m. cons.-stem. foot; gs. —es, M
247; dp. —um, M 119, 171; np.
fēt, S 9. fōt-mǣl, n. foot's length;
as. as adv. M 275.

fracuþ, adj. wicked, shameful, pro-
scribed; gsm. —es, R 10 (as noun,
a criminal's).

fram, prep. w. dat. or instr. from;
B 8; R 69; M 185, 187, 193, 252,
316 (the last clearly w. instr.).

fram, adv. away; M 317.

fram-weard, adj. on the way out,
passing away; dsm. —um, S 71.

franca, wk.m. spear; as. —n, M 140;
ds. —n, M 77. [Originally a spear
favored by the Franks, but in
poetry equated with gār; see Gor-
don's note on M 77.]

frēa, wk.m. (a) lord; as. —n, M 259;
ds. —n, M 12, 16, 184, 289; (b)
the Lord; ns. C 9; as. —n, R 33.

frēfran, wk.v.I. comfort; inf. W 28;
S 26 (MS.feran). [Base-word
frōfor, q.v.]

ġe-fremman, wk.v.I. *perform, bring about, accomplish;* inf. W 16, 114; pret. 3p. ġefremedon, S 84.

fremu, f. *beneficial action; good deed;* dip. —m, S 75 (MS. *fremman*).

frēo, f. ja-stem. *lady;* gs. frīge, D 15.

frēo, adj. ja-stem. *free, noble.* frēomǣġ, m. *(noble) kinsman;* dip. —māgum, W 21.

frēod, f. *peace;* ds. —e, M 39.

frēond, m. nd-stem. *friend, loved one, kinsman;* ns. R 144; W 108; np. —as, R 76; gp. —a, B 41, R 132; ap. frīend, M 229. [Standard West Saxon has nap. frīend, but the analogical -as occurs in some poems, esp. of Anglian origin.]

frēond-lēas, adj. *friendless;* asm. —ne, W 28.

frēoriġ, adj. *cold, frozen;* nsm. W 33. [Cf. FRĒOSAN, v.2, *freeze.*]

frīend, see frēond.

frīge, see frēo, f.

friġnan, v.3. *ask;* pres. 3s. friġneþ, R 112 (future sense). [FRIĠNAN, FRÆĠN, FRUGNON, FRUGNEN; parts 1, 3, and 4 were often spelled without ġ, indicating the pronunciation FRĪN- and FRŪN-.]

ġe-friġnan, v.3. *learn* (by asking); pret. 1p. ġefrugnon, D 14; 3p. R 76.

friþ, m. *peace;* as. M 39; gs. —es, M 41 (instr. *force, at peace*—see healdan); ds. —e, M 179.

frōd, adj. *old, wise, experienced;* nsm. M 140, 317 (frōd feores, *advanced in years*); W 90; nsm.wk. as noun, se frōda, *the old campaigner,* B 37.

frōfor, f. *comfort, help, support;* as. frōfre, W 115.

ġe-frugnon, see ġe-friġnan.

frymdiġ, adj. *asking, desirous;* nsm.

M 179 (iċ eom f. to þē, *I beseech thee*).

fugol, m. *bird;* ns. W 81. [Cf. brimfugol.]

full, adj. w. gen. *full (of);* nsf. S 100; asm. fulne, S 113 (w. gen. fȳres according to MS., but some other gen. beginning with *w* seems to be needed).

full, adv. *wholly, fully, very;* M 153, 253, 311; W 5; S 24.

fundian, wk.v.II, w. prep. or adv. (indicating the goal), *direct one's course (to);* pres. 3s. fundaþ, S 47 (sē-þe on lagu fundaþ, *he that will go to sea*); and w. inf. (indicating purpose), R 103 (hider eft fundaþ ... mann-cynn sēċan, *he will come hither again to seek mankind*).

fundon, see findan.

furðor, adv. comp. *further;* f. gān, *advance,* M 247.

fūs, adj. (a) *eager (to set out, to press on);* nsm. M 281; asm. —ne, S 50; (b) *hastening;* npm. —e, R 57 (as noun); (c) *brilliant, shining;* asn.wk. —e, R 21 (the meaning "mobile, quickly shifting," suggested by Cook, lacks confirmation from other passages —see note in Dickins and Ross). [Related to fundian; the base of fȳsan.]

fylstan, wk.v.I. w. dat., *help;* inf. M 265.

fȳr, n. *fire;* gs. —es, S 113 (MS. — this reading rejected for faulty alliteration and doubtful sense).

fyrmest, adj. superl. *foremost, first;* nsm. M 323.

fȳsan, wk.v.I, trans. *send forth rapidly; speed, shoot;* pret. 3s. fȳsde, M 269. [The intrans. sense, *hasten,* is not here represented; base-word fūs, q.v.; cf. a-fȳsan.]

# G

**gǣstlić,** adj. *ghostly, spectral;* nsn. W 73. [The meaning *ghastly, terrifying* is tempting here and may be correct, but see OED, "ghastly"—the word cannot with certainty be connected with OE **gǣstlić.**]

**gafol,** n. *tribute;* as. M 61; ds. —e, M 32, 46.

**gāl,** adj. *gay, wanton.* See **wīn-gāl.**

**galan,** v.6. *sing;* inf. R 67. [GALAN, GŌL, GŌLON, GALEN.]

**gamen,** n. *entertainment;* ds. —e, S 20.

**gamol,** adj. *old, aged.* **gamol-feax,** adj. *hoary-haired, gray-headed;* nsm. S 92 (as noun).

**gān,** anom.v. *go;* inf. M 247; imper. pl. **gāþ,** M 93 (=*come*) ; pret. 3s. **ēode,** R 54; M 132, 159, 225, 297, 323; 3p. **ēodon,** M 260; 3p. subj. **ēoden,** M 229. [Cf. **ofer-gān.**]

**gang,** m. *going, passage; flow* (of blood), ds. —e, R 23. [Cf. **upp-gang,** and next word.]

**gangan,** v.7. *go, move along, proceed;* inf. M 62; **gangan forþ,** *advance;* inf. M 3, 170; **to scipe gangan,** *embark;* inf. M 40 (w. refl. dat. **ūs,** *take to our ships*) ; pres. 2p. subj. **gangen,** *should embark,* M 56. [GANGAN, ĠEONG, ĠEONGON, GANGEN.]

**ġe-gangan,** v.7. (*go and*) *get, obtain;* inf. M 59.

**ganot,** m. *gannet;* gs. —es, S 20.

**gār,** m. *spear;* ns. M 296; as. M 13, 134, 154, 237, 321; ds. —e, M 138; ap. —as, M 46, 67, 109; dip. —um, B 18. **gār-berend,** m. nd-stem. *spear-bearer, spearman;* np. M 262. **gār-mitting,** f. *encounter of spears;* gs. —e, B 50. **gār-rǣs,** m.

*rush of spears, battle;* as. M 32.

**gāst,** m. *soul, spirit;* as. R 49; ds. —e, M 176; np. —as, R 11; gp. —a, R 152.

**gāþ,** see **gān.**

**ġe-,** prefix, sometimes signifying *together*. With verbs a sign of completed action, often untranslatable but sometimes distinctive. All words beginning with this prefix are listed according to the first letter of their stems.

**ġē,** pron. 2nd pers. pl. *ye;* nom. M 32, 34, 56, 57, 59; dat. **ēow,** M 31, 46, 48; 93; acc. **ēow,** M 41.

**ġēac,** m. *cuckoo;* ns. S 53.

**ġealga,** wk.m. *gallows, cross;* ns. R 10; as. —n, R 40. **ġealg-trēo,** n. wa-stem. *gallows-tree, cross;* ds. —we, R 146. [Mod. pronunciation from Anglian GALGA.]

**ġēar,** n. *year;* gp. in **ġēara ġeō,** adv. *in years gone by, long ago,* R 28; W 22. **ġēar-dagas,** m.pl. *days of yore, former times;* dp. —dagum, W 44. [The sense here develops in accordance with **ġēara** or **ġeāra,** gp. as independent adv. *of yore, formerly.*]

**ġeard,** m. *yard; enclosed field or plot of ground* (sometimes of great extent). See **eard-, middan-ġeard.**

**ġearu,** adj. wa-stem. *ready;* nsm. M 274; npm. **ġearwe,** M 72, 100.

**ġearulīċe,** adv. *readily;* (with verb of perceiving) *clearly;* D 10.

**ġearwe,** or **ġeare,** adv. *readily;* (with verb of knowing) *clearly, for certain, well;* W 69, 71. [The two spellings represent a long and a short stressed syllable respectively and their alternate use here accords with metrical requirements.]

ġeatu, f. wō-stem. *equipment, gear.* See here-ġeatu.

ġeō, adv. *of old, formerly;* R 87; S 83; ġēara ġeō, *in years gone by, long ago,* R 28; W 22. ġeō-wine, m. i-stem. *friend* (or *lord*) *of former days;* ap. S 92. [Often spelled *iu* in the MSS.]

ġēoc, f. *help;* ds. —e, S 101.

ġeoguþ, f. *youth* (as a period of life) ; ds. —e, W 35; S 40.

ġeōmor, adj. *sad, mournful;* disf. wk. ġeōmran, S 53.

ġeond, prep. w. acc. *through, throughout, over;* W 3, 58, 75; S 90; D 31 (wendeþ ġeond, *goes about through*).

ġeond-hweorfan, v.3. *pass through, rove through;* pres. 3s. —hweorfeþ, W 51. [Cf. hweorfan.]

ġeond-scēawian, wk.v.II. *survey;* pres. 3s. —scēawaþ, W 52. [Cf. scēawian.]

ġeond-þenċan, wk.v.I. *consider thoroughly, contemplate;* pres. 1s. —þenċe, W 60; 3s. —þenċeþ, W 89. [Cf. þenċan.]

ġeong, adj. *young;* nsm. R 39; M 210; nsm.wk. se ġeonga, as epithet, M 155; asm. —ne, B 44; npm. —e, B 29.

ġeorn, adj., w. gen. *eager (for);* nsm. M 107; W 69; npm. —e, M 73. [Cf. dōm-, forþ-ġeorn.]

ġeorne, adv. *eagerly,* M 123, 206; W 52; (with a verb of seeing, implying careful observation) *well, clearly;* M 84.

ġeornfull, adj. *eager;* nsm. M 274.

ġeornlīċe, adv. *eagerly,* M 265.

ġēotan, v.2. *pour out, shed* (blood); pres. part. ġeotende, *dripping* (with blood), np. R 70 (emendation adopted by Cook for MS. *reotende;* see grēotan for the alternative here preferred).

[ĠĒOTAN, ĠEAT, GUTON, GOTEN; cf. be-ġēotan and a-ġietan.]

ġicel, m. *piece of ice, icicle.* See hrīm-ġicel.

ġiedd, n. ja-stem. *saying; song, poem.* See cwide-, sōþ-ġiedd.

ġiefa, wk.m. *giver.* See bēag-, gold-, māðum-, sinc-ġiefa.

ġiefan, v.5. *give.* See a-, for-, of-ġiefan. [ĠIEFAN, ĠEAF, ĠĒAFON, ĠIEFEN.]

ġiefu, f. *gift;* gp. ġiefena, S 40 (with gōd, *generous of gifts?* or *well-endowed with natural abilities, generously gifted?* —Mrs. Gordon recommends the first, but the other seems more appropriate) . ġief-stōl, m. *gift-seat* (the high seat or throne, from which gifts were dispensed) ; *the ceremony of gift-giving;* gs. —es, W 44.

ġieldan, v.3. *yield, give, pay.* See for-ġieldan.

ġiellan, v.3. (*yell,*) *cry out loudly;* pres. 3s. ġielleþ, S 62. [ĠIELLAN, ĠEALL, GULLON, *GOLLEN; cf. be-ġiellan.]

ġielp, m. or n. *boasting; a boast;* gs. —es, W 69. ġielp-word, n. *vaunting word;* dip. M 274.

ġielpan, v.3. *boast;* inf. B 44 (w. gen.). [ĠIELPAN, ĠEALP, GULPON, GOLPEN.]

ġieman, wk.v.I, w. gen. *heed, care for;* pret. 3p. ġiemdon, M 192.

ġierwan, wk.v.I. *prepare, dress, adorn;* pret. 3p. ġieredon, R 77. [Base-word ġearu; cf. ġe-, on-ġierwan.]

ġe-ġierwan, wk.v.I. *adorn;* pp. ġe-ġiered, asn. R 16; ġeġierwed, the same, R 23. [The form without w is historically correct, the other analogical, and the alternation metrically sound.]

ġiest, m. i-stem. *stranger;* np. —as,
M 86.

ġiet, adv. *yet.* See þā-ġiet.

ġieta, adv. *yet;* B 66; R 28.

ġietan, v.5. *get.* See be-, on-ġietan.
[ĠIETAN, ĠEAT, ĠĒATON, ĠIETEN.]

ġietan, wk.v.I. *destroy.* See a-ġietan.

ġif, conj. *if,* M 34, 36, 196.

ġifre, adj. ja-stem. *greedy, ravenous;*
nsm. S 62. [Cf. feoh-, wæl-ġifre.]

ġimm, m. *jewel;* np. —as, R 7, 16.
[From Lat. GEMMA.]

-ġinnan, v.3. *begin.* Never without
prefix. See on-ġinnan.

ġisel, m. *hostage;* ns. M 265.

glēaw, adj. *sagacious, sharp-sighted,
wise, prudent;* nsm. W 73.

glēo, n. *joy, merriment; music.* glēo-
stafas, m.pl. *signs of joy, joyful
salutations, songs?* dp. —stafum, W
52. [See stæf.]

glīdan, v.l. *glide;* pret. 3s. glād, B 15.
[GLĪDAN, GLĀD, GLIDON, GLIDEN.]

gnornian, wk.v.II. *mourn, feel sor-
row, lament;* inf. M 315; pres. 3s.
gnornaþ, S 92.

God, m. *God;* ns. R 39, 93, 98, 106,
156; M 94; as. R 51, 60; M 262;
gs. —es, B 15; R 83, 152; S 101.
[GOD, n. (*heathen) god.*]

gōd, n. (*that which is) good;* gs. —es,
M 176.

gōd, adj. *good;* nsm. M 315; S 40
(*well-endowed, excellent? gener-
ous?*) ; asn. M 13, 237; asm.wk.
—an, M 187 (as noun); dsm. —um,
M 4; apm. —e, M 170; asf. in gōde
hwīle, *a good while,* R 70. [Cf.
betera, betst, sēlest.]

gold, n. *gold;* ns. W 32 (see wun-
den); S 101; as. R 18; ds. —e, R 7,
16; M 35; dis. —e, R 77; S 97. gold-
ġiefa, wk.m. *gold-giver;* np. —n, S
83. gold-wine, m. *friendly patron,
bountiful friend* (since the lord

typically gives gold to his loyal re-
tainers); ns. W 35; as. W 22.

grǣdiġ, adj. *greedy;* nsm. S 62; asm.
—ne, B 64.

græf, n. *grave;* as. S 97.

grǣġ, adj. *gray;* asn.wk. grǣġe, B 64.

gram, adj. *fierce;* npm. —e, M 262;
dp. —um, M 100 (as noun, *foes*).

ġe-gremian or -gremman, wk.v.I. *en-
rage;* pp. ġegremed, nsm. M 138;
np. —e, M 296. [Base-word gram.]

grēot, n. *sand, dust;* ds. —e, M 315.

grēotan, v.2. *weep;* pres. part. grēo-
tende, np. R 70 (MS. *reotende,*
from RĒOTAN, v.2, *weep,* lacks al-
literation; see ġēotan for alterna-
tive emendation). [Only the pres-
ent stem of this verb is on record.]

grētan, wk.v.I. *approach; speak to,
hail, greet;* pres. 3s. grēteþ, W 52.
[The base-word *GRŌT has not
survived.]

grimm, adj. *grim, fierce, savage;* nsm.
M 61; D 23.

grimme, adv. *grimly, cruelly;* M 109.

ġe-grindan, v.3. *grind, sharpen;* pp.
ġegrunden, ap. ġegrundne, M 109.
[GRINDAN, GRAND, GRUNDON, GRUN-
DEN; cf. for-grindan.]

griþ, n. *truce, peace;* as. M 35. [A
Scandinavian term for a truce
based on definite conditions; less
general than friþ; see Gordon's
note.]

grund, m. *ground; land, surface of
the earth; bottom, foundation;* as.
M 287 (*the ground*); ap. —as, B 15
(*surfaces of earth; the land*); S
104 (stīðe grundas, *the rocky foun-
dations*). grund-lēas, adj. *bottom-
less; boundless;* npf. —e, D 15.

ġe-grundne, see ġe-grindan.

gryre, m. i-stem. *terror.* gryre-lēoþ, n.
*terrible song;* gp. —a, M 285.

guma, wk.m. *man;* ns. B 18; W 45;

gs. —n, R 49, 146 (generic sing. or late form of pl. **gumena?**); np. — n, M 94; gp. **gumena, B** 50.

**gūþ,** f. *battle;* as. —e, M 325; gs. —e, M 192; ds. —e, B 44; M 13, 94, 187, 285, 296 (or instr.), 321. **gūþ-hafoc,** m. *war-hawk;* as. B 64. **gūþ-plega,** wk.m. *battle-play;* ns. M 61. **gūþ-rinc,** m. *warrior;* ns. M 138.

# H

**habban,** wk.v.III. *have.* (a) as independent v.; inf. M 236; pres. 3s. **hafaþ,** W 31; S 47; pret. 3s. **hæfde,** M 13, 121, 199 *(held);* D 3. —neg. **næbbe** (**ne hæbbe**), pres. 3s. subj. S 42. (b) as aux. w pp.; pres. 1s. **hæbbe,** R 50, 79; S 4; 2s. **hafast,** M 231; 3s. **hafaþ,** M 237 (MS. **hæfþ**); pret. 3s. **hæfde,** R 49; M 22, 197, 289; D 10; 3p. **hæfdon,** R 16, 52. [West Saxon normally has HÆFST, HÆFþ, but it has seemed best to adopt the commoner poetic forms.]

**hæġl,** m. *hail;* ns. S 17, 32; dis. —e, W 48. **hæġl-faru,** f. *shower of hail, hailstorm* (perhaps with analogy to an army on the march; see **faru**) ; as. —fære, W 105.

**hǣlan,** wk.v.I. *heal, save;* inf. R 85. [Base-word **hāl,** q.v.]

**hæle,** or **hæleþ,** m. þ-stem. *man, warrior, hero;* ns. **hæle,** W 73; **hæleþ,** R 39; vs. **hæleþ,** R 78, 95; np. **hæleþ,** M 214, 249; gp. **hæleða,** B 25; M 74; dp. **hæleðum,** W 105. [Originally ns. **hæle,** np. **hæleþ.**]

**Hǣlend,** m. nd-stem. *Healer, Savior* (translation of "Jesus"); gs. —es, R 25. [Cf. **hǣlan** and **hāl.**]

**hǣðen,** adj. *heathen;* npm. **hǣðne,** M 55, 181.

**hafaþ,** see **habban.**

**hafenian,** wk.v.II. *raise aloft;* pret. 3s. **hafenode,** M 42, 309.

**hafoc,** m. *hawk;* as. M 8. [Cf. **gūþ-hafoc.**]

**haga,** wk.m. *hedge, enclosure,* as in **wiġ-haga,** q.v.; in **ān-haga** the wk. ending -a, signifies an agent and **hag-** may signify a hedged dwelling (hence "lone-dweller"), but the sense of narrow confinement is appropriate.

**hāl,** adj. *whole, safe and sound, unhurt;* npm. —e, M 292.

**hāliġ,** adj. *holy;* nsm. C 6; npm. **hālġe,** R 11; —declined wk. as m. noun, **hālga,** *holy one;* ds. —n, S 122 *(God);* dp. **hālgum,** R 143, 154 *(saints).*

**hām,** m. *home, dwelling;* as. R 148; S 117; ds. —e, M 292; ap. —as, B 10; —as. as adv. w. verb of motion, *home(ward),* M 251.

**hama,** wk.m. *covering.* See **flǣsc-hama.**

**hamor,** m. *hammer;* gp. —a, B 6.

**hand,** f. u-stem. *hand;* ns. M 141; as. M 112; S 96; ds. —a, R 59; M 149; ap. —a, W 43; dp. —um, M 4 (see note), 7, 14; W 4. **hand-plega,** wk. m. *hand-to-hand combat;* gs. —n, B 25.

**hār,** adj. *gray; hoary, old;* nsm. B 39; M 169; nsm.wk. —a, W 82.

**hasu,** adj. wa-stem. *dark, dusky.* **hasu-pāda,** wk.m. *dusky-coated one;* as. —n, B 62. (The same in form as a wk. adj. corresponding to strong HASU-PĀD, *dusky-coated.*)

**hāt,** adj. *hot;* npf. **hāt'** for **hāte,** S 11; comp. **hātra,** npm. —n, S 64 (fig.). **hāt-heort,** adj. *hot-tempered;* nsm. W 66.

**hātan,** v.7. (a) *command;* pres. 1s. **hāte,** R 95; pret. 3s. **hēt,** M 2, 62,

74, 101; 3p. **hēton**, R 31; M 30;
—(b) *call, name;* pp. **hāten**, nsm.
M 75, 218. [HĀTAN, HĒT, HĒTON,
HĀTEN.]

ġe-**hātan**, v.7. *promise, vow;* pres. 1s.
ġe**hāte**, M 246; pret. 3s. ġe**hēt**, M
289.

**hē, hēo, hit**, pron. 3d pers. *he, she,
it,* pl. *they.* **hē**, nsm. C 3, 5; B 40;
R 34, etc. (15 times); M 7, etc.
(56 times); W 2, etc. (10 times);
S 8 (*it*), 42, etc. (9 times). **his,** gsm.
C 2; B 2, 38, 40, 42; R 49, 63, 92,
102, 106, 156; M 11, etc. (20
times); W 13, etc. (8 times); S 40,
etc. (11 times). **him,** dsm. R 65,
67, 108, 118; M 7, etc. (15 times;
refl. in 300); W 1, 10 (w. þe, *to
whom*), etc. (7 times); S 13 (w. þe,
*to whom*), etc. (11 times); D 1, 3.
**hine,** asm. R 11, 39, 61, 64; M 164,
181; W 32, 35; S 43, 77, 99; D 5.
**hēo,** nsf. W 96; D 10, 11. **hire,** gsf.
D 8, 9. **hīe,** asf. M 180; S 103
(refl., *itself*); D 16. **hit,** nsn. R 19,
22, 26, 97; M 66, 137, 190, 195,
240; asn. S 102. **hīe,** np. B 8, 48,
51; R 32, 46, 48, 60, 63, 64, 66,
67, 68, 115, 116, 132; M 19, etc.
(19 times); W 61; S 84. **hīe,** ap.
M 82, 127, 209, 283, 320. **hira,** gp.
B 47; R 31, 47, 155; M 20, etc.
(11 times); W 18. **him,** dp. B 7,
60; R 86, 88; M 66, 197, 198, 265;
S 23; refl., B 53; R 31, 63 (see
note), 83, 133; S 67, 84 (mid him,
*amongst themselves*).

**hēafod,** n. *head;* as. W 43; ds. **hēaf-
dum,** R 63. [Campbell, *OE Gram.*
574, 4, regards this form as a
locatival dat. sg., perhaps instr.
in origin; the three recorded in-
stances are all datives with æt;
otherwise we find ds. **hēafde.**]

**hēah,** adj. *high;* nsm. W 98; asm.

**hēanne,** R 40; W 82; apm. wk.
**hēan,** S 34 (*high* or *deep*). **hēah-
fæder,** m. r-stem. *God the Father;*
ds. —e, R 134.

**healdan,** v.7. *hold, grasp, possess;
keep, guard, maintain, control;*
inf. M 14, 19, 74, 102, 236; S 109,
111; pres. 3p. **healdaþ,** S 87; 3s.
subj. **healde,** W 14 (*hold in, keep
to himself*); pret. 3p. subj.
**hēolden,** M 20; —w. instrumental
genitive, **ēow** friðes **healdan** (inf.),
*keep you at peace, remain at
peace with you?* M 41. [HEALDAN,
HĒOLD, HĒOLDON, HEALDEN; cf.
be-**healdan.**]

ġe-**healdan.** v.7. *keep hold of;* inf. M
167; *keep (unbroken)*, pres. 3s.
ġe**healdeþ,** W 112.

**healf,** f. *side;* ds. —e, M 152, 318;
as. —e, R 20.

**heall,** f. *hall;* ds. —e, M 214. [Cf.
**medu-heall.**]

**heals,** m. *neck;* as. M 141.

**hēan,** adj. *lowly, abject, downcast;*
nsm. W 23.

**hēan, hēanne,** inflected forms, see
**hēah.**

**hēanliċ,** adj. *humiliating;* nsn. M 55.

**heard,** adj. *hard; severe, bitter; hard-
fighting, fierce, unyielding;* nsm.
M 130 (wīġes **heard,** *fierce in
battle*); asn. M 214; gsm. —es, B
25; gsn. —es, M 266; asm. —ne, M
167, 236; asf. —e, M 33. —comp.
**heardra,** *harder, more resolute,*
nsm. M 312; superl. **heardost,** *bit-
terest, most severe;* nsn. R 87. [Cf.
**fēol-, for-, wīġ-heard.**]

**heardliċe,** adv. *fiercely;* M 261.

**hearm,** m. *grief, sorrow;* gp. —a, M
223.

**hearpe,** wk.f. *harp;* ds. **hearpan,** S 44.

**hearra,** wk.m. *lord;* ns. M 204. [Cf.
German HERR. The OE word may

have been borrowed from Old
Saxon.]

heaðu-, *battle, war* (a word occurring
only as the first member of com-
pounds). heaðu-lind, f. *battle-
shield (of linden)*; ap. —a, B 6.

hēawan, v.7. *hew;* pret. 3s. hēow, M
324; 3p. hēowon, B 6, 23; M 181.
[HĒAWAN, HĒOW, HĒOWON, HĒA-
WEN; cf. a-, for-hēawan.]

hebban, v.6. *lift, raise;* inf. R 31.
[HEBBAN, HŌF, HŌFON, HAFEN; cf.
a-hebban.]

hefiġ, adj. *heavy, oppressive;* dsn.
wk. —an, R 61; *sad, depressed;*
comp. hefiġran, npf. W 49.

hell, f. *hell.* hell-scaða, wk.m. *fiend
of hell;* np. —n, M 180.

helm, m. *covering, helmet,* etc. See
niht-helm. [Cf. HELAN, v.4, *conceal,
hide.*]

help, f. *help;* as. —e, W 16; ds. —e,
R 102.

ġe-hende, prep. w. dat. *near,* M 294
(postpos.). [Base-word hand.]

hēo, see hē.

heofon, m. *heaven;* as. C 6; gs. —es,
R 64; ap. —as, R 103; gp. —a, R
45; dp. —um, R 85, 134, 140, 154;
M 172; W 107, 115; S 107, 122.
heofon-rīċe, n. ja-stem. *kingdom of
heaven;* gs. —s, C 1; R 91.

heofonlīċ, adj. *heavenly;* asm. —ne,
R 148.

hēolden, see healdan.

heolstor, m. *concealment, darkness;*
dis. heolstre, W 23. [Cf. HELAN, v.4,
*conceal, hide.*]

heonan, adv. *hence, from here;* R
132; M 246; S 37.

-heort, adjectival combining-form of
heorte, *heart.* See hāt-heort.

heorte, wk.f. *heart;* ns. M 312;
heortan, gs. W 49; ds. M 145; as.

S 11, 34 (obj. of cnyssaþ; or gs.
with ġeþōhtas).

heorþ, m. *hearth.* heorþ-ġenēat, m.
*sharer of the hearth, member of
the chief's household troops, his
closest followers;* np. —as, M 204.
heorþ-weorod, n. *the body of
household retainers;* as. M 24.

hēow, hēowon, see hēawan.

hēr, adv. *here,* M 36, 51, 241, 243,
314; *in this world,* R 108, 137,
145; W 108 (twice), 109 (twice);
S 102; *in this year,* B 1 (the
typical introduction to an entry
in the Chronicle; probably not
part of the poem).

here, m. ja-stem. *army;* ds. M 292
(West Saxon variant of herġe, the
usual dative); gs. herġes, B 31.
here-flīema, wk.m. *fugitive* (from
pursuing host); ap. —n, B 23.
here-ġeatu, f. *war-equipment;* in
law a "heriot," "a feudal ser-
vice originally consisting of wea-
pons, horses and other military
equipments, restored to a lord on
the death of his tenant" (see
Gordon's note, taking up a sug-
gestion made by C. Brett); as.
—ġeatwe, M 48. here-lāf, f. *rem-
nant of an army after a battle;
group of survivors;* dp. —um. B
47. [Cf. æsc-here.]

herian, wk.v.I. *praise, extol;* inf. C 1;
pres. 3p. subj. herien, S 77.
[HERIAN (from *H.ERJAN), HEREDE,
HERED.]

hēt, hēton, ġe-hēt, see hātan, ġe-hātan.

hete, m. i-stem. *hate, hostility.* See
ecg-hete.

hettend, m. nd-stem. *enemy;* np. B
10. [Cf. HATIAN, *hate,* and HETTAN,
*persecute.*]

hider, adv. *hither;* B 69; R 103; M
57.

**hīe,** see **hē.**

**hieldan,** wk.v.I. *bend;* inf. R 45 (w. refl. pron.) [Base-word HEALD, adj. *bent, inclined.*]

**hīenan,** wk.v.I. *bring low, lay low, afflict;* inf. M 180; pret. 3s. **hīende,** M 324 (used absolutely: *laid low.*) [Base-word hēan, adj., q.v.]

**ġe-hīeran,** wk.v.I. *hear, perceive, understand;* inf. R 78; pres. 2s. **ġehīerst,** M 45; pret. 1s. **ġe-hīerde,** R 26; M 117; S 18.

**hild,** f. jō-stem. *battle, war;* as. —e, M 33; ds. —e, M 8, 48, 55, 123, 223, 288, 324. **hilde-rinc,** m. *warrior;* ns. B 39; M 169; np. —as, R 61; gp. —a. R 72.

**-hilte,** adjectival combining-form, *hilted,* corresponding to ĠE-HILTE, n. ja-stem, *sword-hilt.* See **fealu-hilte.**

**him,** see **hē.**

**hindan,** adv. *from behind;* B 23. [Cf. **be-hindan.**]

**hine, hira,** see **hē.**

**hīred,** m. *household, body of retainers.* **hīred-mann,** m. *household retainer;* np. —menn, M 261.

**his, hit,** see **hē.**

**hlāford,** m. *lord;* ns. M 135, 189, 224, 240; as. D 39; ds. —e, M 318; *the Lord,* as. R 45. **hlāford-lēas,** adj. *lordless;* nsm. M 251.

**hleahtor,** m. *laughter;* as. S 21 (perhaps for ds. **hleahtre;** see **fore**).

**ġe-hlēapan,** v.7. *leap upon, mount;* pret. 3s. **ġehlēop,** M 189. [HLĒAPAN, HLĒOP, HLĒOPON, HLĒAPEN.]

**hlemm,** m. ja-stem. *noise (of a blow);* but in **inwitt-hlemm,** (q.v.) the meaning appears to be *wound.*

**hlēo,** n. wa-stem. *shelter; protector, lord;* ns. M 74; D 41. **hlēo-mǣġ,**

m. *protecting kinsman; gp.* —māga, S 25.

**ġe-hlēop,** see **ge-hlēapan.**

**hlēor,** n. *cheek, face;* as adjectival combining-form, -**hlēor,** *faced.* See **drēoriġ-hlēor.**

**hlēoðor,** n. *cry, (bird-) call;* as. S 20. [Cf. next word.]

**hlēoðrian,** wk.v.II. *call out, speak;* pret. 3s. **hlēoðrode,** R 26.

**hliehhan,** v.6. *laugh;* inf. B 47; pret. 3s. **hlōg,** M 147. [HLIEHHAN, HLŌG, HLŌGON,——; *cf.* **hleahtor.**]

**hlīfian,** wk.v.II. *tower, rise up;* pres. 1s. **hlīfie,** R 85.

**hlimman,** v.3. *roar, resound;* inf. S 18. [HLIMMAN, *HLAMM, HLUMMON,——.]

**hliþ,** n. *cliff;* see **stān-hliþ.**

**hlōg,** see **hliehhan.**

**ġe-hlystan,** wk.v.I. *listen;* pret. 3p. **ġehlyston,** M 92.

**ġe-hnǣġan,** wk.v.I. *bring low, abase, humble;* pp. **ġehnǣġed,** nsm. S 88. [Base-word HNĀG, adj. *low; cf.* **hnīgan.**]

**hnāg,** see **hnīgan.**

**ġe-hnāst,** n. *collision* (in battle). See **cumbol-ġehnāst.**

**hnīgan,** v.1. *bow down;* pret. 1s. **hnāg,** R 59. [HNĪGAN, HNĀG, HNIGON, HNIĠEN; *cf.* **ġe-hnǣġan.**]

**hogode, hogodon,** see **hycgan.**

**ġe-hola,** wk.m. *protector;* gp. **ġe-holena,** W 31.

**hold,** adj. *kind, friendly, gracious;* nsm. S 41; asm. —ne, D 39; superl. **holdost,** *most loyal, devoted;* asn. M 24. [Describes a lord's regard for his followers and also theirs for him; hence the two shades of meaning.]

**holm,** m. *wave, (high) sea;* pl. *seas, ocean;* as. W 82; gp. —a, S 64.

**holt,** n. *forest, wood; wooden shaft;*

gs. —es, R 29; M 8. holt-wudu, m.
u-stem, *trees of the forest;* as. R
91 (MS. *holm wudu*). [Cf. æsc-
holt.]

hōn, contr.v.7. *hang.* See be-hōn.

hord, n. *treasure, hoard;* as. or ap.
B 10. hord-cofa, wk.m. *treasure-
chest* (i.e. the breast as container
of thoughts) ; as. —n, W 14. [Cf.
brēost-hord.]

hors, n. *horse;* as. M 2.

hræd, adj. *quick, swift, sudden,
hasty.* hræd-wyrde, adj. ja-stem.
*hasty of speech;* nsm. W 66.

hræfn, m. *raven;* as. B 61; np. —as,
M 106.

hræðe, adv. *quickly, soon;* M 30,
164, 288.

hrǣw, n. *corpse;* ns. R 72; as. R 53;
ap. B 60.

hrēam, m. *outcry, clamor;* ns. M 106.

hrēman, wk.v.I. *exult;* inf. B 39 (w.
gen.) [Cf. Old Saxon HRŌM, *glory;*
German RUHM.]

hrēmiġ, adj. *exultant;* npm. hrēmġe,
B 59 (w. gen.) .

hrēoh, adj. *rough, troubled;* nsm. wk.
hrēo, (= *HRĒOHA), W 16; asf.
hrēo, (= *HREŌHE) , W 105.

hrēosan, v.2. *fall;* inf. W 48; pres.
part. hrēosende, nsf. W 102.
[HRĒOSAN, HRĒAS, HRURON, HROREN;
cf. be-hroren.]

hrēow, f. wō-stem. *sorrow, (rue) .*
hrēow-ċeariġ, adj. *sorrowful,
troubled;* nsm. R 25.

hrēran, wk.v.I. *stir (up) , move;* inf.
W 4. [Base-word HRŌR, adj.
*vigorous, active;* cf. on-hrēran.]

hreðer, m. or n. *breast, bosom* (esp.
as the seat of feelings); *heart;* as.
S 63; gp. hreðra, W 72. hreðer-
loca, wk.m. *enclosure of the breast
or heart: the breast;* as. —n, S 58.

hrīm, m. *rime, (hoar-)frost;* ns. S 32;

as. W 48; dis. —e, W 77. hrīm-
ċeald, adj. *frost-cold;* asf. —e, W 4.
hrīm-ġicel, m. *icicle;* dip. —um, S
17.

hring, m. *ring;* ap. —as, M 161 (*gold
rings, ornaments*). hring-loca, wk.
m. *linked ring* (of corselet); ap. —
n, M 145. hring-þegu, f. *receiving
of (gold) rings* (by a liegeman
from his lord); ds. —þeġe, S 44.

hriþ. f. *snowstorm;* ns. W 102. [The
only occurrence of the word in
OE; the meaning inferred from
the context and from Old Norse
HRĪÐ, f. *tempest.*]

hrīðiġ, adj. *snow-covered? storm-
beaten?* npm. hrīðġe, W 77. [Only
occurrence; see preceding word.]

hrōf, m. *roof;* ds. —e, C 6.

hrūse, wk.f. *earth, ground;* gs. hrū-
san, W 23; as. W 102 (MS. has
nom. *hruse*) ; S 32.

hryre, m. i-stem. *fall, ruin;* ds. hryre,
W 7. [One would expect hryres,
parallel to the two preceding gen-
itives dependent on ġemyndiġ, 6;
but perhaps a dat. of accompani-
ment modifying wæl-sleahta, "at-
tended by the fall of kinsmen."
For the word, cf. hroren, pp. of
hrēosan.]

hū, interr. adv. and conj. *how;* (a)
introducing subord. cl., M 19; W
30, 35, 61, 73; S 2, 14, 29, 118;
D 12; (b) introducing an exclama-
tion, W 95.

hungor, m. *hunger;* ns. S 11.

hūru, adv. *certainly,* R 10.

hūs, n. *house.* See feorh-hūs.

hwā, hwæt, pron. (1) interr. *who
what;* (a) in indirect questions,
nsm. hwā, M 95, 124, 215; asn.
hwæt, R 116; isn. hwon, S 43 (to
hwon, *to what:* scil. *what end,
what service, what fate*); (b) as a

relative, asn. **hwæt**, R 2 (MS. **hæt**); M 45; S 56. (2) indef. pron. *someone, something;* nsm. **hwā**, M 71. (3) indef. pron. *each* (normally ġe-hwā); asm. **hwone**, M 2.

ġe-**hwā**, ġe-**hwæt**, pron. w. part. gen. *each;* gsn. **ġehwæs**, C 3; dsm. ġe-**hwǣm**, W 63; S 72; asm. **ġehwone**, B 9.

**hwæl**, m. *whale;* gs. —es, S 60. **hwæl-weġ**, m. *whale's way, ocean;* as. S 63 (MS. *wæl weg*).

**hwǣr**, adv. and conj. *where;* (a) interr. adv. R 112; W 92, 93 (five times); (b) rel. conj. *(there) where,* W 26; S 117.

**hwæt**, adj. *quick, vigorous, active;* nsm. S 40; in certain compounds, *quick at producing, abounding in.* See **ār-hwæt**.

**hwæt**, interj. *lo!* R 1, 90; M 231.

**hwæt**, pron. see **hwā**.

ġe-**hwæðer**, adj. *either;* asf. —e, M 112.

**hwæð(e)re**, adv. conj. *nevertheless, but;* R 18, 24, 38, 42, 57, 59, 70, 75, 101.

ġe-**hwelċ**, pron. w. part. gen. *each;* nsm. M 128, 257; S 90, 111; dsm. —um, R 108 (ānra ġ., *each one*); S 68 (MS. isn. —e) ; ism. —e, R 136; W 8; S 36. [Fusion of ġe-hwā and liċ; cf. ǣġhwelċ.]

**hweorfan**, v.3. *turn, go, take* (or *change*) *one's course;* inf. W 72; pres. 3s. **hweorfeþ**, S 58, 60 (w. comparison to a bird: *flies, takes its flight*). [HWEORFAN, HWEARF, HWURFON, HWORFEN; cf. ġeond-hweorfan.]

**hwettan**, wk.v.I. *whet, incite;* pres. 3s. **hweteþ**, S 63. [Base-word **hwæt**, adj., q.v.]

**hwider**, interr. conj. *whither,* W 72.

**hwīl**, f. *(an indefinite period of)*

*time, while.* (a) as. —e as adv. *for a time,* R 64, 84; D 36; **ealle h.** *all the time, continually,* M 304; **gōde h.** *for a good while,* R 70; **lange h.** *for a long time,* R 24. (b) dp. —um as adv. *at times, sometimes;* W 43; S 19; correl. *at one time . . . at another time; now . . . now,* R 22, 23; M 270. (c) **þā hwile þe,** conj. *while;* M 14, 83, 235, 272. [Cf. **earfoþ-, langunghwil.**]

**hwilpe**, wk.f. *whaup* (English and Scottish dialect) , *curlew;* gs. —n, S 21. (See Mrs. Gordon's note.)

**hwilum**, adv. see **hwil**.

**hwīt**, adj. *white;* asm. uninflected (because parenthetical?), B 63. [On the grammar, see Campbell's ed., p. 119. He says **earn æftan hwīt** is parenthetical and therefore ns.]

**hwon**, instr. of **hwæt**, see **hwā** and **for-hwon** under **for**.

**hwōn**, pron. w. gen. *little, few;* as. S 28.

**hwone**, see **hwā**.

**hwonne**, interr. adv. *when;* as rel. conj. w. subj. *(the time) when,* R 136; M 66 (w. **tō lang**, *too long until the time when*) .

**hycgan**, wk.v.III (and II) . *think, consider, be intent* (*on*) *, intend, purpose;* inf. M 4; S 117; pres. 3s. subj. **hycge**, W 14; pret. 3s. **hogode**, M 133 (w. gen., *was intent on, purposed*) ; 3s. subj., M 128; 3p. **hogodon**, M 123. [HYCGAN, HOGDE or HOGODE, HOGD or HOGOD; cf. for-hycgan, stīþ-hycgende.]

**hȳdan**, wk.v.I. *hide, hoard;* pres. 3s. **hȳdeþ**, S 102.

ġe-**hȳdan**, wk.v.I. *hide, bury;* pret. 3s. **ġehȳdde**, W 84.

ġe-**hyġd**, f. and n. i-stem. *thought,*

*intention; conception;* ns. W 72; S 116.

**hyġdiġ,** adj. *mindful;* in composition, *minded, disposed.* See **an-, wan-hyġdiġ.**

**hyġe,** m. i-stem. *mind, thought; soul, spirit; purpose, courage;* ns. M 312; W 16; S 44, 58; ds. M 4; S 96.

**hyht,** m. i-stem. *joyous expectation, pleasure, bliss;* ns. R 126, 148; S 45, 122.

**hyrned,** pp. adj. *horned.* **hyrned-nebba,** wk.m. *horny-beaked one,* as. **−n,** B 62. [The same in form as a wk. adj., corresponding to strong HYRNED-NEBB, *horny-beaked;* cf. **isig-, ūriġ-feðra.**]

**hyse,** m. i-stem, inflected according to ja-stems (with gemination), **hyss-,** *young man, young warrior;* ns. M 152; gs. **hysses,** M 141; np. **hyssas,** M 112, 123; ap. **hyssas,** M 169; gp. **hyssa,** M 2, 128.

## I

**iċ,** pron. 1st pers. sg. *I;* ns. R 1, etc. (43 times); M 117, etc. (14 times); W 8, etc. (8 times); S 1, 2, etc. (9 times); D 35, 36, 38. **mīn,** gs., only in the rejected emendation, **mīn myne wisse,** W 27 (but see **mīn,** poss. adj.). **mē,** ds. R 2, 4, 46, 83, 86, 126, 129, 135, 144; M 55, 220, 223, 249, 318 (refl.); S 1, 20 (refl.), 61, 64; D 35, 37, 41. **mē,** as. R 30, 31, 32 (twice), 33, 34, 42, 45, 46, 61, 75, 77, 81, 90, 122, 136, 139, 142; M 29, 252. **meċ,** as. W 28; S 6. [See **wē, wit.**]

**īdel,** adj. *empty, vain;* nsn. W 110; npn. **īdlu,** W 87.

**ielde,** m. i-stem, pl. *men* (conceived

as the successive generations, or men of old); gp. **ielda,** C 5; W 85; S 77. [Base-word **eald,** *old.*]

**ieldu,** f. īn-stem. *age, old age;* ns. S 70, 91.

**ielfetu,** f. *(wild) swan;* gs. **ielfete,** S 19.

**ierġþu,** f. iþō-stem. *slackness;* as. **ierġþe,** M 6. [Base-word **earg,** q.v.]

**ierre,** adj. ja-stem. *angry, wrathful;* nsm. M 44, 253.

**īeðan,** wk.v.I. *lay waste, depopulate, destroy;* pret. 3s. **īeðde,** W 85. [Cf. the rare adj. **īEðE,** *empty, waste,* cognate w. German ÖDE.]

**īġ,** f. jō-stem (alt. sp. **īeġ,** from *ĒA-JŌ-;* see **ēa,**), *watery place, island.* **īġ-land,** n. *island;* is. **−e,** B 66. [Mod. "island" from native ME ILAND, influenced by OF ILE from Lat. INSULA, respelled ISLE by Renaissance scholars.]

**in-dryhten,** adj. *noble, excellent;* nsm. W 12. [This adj. is probably formed from **in-dryhtu,** next below, the prefix indicating a quality inherent in a noble **dryht,** though it is sometimes regarded as an intensive.]

**in-dryhtu,** f. īn-stem. *nobility;* ns. S 89. [Cf. preceding word.]

**inn,** adv. *in,* M 58, 157.

**innan,** adv. *(from) within,* S 11.

**inwitt,** n. *malice, fraud.* **inwitt-hlemm,** m. *malicious wound;* np. **−as,** R 47. [It is uncertain whether **inwitt** is borrowed from Lat. INVIDIA or of Germanic origin; for the odd meaning of the second element see **hlemm.**]

**inwitta,** wk.m. *malicious or deceitful one;* ns. B 46. [Cf. preceding word.]

**īren,** n. ja-stem, *iron, iron blade;* ns. M 253 (**ord and iren** as variation of **wǣpen**: *point* [*of spear*] *and iron blade;* or, as hendiadys, *iron point* or *pointed iron?*) .

**is**, see **bēon-wesan**.

**īs**, n. *ice*. **īs-ċeald**, adj. *ice-cold;* asm. —**ne**, S 14, 19.

**īsiġ**, adj. *icy*. **isiġ-feðra**, wk.m. *icy-feathered one;* ns. S 24. [Usually regarded as a wk. adj., but like **ūriġ-feðra**, q.v., it is placed as if in apposition and can be taken as a characterizing noun like **hyrned-nebba**, q.v. The corresponding strong adj. would be **ISIĠ-FEÐER**.]

## L

**lā**, interj. *lo!* — see **eā-lā**.

**ġe-lāc**, n. *tossing, play; tumult;* as. S 35.

**lād**, f. *way, course*. See **brim-, lagu-lād**. [Cf. **līðend, lid, lida**.]

**lǣdan**, wk.v.I. *lead;* inf. R 5 (*extend*: possibly an error for **LĒODAN**, v.2, *spring up*); M 88. [Base-word **lād**, as above.]

**lǣġ**, see **licgan**.

**lǣne**, adj. ja-stem. *transitory, brief, fleeting;* ns. W 108 (n. and m.), 109 (m. and f.) ; nsn. S 66; dsn.wk. **lǣnan**, R 109 (MS. —*um*), 138. [Lit. *on loan*: **LǢN**, f. *a loan*.]

**lǣran**, wk.v.I. *instruct;* pret. 3s. **lǣrde**, M 311. [Base-word **lār**, f., q.v.]

**lǣriġ**, m. *rim (of shield)*? ns. M 284. [Perhaps a borrowing from Lat. **LŌRĪCA**, *corselet*, by way of Old Welsh, with shift of meaning; see Gordon's note.]

**ġe-lǣstan**, wk.v.I, w. dat. *support, help;* inf. M 11; w. acc., *fulfill;* pret. 3s. **ġelǣste**, M 15. [Base-word **lāst**, m., q.v.]

**lǣtan**, v.7, w. inf. *let, cause to;* pret. 3s. **lēt**, M 7, 140; 3p. **lēton**, B 60; M 108. [**LǢTAN, LĒT, LĒTON, LǢTEN**; cf. **for-lǣtan**.]

**lāf**, f. *remnant;* **hamora lāf**, *what is left by the hammers of the smith: a sword;* dip. —**um**, B 6; **daroða lāf**, *what is left by the spears: the remnant that survives after a battle;* ns. B 54. [Cf. **here-lāf**.]

**lāge, lāgon**, see **licgan**.

**lagu**, m. u-stem. *sea, water;* as. S 47 (**on l.**, *to sea*). **lagu-lād** f. *water-way, sea;* as. —**e**, W 3. **lagu-strēam**, m. *sea-stream;* np. —**as**, M 66 (tidal streams, coming up the river) .

**ġe-lagu**, n.pl. (uniquely recorded, apparently an inflected form of *ġE-LǢĊ, n. lay, layer, material spread out*), *stretches, expanse;* ap. in **holma ġelagu**, *expanse of the seas*, S 64. [Etymologically distinct from **lagu**, m.; cf. **licgan**.]

**land**, n. *land;* as. B 9, 27, 56, 59; gs. —**es**, M 90, 275; ds. —**e**, M 99; S 66. **land-riht**, n. *land-right* (the rights and privileges of an estate); as. D 40. [Cf. **īġ-land**.]

**lang**, adj. *long; (in duration)* nsn. M 66; asf. —**e**, R 24; *(in stature)* nsm. wk. **se langa** (as distinguishing epithet), *the tall*, M 273. [Cf. **ealdor-lang**; also **lenġ**.]

**ġe-lang**, adj. w. prep. **on** (Anglian **IN**), *comprehended in, inseparable from;* nsn. S 121.

**lange**, adv. *for a long time*. W 3, 38.

**langoþ**, m. *longing;* as. D 3.

**langung**, f. *longing, restless desire, anxiety;* as. —**e**, S 47. **langung-hwīl**, f. *time of longing;* gp. —**a**, R 126 (according to Dickins and Ross, times of weariness of spirit, *accidia;* but the dreamer seems hardly to be blaming himself here).

**lār,** f. *lore, instruction, knowledge.*

**lār-cwide,** m. i-stem, *speech of instruction, counsel;* dip. — cwidum, W 38. [Cf. **lǣran.**]

**lāst,** m. *footstep, track, path;* as. B 22; ds. —e, W 97 (on l., w. dat. *on the track of, behind, after*) ; dip. —um, S 15 (wreċċan l., *in the paths of an exile*). **lāst-word,** n. *reputation left behind* (after death); gp. —a, S 73 (Mrs. Gordon's definition). [Cf. **wrǣc-lāst.**]

**lāþ,** adj. *hostile, hateful, hated;* asm. —ne, S 112 (as noun) ; dsf. —re, M 90; npm. —e, M 86; gp. —ra, B 9 (as noun, *enemies*) ; dp. —um, B 22; comp. **lāðre,** asn. M 50; superl. **lāðost,** nsm. R 88.

**lēan,** n. *recompense.* Cf. **wiðer-lēan.**

**lēas,** adj. *lacking, deprived of;* npn. —e, W 86 (analogical -e, generalized from the npm.; the npn. of long monosyllables usually has no ending, having lost its original -u; but the extra syllable is metrically necessary; possibly the original version had an archaic -u, but the analogical -e of the MS. is probably authentic); —as suffix, -less; see **ende-, frēond-, grund-, hlāford-, wine-lēas.**

**leċgan,** wk.v.I. *lay;* pres. 3p. leċgaþ, S 57; 3s. subj. leċge, W 42; pret. 3s. leġde, D 5; 3p. leġdon, B 22 (elliptically w. on **lāst,** *pursued*). [LECGAN, LEĊDE, LEĊ(E)D; baseword LǢĠ; cf. **liċgan;** also **a-leċgan.**]

**lenġ,** comp. adv. *longer;* M 171. [Cf. **lang.**]

**lēode,** m. i-stem, pl. *people;* np. B 11; ap. M 37; dp. **lēodum,** R 88; M 23, 50. [Cf. LĒOD, m. *man, leader;* LĒOD, f. *people, nation.* The plural

**lēode** is usually assigned to the former.]

**lēof,** adj. *dear, beloved;* gsm. —es, W 38; dsm. —um, M 319; asm. —ne, M 7, 208 (as noun) ; S 112 (as noun); dsf. —re, W 97; vsm.wk. —a, R 78, 95; gp. —ra, W 31; superl. **lēofost,** nsn. M 23 (see note).

**leofaþ,** see **libban.**

**lēoht,** n. *light;* dis. —e, R 5.

**lēoþ,** n. *song.* **lēoþ-cræftiġ,** adj. *skilled in song;* nsm. D 40. [Cf. **gryre-, sorg-lēoþ.**]

**lēt, lēton,** see **lǣtan.**

**ġe-lettan,** wk.v.I. *hinder;* pret. 3s. ġelette, M 164.

**libban,** wk.v.III. *live;* pres. 3s. leofaþ, S 102, 107; 3p. libbaþ, R 134; 3s. subj. libbe, S 78; pret. 3p. lifdon, S 85; —pres. part. libbende, m.pl. as noun, *the living;* gp. libbendra, S 73.

**liċ,** n. *body;* gs. —es, R 63.

**-līca,** wk. m. *image, likeness;* see **wyrm-līca.**

**liċgan,** v.5. *lie, lie dead;* pres. part. liċgende, nsm. R 24; pres. 3s. liġeþ, M 222, 232, 314; 3p. liċgaþ, W 78; pret. 3s. læġ, B 17; M 157, 204, 227, 276, 294; 3p. lāgon, B 28; M 112, 183; pret. 3s. subj. lāge, M 279; w. refl. dat., *lie down;* inf. M 319; pret. 3s. subj. lāge, M 300 (see note). [LICGAN, LÆĠ, LĀGON, LEĠEN.]

**lid,** n. *ship;* gs. —es, B 27, 34. **lid-mann,** m. *shipman, sailor* (*viking*); np. —menn, M 99; gp. —manna, M 164. [Cf. LIÐAN, v.l, *sail;* and next word.]

**lida,** wk.m. *sailor.* See **sǣ-lida.**

**liefan,** wk.v.I, *allow, permit.* See **a-liefan.**

**ġe-liefan,** wk.v.I. *believe;* (a) w. subordinate clause as object, pres.

1s. ġelīefe, S 66; 3s. ġelīefeþ, S 27
(w. refl. him, *admits to himself*);
(b) w. on and dat. (or acc.), *be-
lieve in, trust in*; pres. 3s.
ġelīefeþ, S 108. [Base-word LĒAF, f.
*leave, permission*; cf. a-līefan;
also ĠELĒAFA, wk.m. *belief*.]

līehtan, wk.v.I. *alight*; pret. 3s. līehte,
M 23. [Cf. LĪOHT, later LĒOHT, adj.
*light in weight*.]

līesan, wk.v.I. *liberate, redeem,
ransom*; inf. R 41; M 37. [Cf.
lēas, adj.; also on-līesan.]

līf, n. *life*; ns. S 65, 121; as. R 147;
M 208; W 60, 89; gs. −es, R 88,
126; S 27, 79; ds. −e, R 109, 138.

lifdon, see libban.

liġeþ, see licgan.

lim, n. *limb*. lim-wēriġ, adj. *weary of
limb*; asm. −ne, R 63.

limpan, v.3. impersonal, w. dat.
*befall*; pres. 3s. limpeþ, S 13.
[LIMPAN, LAMP, LUMPON, LUMPEN.]

lind, f. *linden-wood; shield (of
linden-wood)*; as. −e, M 244; ap.
−a, M 99. [Cf. heaðu-lind.]

līðend, m. nd-stem. *sailor.* See
brim-līðend.

loca, wk.m. *lock, link*; see hring-loca;
*enclosure, locker*; see ferhþ-,
hreðer-loca. [Cf. lūcan.]

lof, n. and m. *praise*; ns. S 73, 78.

losian, wk.v.II. *be lost, fail*; pres. 3s.
losaþ, S 94.

lūcan, v.2. *lock, unite, join*; pret.
3p. lucon, M 66. [LŪCAN, LĒAC,
LUCON, LOCEN.]

lufu, f. *love* (often inflected, as here,
according to the wk. decl. as if
from the rare nom. LUFE); ds.
lufan, S 121; as. lufan, S 112 (not
in MS.). [Cf. sorg-lufu.]

lust, m. *desire*; ns. S 36.

lyft, f. i-stem (also m. and n.) *air*;
as. R 5 (on lyft, *aloft, on high*).

lȳt, indecl. subst., adj. and adv.
*little, few*; as subst., w. part. gen.,
as. W 31; as adv., S 27.

lȳtel, adj. *little*; isn. lȳtle, B 34.

lytiġian, wk.v.II. *use guile*; inf. M
86.

lȳtlian, wk.v.II. *grow less, dwindle,
diminish*; pres. 3s. lȳtlaþ, M 313.

## M

mā, n., w. part. gen. *more*; M 195;
as adv. *more*, B 46. [Cf. mǣst.]

mæcg, m. ja-stem. *man*; gp. −a, B
40 (alt. reading for mēċa).

mæġ, mæġe, see magan.

mæġ, f. þ-stem (gds. and nap. mæġþ),
*maiden, woman*; ns. W 109.
[Some scholars regard this word
as mǣġ, f. *kinswoman, woman*;
but all instances are in nom. sg.,
so that association with mæġþ, rep-
resented in other cases, is prob-
able. Cf. the variation of hæle
and hæleþ.]

mǣġ, m. *kinsman*; ns. M 5, 114, 224,
287; gp. māga, B 40; W 51. [Cf.
cnēo-, frēo-, hlēo-, wine-mǣġ.]

mæġen, n. *strength*; ns. M 313.

mǣl 1, n. (a) *measure*; see fōt-mǣl;
(b) *time, occasion*; gp. −a, S 36.

mǣl 2, n. *speech*; gp. −a, M 212.
[Unique occurrence with this
meaning, but cf. mǣlan and
mæðel. Gordon's emendation of
MS. þa to gen. pl. þāra permits us
to regard mǣl as neuter in-
stead of feminine, a gender which
is improbable on other grounds.]

mǣlan, wk.v.I. *speak*; pret. 3s.
mǣlde, M 26, 43, 210. [Cf.
maðelian.]

ġe-mǣlan, wk.v.I. *speak*; pret. 3s.
ġemǣlde, M 230, 244.

mǣre, adj. ja-stem. *glorious, famous*;
nsf. wk. R 12, 82; W 100 (*Wyrd*

*the mighty?*); nsn. (or m.), B 14 (**tungol** is usually neuter in the poetry but once masc.); dsm.wk. **mǣran**, R 69.

**mǣrðu**, f. iþō-stem. *glorious deed;* gp. —a, S 84.

**mǣst**, adj. superl. *most, greatest;* asf. —e, M 175; — as noun, n., w. part. gen. *the greatest* (*of*); ns. M 223; *the greatest number* (*of*); as. S 84. [Cf. **micel, mā, māra**.]

**ge-mǣtan**, wk.v.I, impers. w. dat. of person. *dream;* pret. 3s. **gemǣtte**, R 2.

**mǣte**, adj. ja-stem. *small, limited;* isn. R 69, 124. [Cf. METAN, v.5, *measure*.]

**mǣþ**, f. *proper measure, fitness;* ns. M 195.

**mæðel**, n. *assembly; speech.* **mæðel-stede**, m. i-stem. *meeting-place;* ds. M 199.

**mǣw**, m. i-stem. *mew; seagull;* as. S 22.

**māg-**, see **mǣg**.

**magan**, pret.-pres. v. *be able, can, may.* — (a) w. inf., pres. 1s. **mæg**, R 85; W 58; S 1; 2s. **meaht**, R 78; 3s. **mæg**, R 110; M 215 (subjectless **mæg cunnian**, *one can find out, it can be tested*), 258, 315; W 15, 64; S 94; D 31; impers. w. **ofergān** understood, *it may pass over*, D 7, 13, 17, 20, 27, 42; 3s. subj. **mæge**, M 235; pret. 1s. **meahte**, R 18, 37; 3s. **meahte**, M 9, 14, 70, 124 (subj.?), 167, 171; S 26; D 11; 1s. subj. (?) **meahte**, W 26. (b) w. prep. phrase implying an inf. of being or of motion, pres. 3s. **mæg** (*can be*), S 100; pret. 3s. **meahte** (*could go*), M 64. [MAGAN, MÆG, MAGON, MEAHTE.]

**magu**, m. (*son;*) *young man, warrior;* ns. W 92. **magu-þegn**, m. (*young*) *retainer;* np. —as, W 62.

**man**, m. (weakly stressed form of **mann**), indef. pron. *one* (used in ns. only), R 73, 75; M 9; S 109. [Normally spelled with single *n* in the MSS., but the same spelling sometimes serves for the stressed form.]

**ge-man**, see **ge-munan**.

**mān**, f. *moan, lamentation;* np. —a, D 14. [The base-word of MǢNAN, wk.v.I, *lament,* and ancestor of mod. "moan," but unrecorded in OE; conjectured by Malone in the form of a nom.pl. MŌNE, for the improbable *monge* of the MS.]

**ge-māna**, wk.m. *fellowship, meeting;* gs. (or dis.?) —n, depending on **hrēman**, B 40. [GEMǢNE, adj. *common;* German GEMEIN.]

**manian**, wk.v.II. *exhort, remind, urge;* inf. M 228; pres. 3s **manaþ**, S 36 (w. clause), 53 (used absolutely).

**ge-manian**, wk.v.II. *exhort, admonish, remind;* pres. 3p. **gemaniaþ**, S 50 (w. **to** and dat.); pp. **ge-manod**, apm. —e (agreeing w. **þegnas**, obj. of **hafast**), M 231.

**manig**, adj. and pron. *many* (*a*); — as adj., nsm. B 17; M 282; D 24; dsm. —um, D 33; asm. —ne, M 188, 243; dp. —um, R 99; — as pron., npm. —e, M 200; gp. —ra, R 41; dp. —um, D 19. [Cf. **for-manig**.]

**mann**, m. cons.-stem. *man;* ns. R 112; M 147, 239; W 109; S 12, 39; D 40; as. M 77, 243; D 6; gs. —es, S 116; ds. **menn**, M 125, 319; np. **menn**, R 12, 82, 128; M 105, 206; ap. **menn**, R 93; gp. **manna**, M

195; S 90, 111; dp. **mannum, R** 96, 102. **mann-cynn,** n. ja-stem. *mankind;* as. R 41, 104; gs. —**es,** C 7; R 33, 99. **mann-dryhten,** m. *(liege) lord;* as. W 41. (For this meaning see Klaeber's glossary to *Beowulf.*) [Cf. **brim-, ealdor-, hired-, lid-, sǣ-mann;** and **Norþ-mann,** pr. n.; also **man,** pron.]

**māra,** comp. adj. *more, greater;* nsn. **māre,** B 65; M 313. [Cf. **micel, mā,** and **mǣst.**]

**maðelian,** wk.v.II. *make a speech, speak;* pret. 3s. **maðelode,** M 42, 309.

**māðum,** m. *gift, treasure, precious object;* dip. **māðmum,** S 99. **māð-um-ġiefa,** m. *giver of treasure;* ns. W 92.

**mē,** see **iċ.**

**meaht,** f. i-stem. *might, power;* dis. **meahte,** R 102; ds. S 108 (less probably as., which should have no ending; possibly ap. *powers,* since **ġelīefan on** takes acc. more often than dat.); ap. —**a,** C 2 (Northumbrian *-i;* the West Saxon *-e* may be as.) . [The parallel form MIHT gives mod. "might"; cf. **ma-gan.**]

**meaht, meahte,** see **magan.**

**mearh,** m. *horse, steed;* ns. W 92; as. M 188; ds. **mēare,** M 239.

**meċ,** see **iċ.**

**mēċe,** m. ja-stem. *sword;* as. M 167, 236; gp. **mēċa,** B 40 (alt. reading MÆCGA, see **mæcg**); dip. **mēċum,** B 24. [A poetical word appearing only in this Anglian form; West Saxon *MĒĊE.]

**medu,** m. u-stem. *mead;* ds. M 212. **medu-drinc,** m. *(mead-drink,) mead;* ds. —**e,** S 22. **medu-heall,** f. *mead-hall;* ds. —**e,** W 27.

**ġe-menġan,** wk.v.I. *mingle;* pp. **ġe-**

**menġed,** W 48 (uninflected; one might expect apm. ĠEMENĠDE). [Base-word ĠE-MANG, n. *mixture, throng.*]

**meniġu,** f. īn-stem. *multitude;* ds. **meniġe,** R 112, 151.

**menn,** see **mann.**

**mere,** m. i-stem. *sea* (elsewhere also *lake*); as. B 54. **mere-flōd,** m. *ocean-stream;* ds. —**e,** S 59. **mere-wēriġ,** adj. *sea-weary;* gs. —**werġes,** S 12 (as noun).

**ġe-met,** n. *measure;* ds. S 111 (mid **ġemete,** with moderation).

**metod,** m. *the measurer,* originally *fate,* but in these and most other poems, God (as ordainer of fate or creator); ns. S 108, 116; vs. M 175; gs. —**es,** C 2; W 2; S 103; ds. —**e,** M 147. [Cf. METAN, v. 5, *mete, measure.*]

**mēðe,** adj. ja-stem. *weary;* nsm. R 65; npm. R 69. [From *MŌÐJA-.]

**micel,** adj. *much, great;* nsm. R 130; S 103; nsf. R 139; gsn. **micles,** M 217; ds.wk. **miclan,** R 65, 102; ism. **micle,** R 34, 60, 123 (w. **elne**). [Cf. **mā, māra, mǣst.**]

**micle,** isn. of **micel,** n., adv. w. comp., *much;* M 50.

**mid,** prep. *with, amid, by,* etc. (1) w. dat. (instr.) ; (a) of persons act-ing, moving, or being together: *(in company) with, together with, accompanied by;* B 26, 47; R 121, 134, 143, 151; M 51, 79, 101a, 191; and with latent personification, S 59 (mid **mere-flōde**). (b) of asso-ciated abstractions: *(in conjunc-tion) with,* R 149 (twice). (c) *hav-ing in hold, taking;* M 40, 56. (d) *amid, among;* M 23, 76; S 78, 80, 84 (mid him, *amongst themselves*) . (e) of instrumentality: *with, by means of;* R 7, 14, 16, 20, 22, 23

(twice), 46, 48, 53, 59, 62, 102; M
14, 21, 32, 77, 101b, 114, 118, 124,
126, 136, 138, 226, 228; W 4, 29
(or manner); S 96. (f) of manner:
*with, in;* B 37; M 68, 179; W 114;
S 111. (2) w. acc., *along with,* S 99
(postpos.).

**mid,** adv. *in attendance, at the
same time* (an extension of the
preposition), R 106.

**midd,** adj. *middle, mid;* dsf. **midre,**
R 2.

**middan-ġeard,** m. *(this) world, the
earth;* ns. W 62; as. C 7; R 104;
W 75; S 90. [Gothic MIDJUN-
GARD-S, OHG MITTIN-GART; the
the first element related to **midd,**
adj.; cf. Old Norse MIÐ-GARÐR.]

**mierran,** wk.v.I. *hinder.* See **a-
mierran.**

**mihtiġ,** adj. *mighty;* nsm. R 151;
comp. **mihtiġra,** nsm. S 116. [Cf.
**ælmihtiġ.**]

**milde,** adj. ja-stem. *merciful;* vsm.
M 175.

**milds,** f. jō-stem. *mildness, mercy,
favor;* as. —e, W 2.

**min,** poss. adj. *my, mine;* nsm. M
218, 222, 224 (twice), 250; W 59;
S 58, 59; vsm. R 78, 95; nsf. R
130; M 177; gsm. —es, M 53; dsm.
—um, R 30; M 176, 318; asm. —ne,
M 248; W 10, 19, 22; asf. —e, W
9; npm. —e, S 9; apm. —e, W 27
*(my [people]);* apn. —e, M 216.
[Cf. **iċ.**]

**misliċ,** adj. *various, diverse;* dip.
—um, S 99.

**missenliċe,** adv. *variously,* W 75 *(in
various places or forms);* or
**missenliċ,** adj. *various,* npm. —e.
[If the word is taken as an adv.,
its relation to the following
phrase is closer and the flow of

the sentence easier. The alternate
form MISLĪĊE would be metrically
more regular.]

**mittung,** f. *encounter.* See **ġār-
mittung.**

**mōd,** n. *mind, heart, spirit, mood;*
ns. M 313; as. W 51; S 12, 108;
gs. —es, S 36, 50; ds. —e, R 130;
W 41, 111; S 109; is. —e, R 122.
**mōd-ċeariġ,** adj. *sad, troubled in
spirit;* nsm. W 2. **mōd-ġeþanc,** m.
or n. *(mind's) purpose, counsel;*
as. C 2. **mōd-sefa,** wk. m. *heart,
soul, mind, inmost thoughts;* ns.
R 124; W 59; S 59; as. —n, W 10,
19. **mōd-wlanc,** adj. *proud in spirit;*
nsm. S 39. [Cf. **æwisc-, ēaþ-, ofer-,
stīþ-, wēriġ-mōd.**]

**mōdiġ,** adj. *bold, courageous, spirit-
ed;* nsm. R 41; M 147; npm.
**mōdġe,** M 80; W 62.

**mōdiġliċe,** adv. *boldly, with a show
of courage;* M 200.

**mōdor,** f. r-stem. *mother;* as. R 92.

**molde,** wk.f. *earth;* ns. S 103; as.
**moldan,** R 12, 82. **mold-ærn,** n.
*earth-house, sepulchre;* as. R 65.

**morgen,** m. *morning.* **morgen-tīd,** f.
i-stem. *morningtide;* as. B 14.

**mōst, mōste, mōston,** see **mōtan.**

**ġe-mōt,** n. *meeting, encounter;* ns.
M 301; as. M 199; gs. —es, B 50.

**mōtan,** pret.-pres. v. *be permitted,
may, must;* pres. 1s. **mōt,** R 142;
2s. **mōst,** M 30; 1s. subj. **mōte,**
R 127; 3s. subj. **mōte,** M 95, 177;
1p. subj. **mōten,** S 119 (tō mōten,
*may go thither);* 3p. subj. **mōten,**
M 180; pret. 3s. **mōste,** M 272; 3p.
**mōston,** M 83; 3p. subj. **mōsten,**
M 87, 263. [MŌTAN, MŌT, MŌTON,
MŌSTE.]

**ġe-munan,** pret.-pres. v. *remember,
be mindful of;* — w. acc., pres. 1s.
**ġeman,** R 28; 3s. **ġeman,** W 34,

90; pret. 3s. ġemunde, M 225 (acc. or gen.) ; 3p. subj. ġemunden, M 196; — w. gen., imper.pl. ġemunaþ, M 212 (emendation; E's transcript has *gemunu þa mæla,* which might indicate acc. originally). [MUNAN, MAN, MUNON, MUNDE.]

mund, f. *hand, protection.* mund-byrd, f. i-stem, *protection* (as a social or legal obligation, such as a king owes to his subjects) ; ns. R 130 *(hope of protection).*

murnan, v.3. *mourn; w.* for, *trouble about, care for;* inf. M 259; pret. 3p. murnon, M 96. [MURNAN, MEARN, MURNON, MURNEN.]

mylen, m. *mill; place where weapons were ground? grindstone?* mylen-scearp, adj. *sharp from the grinding?* dip. —um, B 24. [On the various possibilities offered by this uniquely recorded extension of the ordinary meaning of mylen (from Lat. MOLĪNA, a mill for grinding grain), see note in Campbell's ed. of B, p. 105.]

ġe-mynd, f. i-stem (or n.) . *memory;* ns. W 51. [Cf. ġe-munan.]

ġe-myndiġ, adj. *mindful;* nsm. W 6.

myne, m. *thought, intention; remembrance, favor, affection;* as. W 27 (according to the traditional emendation, [min] myne wisse, *might show me favor, feel affection for me*—an adaptation of *Beowulf* 169, itself of doubtful meaning; here the MS. reading is taken as mine wisse; see mīn and witan.)

## N

nā (ne ā), adv. *never, not (at all);* M 21, 258, 268, 325; W 54, 66, 96; S 66.

naca, wk.m. *boat, ship;* gs. —n, S 7.

næbbe (ne hæbbe), see habban.

næfre (ne æfre), adv. *never;* W 69, 112.

næġl or næġel, m. *nail;* dip. næġlum, R 46.

næġled, pp. adj. *nailed, studded.* næġled-cnearr, m. *nailed ship;* dip. —um, B 53.

næniġ (ne æniġ), pron. and adj. *not any, none;* as pron. w. part. gen., nsm. S 25.

næs (ne wæs), see bēon-wesan.

nāg (ne āg), see āgan.

nama, wk.m. *name;* ns. M 267; D 37; ds. —n, R 113 (in a phrase imitative of the Bible, for dryhtnes naman, *for the Lord's* [name's] *sake*).

ġe-nāme, ġe-nāmon, see ġe-niman.

nān (ne ān), pron. (and adj.) , *not one, none;* as pron. w. part. gen., nsm. W 9; dp. —um, B 25.

nāp, ġe-nāp, see nipan, ġe-nīpan.

ne or nē, negative particle. *not, nor.* (a) as adv., *not;* B 24, etc. (5 times) ; R 10, etc. (7 times) ; M 21, etc. (18 times) ; W 15, etc. (5 times) ; S 12, etc. (8 times) ; D 8, 11; at head of series, *neither,* W 66a, S 95a. (b) as conj., *nor;* B 46; M 259; W 16, 66b-69 (7 times) ; S 40 (twice), 41 (twice), 44b, 45 (twice), 46, 82, 83, 95b, 96 (twice) . [Negative affix in nā, næbbe, næfre, etc.]

nēah, adv. *near;* M 103; W 26.

ġe-neahhe, adv. *frequently;* M 269; W 56; D 25, 32.

nealles (ne ealles), adv. *not at all;* W 32, 33.

nearon (ne earon), see bēon-wesan.

nearu, adj. wa-stem. *narrow, close;* (fig.) *anxious;* nsf. S 7.

ġe-nēat, m. *follower, retainer;* ns. M 310. [Cf. heorþ-ġenēat.]

-nebba, wk.m. *beaked one,* formed from adjectival -NEBB, *beaked,* corresponding to NEBB, n. ja-stem. *bill, beak, nose, face.* See hyrned-nebba.

nefne (ne efne), conj. (following a negative). *unless,* W 113; *except, but,* S 46.

nēotan, v.2, w. gen. *make use of;* inf. M 308. [NĒOTAN, NĒAT, NUTON, NOTEN.]

ġe-nerian, wk.v.I. *save;* pret. 3s. ġenerede, B 36.

nied, f. i-stem. *need, (dire) necessity;* dis. —e, B 33; pl., *constraints, fetters;* ap. —a, D 5.

ġe-niewian, wk.v.II. *renew;* pp. ġeniewod, nsm. R 148; nsf. W 50, 55.

niht, f. (orig. a cons.-stem). *night;* ds. —e, R 2. niht-helm, m. *cover of night;* as. W 96. niht-scua, wk. m. *shadow of night;* ns. W 104; S 31. niht-wacu, f. *night-watch;* ns. S 7.

niman, v.4. *take; receive,* inf. M 39; *take off, kill,* inf. M 252; w. dat. or instr. *take on, assume,* pres. 3p. nimaþ, S 48 (bearwas blostmum nimaþ, *the groves take on blossoms, burst into bloom*—for the idiom, Mrs. Gordon compares fōn w. dat.; see her note). [NIMAN, NAM, NĀMON, NUMEN; cf. be-, for-niman.]

ġe-niman, v.4. *take; lay hold of,* pret. 3p. ġenāmon, R 30, 60; *receive,* pret. 3s. subj. ġenāme, M 71.

nipan, v.1. *grow dark, darken;* pres. 3s. nipeþ, W 104; pret. 3s. nāp, S 31. [NĪPAN, NĀP, NIPON, NIPEN.]

ġe-nipan, v.1. *become dark, vanish;* pret. 3s. ġenāp, W 96.

nis (ne is),'see bēon-wesan.

niþ, m. *violence, enmity, malice;* as. S 75.

ġe-nōg, adj. *enough;* npm. —e, R 33; (by understatement, *many*).

nolde, noldon, nolden, see nyllan.

norþ, adv. (*in, to the*) *north;* B 38.

norðan, adv. *from the north;* W 104; S 31.

norðerne, adj. ja-stem. *northern;* nsm.wk. norðerna, B 18.

nū, adv. *now,* C 1; R 78, 80, 84, 95, 126, 134; M 93, 175, 215, 316; W 9, 75, 97; S 33, 58, 82, 90; D 39; —conj. *now that,* M 57, 222, 232, 250.

nyllan (ne willan), anom.v. *will not;* pres. 1s. nylle, M 246; 3s. nyle, S 99 (MS. wille) ; pret. 3s. nolde, M 6, 9, 275; 3p. noldon, M 81, 185; 3p. subj. nolden, M 201.


O

of, prep. w. dat. *from, of, out of;* R 30, 49, 61, 66, 120, 133; M 7, 108, 149, 150, 154, 162, 221; W 113; S 107.

ofer, prep. w. acc. *over.* (a) of motion: *over, across, through;* B 15, 19, 26, 55, 71; M 88, 91, 97, 98; W 24, 57, 82; S 60, 64; *over, beyond,* S 58; ofer bæc, *to the rear, back,* M 276. (b) of distribution or extent: *throughout,* R 12, 82; S 39. (c) of intensity and extent: ofer eall, *over all* (louder than all else and to all parts: so all could hear) , M 256. (d) of degree: *above, more than,* R 91, 94. (e) of crossing someone's will or command: *contrary to, in disregard of,* R 35.

ōfer, m. *bank, shore;* ds. ōfre, M 28.

ofer-cuman, v.4. *overcome;* pret. 3p. ofercōmon, B 72; —impers. w. gen., *pass over;* pp. ofercumen, nsn. D 26 (þæt þæs cyneriċes o. wǣre,

*that it had passed over with
respect to that kingdom: that that
kingdom were no more*—cf. the
similar impersonal use of ofergān,
D 7, etc.) . [Cf. **cuman**.]

**ofer-gān**, anom. v., impers. w. gen.
*pass over, go by;* pret. 3s. **ofer-
ēode**, D 7, 13, 17, 20, 27, 42
(þæs o., *it passed over with re-
spect to that: that has passed*—
cf. **ofer-cuman**, above, at D 26) .
[Cf. **gān**.]

**ofer-mōd**, n. *great pride, overcon-
fidence;* ds. **-e**, M 89. [Cf. **mōd**.]

**of-ġiefan**, v.5. *give up, relinquish,
leave;* pret. 3p. **ofġēafon**, W 61.
[Cf. **a-**, **for-ġiefan**.]

**ofostlīċe**, adv. *speedily*, M 143. [Cf.
**efstan**.]

**of-scēotan**, v.2. *kill by shooting or
hurling a weapon;* pret. 3s. **ofscēat**,
M 77, *struck dead* (with a cast of
his spear) . [Cf. **scēotan**.]

**oft**, adv. *often;* B 8; M 188, 212, 296,
321; W 1, 8, 17, 20, 40, 53 (MS.
—emended to **eft**), 90; S 3, 6, 24,
29; D 4; —comp. **oftor**, R 128.

**on**, prep. *in, on*, etc.

1. w. dat. or instr. (a) of
position: *in, on;* B 27, etc. (8
times) ; R 9, etc. (28 times; post-
pos. at 98) ; M 25, etc. (37 times) ;
W 12, etc. (11 times—either dat.
or acc. at 42) ; S 5, etc. (9 times) ;
D 9, 29; *in* (transl. *from*) , M 125;
*in* (transl. *of*) , M 142; *in* (transl.
*among*) , M 217, 266. — (b) of
condition, state: *in,* S 85; D 25. —
(c) of respect: *in,* S 41. — (d) of
hostile action: *on, at the expense
of,* M 129, 259. — (e) of an inclu-
sive source: **gelang on**, *compre-
hended in, inseparable from,* S
121. — (f) of trust: *in,* S 108 (or
acc. —see **meaht**) . — (g) of con-

trolling mood: *in, with,* W 105.
— (h) of time: *in,* W 35, 44; S 40;
*on,* R 105.

2. w. acc. (a) of motion: *into,
to, on, onto, upon, toward;* B 36,
38, 54; R 5, 32b, 34 (postpos.) ,
40, 103, 104, 125 (MS. dat.) , 152;
M 58, 78, 163, 178, 194, 270,
291, 322; W 81 (MS. dat.) ; S 32,
47, 52, 63, 120; D 5, 6. — (b) of
time: *in,* B 14; R 68; **on ealle tīd**,
*during (for) all time,* S 124; **on
dæġ**, *on a (certain) day,* M 198.
— (c) in various phrases where
motion is sometimes but not al-
ways clearly implicit: **on bēot**,
*threateningly,* M 27 (see Gordon's
note) ; **on ellen**, *valiantly,* M 211;
**on flot**, *afloat, into (deep) water,
to sea,* B 35; M 41; **on . . . hand**,
*on . . . hand,* M 112; **on . . .
healfe**, *on . . . side,* R 20; **on lāst**,
*on the track, in pursuit,* B 22; **on
hira selfra dōm**, *as they themselves
shall decide,* M 38. — (d) **bēodeþ
sorge on brēost-hord**, *forebodes
sorrow in the heart* (implying
that sorrow will enter into the
heart?), S 55.

**on-weġ**, prep. phrase as adv.
*away;* W 53; S 74.

**on**, adv. *on, onward;* S 91 (**ieldu
him on fareþ**, *old age catches up
to him, overtakes him:*—Mrs. Gor-
don points out that if **on** were the
postpos. prep. it ought to be pre-
ceded by acc. **hine**).

**on-bierġan**, wk.v.I, w. gen. *taste (of),
partake (of)* ; inf. R 114. [Cf. **bier-
ġan**.]

**on-ċierran**, wk.v.I. *turn, change;* refl.,
*turn aside or be changed;* pres.
3s. **onċierreþ**, S 103 (**for þon hīe
sēo molde onċierreþ**, *before which
[the terrible power of God] the*

*earth will turn aside;* — so Mrs. Gordon, citing *Apocalypsis* xx, 11: *a cuius conspectu fugit terra*).

on-cnāwan, v.7. *perceive;* inf. M 9. [CNĀWAN, CNĒOW, CNĒOWON, CNĀWEN.]

on-cweðan, v.5. w. dat. of person, *reply to, answer;* pret. 3s. oncwæþ, M 245; S 23. [Cf. cweðan.]

on-drǣdan, v.7, w. refl. dat. and acc. *dread;* pres. 3s. ondrǣdeþ, S 106. [-DRǢDAN, DRĒD (DREORD), DRĒDON, DRǢDEN.]

on-efen, prep. w. dat. *close by, beside,* M 184.

ōnettan, wk.v.I. *hasten on;* pres. 3s. ōnetteþ, S 49. [From Gmc. *ONHAITJAN; stress on first syll. early obscured the compound.]

on-fand, see on-findan.

on-fēng, see on-fōn.

on-findan, v.3. *find, find out, perceive;* pret. 3s. onfunde, M 5; *experience, come to know;* pret. 3s. on-fand, D 4. [Cf. findan.]

on-fōn, contr. v.7. *receive;* pret. 3s. onfēng, M 110 (w. acc.). [Cf. fōn.]

on-funde, see on-findan.

on-gann, see on-ginnan.

on-gēan, adv. *again; in return,* M 49; *back, out again,* M 137; eft o., *back again,* M 156.

on-gēan, prep. w. dat. *against,* M 100.

on-gēaton, see on-ġietan.

on-ġierwan, wk.v.I. *unclothe, strip;* pret. 3s. (refl.), onġierede, R 39. [The prefix here is negative; cf. ġierwan.]

on-ġietan, v.5. *perceive, apprehend, realize;* inf. R 18; W 73; pret. 3p. onġēaton, M 84; pp. onġieten, uninfl., D 10. [ĠIETAN, ĊEAT, ĊEATON, ĊIETEN; cf. be-ġietan.]

on-ġinnan, v. 3. *begin, undertake;* pres. 3p. subj. onġinnen, R 116; pret. 3s. ongann, R 19, 27, 73; M 12, 17, 89, 91, 228, 265; pret. 3p. ongunnon, R 65, 67; M 86, 261. [-ĠINNAN, GANN, GUNNON, GUNNEN; recorded only with be- or on-.]

on-hrēran, wk.v.I. *stir, move;* inf. S 96. [Cf. hrēran.]

on-liesan, wk.v.I. *liberate, redeem;* pret. 3s. onliesde, R 147. [Cf. liesan.]

on-sendan, wk.v.I. *send on, send forth;* pres. 3s. onsendeþ, W 104; pp. onsended, uninfl., R 49 (*yielded up*). [Cf. sendan.]

on-stellan, wk.v.I. *establish;* pret. 3s. onstealde, C 4 (var.). See a-stellan.

on-wæcnan, v.6 (irreg.). *wake up;* pres. 3s. onwæcneþ, W 45. [WÆCNAN, WŌC, WŌCON, WÆCNED.]

on-weġ, adv., see on.

on-wendan, wk.v.I, trans. *change;* pres. 3s. on-wendeþ, W 107. [Cf. wendan.]

on-wrēon, contr.v.I. *uncover, disclose;* imper.sg. onwrēoh, R 97. [The prefix here is negative; cf. be-wrēon.]

open, adj. *open;* npm. opene, R 47.

ōr, n. *beginning;* as. C 4.

ord, m. *point; point of origin, beginning,* as. C 4 (var.); *point of a weapon* (usually a spear), ns. M 60, 146, 157, 253 (ord and iren—see īren); as. M 47, 110; ds. —e, M 124, 226; *battle-line,* ns. M 69 (or *the flower, pick?*); *forefront of the battle,* ds. —e, M 273.

orne, adj. ja-stem. *not mean; excessive.* See un-orne.

oþ, conj. *until;* B 16.

oþ, prep. *to, up to, till.* oþ-þæt, conj. *until,* R 26, 32; M 278, 324; W 71, 86; D 39.

oþ-beran, v.4. *carry off;* pret. 3s. oþbær, W 81. [oþ- here has the sense of *away; cf.* beran.]

ōðer, adj. and pron. *other, another.* (a) adj., asm. —ne, M 234; dsn. ōðrum, M 64. (b) pron., nsm. M 282; asm. —ne, M 143; dsm. ōð-rum, M 70, 133; ōðer, (asn.) twēga, *one of two things,* M 207.

oþþe, conj. *or,* R 36; M 208, 292; W 26, 28; S 70 (twice), 114.

oþ-þringan, v.3. *wrest away;* pres. 3s. oþ-þringeþ, S 71. [Cf. ġe-þringan.]

P

-pāda, wk. m. *coated one,* formed from adjectival -PĀD, *coated,* corresponding to PĀD, f. *coat.* See hasu-, sealwiġ-pāda; also hyrned-nebba, isiġ-feðra, ūriġ-feðra.

plega, wk.m. *play, sport, fight.* See gūþ-, hand-, wiġ-plega.

plegian, wk.v.II. *play;* pret. 3p. pleg-odon, B 52.

prass, m. *proud array;* ds. —e, M 68.

R

rād, see rīdan.

ġe-rǣcan, wk.v.I. *reach;* pret. 3s. ġe-rǣhte, *reached with a weapon, pierced,* M 158, 226; feorh ġ., *reached the life, pierced fatally,* M 142.

rǣdan, wk.v.I. *give counsel, instruct;* pret. 3s. rǣdde, M 18. [Cf. ĠE-RĀD, adj. *wise, skillful;* also RǢD, n. *counsel, advice:* and R.ǢDAN, v.7 (pret. RĒD or REORD), *advise,* etc.]

ġe-rǣdan, wk.v.I. *decide;* pres. 2s. ġerǣdest, M 36.

ġe-rǣdu, n. ja-stem pl. *trappings;* dp. —m, M 190. [Cf. RĀD, f. *riding: harness;* and rīdan, v.1.]

rǣran, wk.v.I. *rear, raise.* See a-rǣran.

rǣs, m. *rush, onset, attack.* See beadu-, gār-rǣs.

rand, m. *boss of a shield* (the metal center); *shield;* ap. —as, M 20.

rēaf, n. *raiment;* as. M 161 (coat of mail:) [Another meaning, *spoil, booty,* seems less appropriate.]

rēċan (later reċċan), wk.v.I, w. gen. *care about;* pret. 3p. rōhton, M 260. [RĒĊAN (from *RŌCJAN), RŌHTE, RŌHT.]

recene, adv. *quickly,* M 93; W 112.

ġe-reġnian, wk.v.II. *adorn, orna-ment;* pp. ġereġnod, asn. M 161.

reord, f. (or n.) *voice, speech;* dis. — e, S 53 (of a bird). reord-berend, m. nd-stem. *speech-bearer* (a peri-phrasis for a human being as one endowed with speech; it appears in several of the religious poems, sometimes, as here, with point); np. R 3; dp. —um, R 89. [Cf. RǢDAN, v.7. *advise,* redupl. pret. s. REORD.]

rest, f. jō-stem. *resting-place, bed;* as. —e, R 3 (obj. of wunodon: *were in bed*) [Cf. wæl-rest.]

restan, wk.v.I. *rest, lie, remain;* pret. 3s. reste, R 64 (refl.), 69 (intrans.).

rīċe, n. ja-stem. *realm, kingdom;* ns. W 106; as. R 119, 152; gs. —s, S 81; D 23. [Cf. cyne-, heofon-, weorold-rīċe.]

rīċe, adj. ja-stem. *powerful;* as. rīċne, R 44; gp. rīċra, R 131; rīċost, superl., nsm. M 36.

rīdan, v.1. *ride;* inf. M 291; pret. 3s. rād, M 18, 239. [RĪDAN, RĀD, RIDON, RIDEN.]

**riht**, n. *right, privilege, just title.*
See **land-riht**.

**riht**, adj. *right, proper, true;* nsn.
M 190; asm. —**ne**, R 89.

**ġe-rihtan**, wk.v.I. *direct;* pp. **ġeriht**,
nsf. R 131.

**rihte**, adv. *rightly, correctly,* M 20.

**rinc**, m. *warrior, man;* dp. —**um**, M
18. [Cf. **fierd-**, **gūþ-**, **hilde-**, **sǣ-rinc**.]

**risan**, v.l. *rise.* See **a-rīsan**.

**rōd**, f. *rood, cross;* ns. R 44, 136;
ds. —**e**, R 56, 131; as. —**e**, R 119.
[Original sense *twig, branch,
pole.*]

**rodor**, m. *the heavens, sky.* See **upp-rodor**.

**rōhton**, see **rēċan**.

**rūn**, f. *(private) counsel;* ds. in **sundor æt rūne**, (*apart at counsel;* or,
*apart in private meditation*), W
111.

**ġe-rȳman**, wk.v.I. *open* (a way); pret.
1s. **ġerȳmde**, R 89; pp. **ġe-rȳmed**,
nsn. M 93. [Base-word **RŪM**, adj.
*spacious.*]

## S

**sǣ**, m. or f. i-stem. *sea* (applied to
large bodies of water, usually salt
but occasionally fresh); as. (f.) W
4; (m.) S 14, 18. **sǣ-fōr**, f. *sea-voyage;* gs. or ds. —**e**, S 42. **sǣ-lida**,
wk. m. *seafarer;* vs. M 45; as. —**n**,
M 286. **sǣ-mann**, m. *seaman;* dp.
—**um**, M 38, 278; np. —**menn**, M
29. **sǣ-rinc**, m. *sea-warrior, viking;*
ns. M 134.

**sæċċ**, f. jō-stem. *strife, battle;* ds. —
**e**, B 4, 42.

**sæd**, adj. *sated;* nsm. B 20 (w. gen.,
*sated with*). [Cognate w. Lat.

SATIS; mod. "sad" has shifted its
meaning.]

**sǣġde**, **ġe-sǣġde**, **sæġe**, **sæġeþ**, see
**secgan**, **ġe-secgan**.

**sæl**, n. *hall.* See **win-sæl**.

**sǣl**, m. i-stem (or f.). *time, occasion;*
ns. R 80; (*happy time,*) *joy,
pleasure,* dip. —**um**, D 28.

**sǣlan**, wk.v.I. *fasten, bind, tie;* inf.
W 21. [From **SĀL**, m. or f. *rope.*]

**ġe-sǣliġ**, adj. *prosperous, fortunate;*
see **weorold-ġesǣliġ**.

**sæt**, see **sittan**.

**ġe-sæt**, see **ġe-sittan**.

**sāg**, see **sīgan**.

**samod**, adv. *together, jointly, in
unison;* W 39.

**sang**, m. *song;* as. S 19.

**sang**, v. see **singan**.

**sār**, n. *pain;* as. S 95.

**sār**, adj. *sore, painful, grievous;* nsm.
D 9; npf. —**e**, W 50 (**sāre æfter**,
*sore with longing for*); gp. —**ra**,
R 80.

**sāre**, adv. *sorely,* R 59.

**ġe-sāwe**, see **ġe-sēon**.

**sāwol**, f. *soul;* ns. R 120; M 177;
ds. **sāwle**, S 100.

**ġe-sāwon**, see **ġe-sēon**.

**scacan**, v.6. *shake;* see **a-scacan**.

**scadu**, f. wō-stem. *shadow, darkness;*
ns. R 54.

**scaða**, wk.m. *one who does harm;
ravager, enemy, warrior.* See **fǣr-**,
**hell-scaða**.

**scēaf**, see **scūfan**.

**sceaft**, m. *shaft* (of spear); ns. M
136.

**ġe-sceaft**, f. i-stem. *creature, creation;*
ns. B 16; R 12, 55, 82; **wyrda
ġesceaft**, *the operation of the
fates,* ns. W 107. [Cf. **forþ-ġesceaft**; related to **SCEAP-**, base
of **scieppan**, q.v.]

-sceaftiġ, adjectival component, *having possessions* (?). See **fēa-sceaftiġ.**

**sceal,** see **sculan.**

**scealc,** m. *retainer, warrior;* np. —**as,** M 181.

**sceard,** adj., w. gen. *bereft (of)* ; nsm. B 40.

**scearp,** adj. *sharp.* See **mylen-scearp.**

**scēat,** m. *surface, region, expanse;* ap. —**as,** R 37; S 61, 105; dp. —**um,** R 8, 43. [The meaning in R is sometimes taken to be *corner,* but *surface* is appropriate at all three places.]

**scēat,** v. see **scēotan.**

**sceatt,** m. *coin; tax;* dp. —**um,** M 40, 56 (*tribute-money*).

**scēaþ,** f. *sheath;* ds. —**e,** M 162.

**scēawian,** wk.v.II. *see, behold; look at;* pret. 1s. **scēawode,** R 137. [Cf. **ġeond-scēawian.**]

**ġe-scēawian,** wk.v.II. *show, display;* pres. 3s. **ġescēawaþ,** D 33.

**scēotan,** v.2. *shoot, hurl; hit with a missile;* pret. 3s. **scēat,** M 143 (*pierced* with a spear), 270 (*shot* an arrow); pp. **scoten,** nsm. B 19 (*shot* by an arrow or *pierced* by a dart). [SCĒOTAN, SCĒAT, SCUTON, SCOTEN; cf. **of-scēotan.**]

**scield,** m. *shield;* as. B 19; ds. —**e,** M 136; ap. —**as,** M 98. **scield-burg,** f. cons.-stem. *wall of shields;* ns. M 242.

**scieppan,** v.6. w.dat. *create;* pret. 3s. **scōp,** C 5 (var. **ġescōp**). [SCIEPPAN, SCŌP, SCŌPON, SCEAPEN.]

**scieppend,** m. nd-stem. (*the*) *Creator;* ns. C 6; W 85.

**scieþþan,** v.6. *injure;* inf. R 47. [SCIEÞÞAN, SCŌD, SCŌDON, SCEADEN. The present stem is recorded only as SCEÞ- (seemingly an Anglian spelling) and, once,

LWS. SCYÞ- (corresponding to EWS.*SCIEÞ-) . The past participle is recorded only once, in *Genesis* 869, where it is *sceaþen* instead of the expected SCEADEN.]

**scīma,** wk.m. *light, radiance;* as. —**n,** R 54.

**scīnan,** v.1. *shine;* inf. R 15. [SCĪNAN, SCĀN, SCINON, SCINEN.]

**scip,** n. *ship;* ds. —**e,** M 40, 56. **scip-flota,** wk.m. *sailor, seaman;* np. —**n,** B 11.

**scīr,** adj. *bright, clear;* asn. M 98; asm. —**ne,** R 54.

**scolde, scolden, scoldon,** see **sculan.**

**scop,** m. *court poet and singer;* ns. D 36.

**scōp,** see **scieppan.**

**scoten,** see **scēotan.**

**scræf,** n. *pit, cavern, grave.* See **eorþ-scræf.**

**scua,** wk.m. *shade, shadow.* See **niht-scua.**

**scūfan,** v.2. *shove, thrust;* pret. 3s. **scēaf,** M 136. [SCŪFAN, SCĒAF, SCUFON, SCOFEN.]

**sculan,** pret.-pres. v. *shall, must, have to, be destined to;* w. inf. except as indicated; pres. 3s. **sceal,** R 119; M 60, 252; W 37, 56, 70, 73, 112; S 109; —w. **bēon** understood, *must be,* M 312, 313; W 65, 66; —1p. **sculon,** C 1; 2p. **scule** (**ġē**), M 59; 3p. **sculon,** M 54, 220; 3s. subj. **scyle,** S 74 (v. of motion understood: *must go*). 111 (*should, ought to*); pret. 1s. **scolde,** *had to,* R 43; W 8, 19; S 30; 3s. **scolde,** M 16 (*had occasion to, was called upon to*); 3s. subj. **scolde,** W 3 (*may have had to*); D 12 (v. of action understood: *ought to act*); pret. 3p. **scoldon,** M 19 (*should, ought to*), 105 (*were to, were destined to*);

3p. subj. **scolden**, M 291, 307 (*should*). [SCULAN, SCEAL, SCULON, SCOLDE.]

**scūr**, m. *shower;* dip. —**um**, S 17.

**scyle**, see **sculan**.

**sē, sēo, þæt**, dem. adj., def. art. and pron. *that, the, that one.* (a) as adj. and def. art., **sē** or (weakly stressed) **se**, nsm. B 37; R 13, etc. (7 times); M 6, etc. (15 times); W 16, 82; S 12, etc. (5 times);— **sēo**, nsf. B 16; M 104, 144, 284; W 95, 100, 115; S 103, 107; D 16; —**þæt**, nsn. R 6; S 94; asn. B 64; R 18, 21; M 22, 102, 137, 168, 194; S 108; —**þæs**, gsm. R 49; M 131, 141, 160, 165; gsn. M 8, 148, 202; D 26; —**þǣre**, gsf. M 95; dsf. R 21, 112, 131; M 8, 220; S 100;— **þām** or **þam**, dsm. or dsn. B 29; R 9, etc. (11 times); M 10, etc. (19 times); S 122; dp. R 59, 143, 154; M 40, 190, 278; —**þone**, asm. B 61, 62; R 127; M 19, etc. (10 times) ; —**þā**, asf. R 20, 68, 119; M 48, 72, 74, 78, 139, 163, 325; W 113; S 120; in **þā hwīle þe**, M 14, 83, 235, 272 (see **hwīl**); np. B 53, 57; R 46, 61; M 96, 182, 261, 305; W 77, 78; S 10, 56, 87; ap. M 82, 145, 196, 277, 322; S 57; — **þāra**, gp. M 174, 212. (b) as dem. pron. *that (one), those, (he, she, it, they)* etc., **sē**, nsm. M 75, 150, 157, 227, 310; S 104; —**þæt**, nsn. R 28a, 39, 74; M 76, 223, 325; S 99; D 19, 23 (pointing to a person); asn. R 28b, 58, 66; M 5, 36, 84, 246; S 12, 24, 55, 74 (obj. of ġewyrċe, anticipating clause at 77), 109; D 12, 35; —**þæs**, gsn. M 120 (w. **þanc**, *for that*), 239; S 122 (w. **þanc**); *as to that, with respect to that*, D 7, 13, 17, 20, 27, 42; **to þæs**, *to that extent*, S 40b, 41

(twice); alone as adv., *to that extent*, S 39, 40a; —**þām**, dsm. R 129; dsn. M 9, 34; —**þā**, np. M 81; S 50; —**þ̄y**, isn. as adv. w. comp., *by that, the,* B 46; M 146; W 49; correlatively, M 312, 313 (3 times w. comp., once as conj., *the . . . as*). (c) as rel. pron., *who, which,* etc., **sē**, nsm. R 107; M 27, 153; —**þæt**, asn. M 289 (=þæt þæt, *that which*); D 41; —**þæs**, gsn. B 51 (=þæs-þe; see note); —**þā**, np. M 184; — **þon**, isn. S 103 (w. **for**, *before which, for which*). (d) as indef. pron. *he who, whoever,* **sē**, nsm. W 88. (e) w. **þe**, as compound rel. pron. *he who,* etc., **sē-þe**, nsm. R 98, 113, 145; M 258, 316; W 29, 37, 112; S 27, 47, 106a, 107; — **sēo-þe**, nsf. R 121; —**þām- þe**, dsm. W 31, 56, 114; S 51; dp. R 149, 154; —**þone-þe**, asm. W 27; — **þāra-þe**, gp. B 26; R 86. (f) **þæs-þe**, gsn. as conj., *according to what, as,* B 68.

**ġe-seah**, see **ġe-sēon**.

**sealde, ġe-sealde, ġe-sealdon**, see **sellan, ġe-sellan**.

**sealt**, n. *salt.* **sealt-ȳþ**, f. jō-stem. *salt seawave;* gp. —**a**, S 35.

**sealwiġ**, adj. *dark-colored.* **sealwiġ-pāda**, wk.m. *dark-coated one;* ap. —**n**, B 61 (referring to the raven, the eagle, and the wolf; stylistically less satisfactory if treated as as., referring only to the raven). [On the form, see **pāda**.]

**sēarian**, wk.v.II. *grow sere, wither, fade;* pres. 3s. **sēaraþ**, S 89.

**sēaþ**, m. *pit;* ds. —**e**, R 75.

**sēċan**, wk.v.I. *seek;* —(a) *set out for, seek out, go to, come to;* inf. B 55; R 104, 127 (*resort to*) ; pret. 3p. **sōhton**, B 58, 71 (*invaded*) ; R 133; ·M 193; —(b) *search for, try* *to find;* pret. 1s. sōhte, W 25; —(c) *try to obtain;* pres. 3s. sēċeþ, W 114. [SĒCAN (from \*SŌCJAN), SŌHTE, SŌHT.]

ġe-sēċan, wk.v.I. *seek, go to, come to;* inf. R 119; M 222; pres. 1s. subj. ġesēċe, S 38; pret. 3s. ġe-sōhte, M 287 *(sank to);* 3p. ġe-sōhton, B 27.

seċg, m. ja-stem. *retainer, man, warrior;* ns. B 17; M 159; S 56; D 24; ap. —as, M 298; gp. —a, B 13; W 53; dp. —um, R 59. [From \*SAGJA-, cognate w. Lat. SOCIU-S. Cf. sele-secg.]

secgan, wk.v.III. *say, tell, relate;* inf. R 1; M 30; S 2; D 35; imper. sg. sæġe, M 50; pres. 3s. sæġeþ, M 45; 3p. secgaþ, B 68; 2s. subj. secge, R 96; pret. 3s. sæġde, M 147. [SEC-GAN, SǼĠDE, SǼĠD; cf. a-secgan.]

ġe-secgan, wk.v.III. *say;* pret. 3s. ġe-sæġde, M 120 (w. þanc, *gave thanks*).

sefa, wk. m. *mind, spirit, heart;* as. —n, W 57; S 51; ds. —n, D 9, 29. [Cf. mōd-sefa.]

sēft-, combining-form corresponding to SĒFTE, adj. *soft.* sēft-ēadiġ, adj. *blessed with comfort;* nsm. S 56 (Grein's emendation, for MS. *eft eadig*).

seld, n. *hall.* See cear-seld.

ġe-selda, wk.m. *companion, fellow-retainer;* ap. —n, W 53 (or *familiar spirit?*) [Lit. "one of the same dwelling"; V. Salmon suggests an allusion to an old belief that men's spirits, though normally in the same dwelling, the body, could be sent out alone in quest of friends or enemies.]

seldliċ, adj. *rare, wonderful;* nsm. R 13: comp. seldlīcre, asn. R 4 *(exceedingly rare?).*

sele, m. i-stem. *hall;* perhaps as separate word, as. W 25; but see sele-drēoriġ below. sele-drēam, m. *hall-joy, festivity in the hall;* np. —as, W 93. sele-drēoriġ, adj. *sad for want of a hall, homesick,* nsm. W 25 (see note). sele-secg, m. *hall-warrior, retainer;* ap. —as, W 34.

sēlest, adj. superl. *best;* asn. (w. part. gen.), R 118; nsm.wk —a, R 27. [Comp. SĒL, adv., sēlra,´ adj.; positive lacking; from \*SŌLI-.]

self, adj. *self;* nsm. S 35; nsm.wk. —a, R 105; asf. —e, R 92; gsf. —re, D 9; dsm. —um, S 1; D 29 (him understood), 35; gp. —ra, M 38.

sellan, wk.v.I. *give;* inf. M 38, 46 *(hand over, pay)* ; pres. 1p. subj. sellen, M 61 *(pay);* pret. 3s. sealde, M 271 *(gave, inflicted).* [SELLAN, SEALDE, SEALD.]

ġe-sellan, wk.v.I. *give;* pret. 3s. ġe-sealde, M 188 *(gave, presented)* ; D 41 (the same); pret. 3p. ġe-sealdon, M 184 *(gave, yielded up)* .

sēlra, adj. comp. *better;* asm. —n, D 6. [Cf. sēlest.]

ġe-sēman, wk.v.I. *reconcile, decide the terms between;* inf. M 60. [Base-word SŌM, f. *agreement.*]

sendan, wk.v.I. *send;* inf. M 30; W 56; pret. 3s. sende, M 134; 3p. sendon, M 29. [SENDAN, SENDE, SENDED; base-word SAND, f. *a sending, message;* cf. on-sendan.]

sēo, see sē.

seofian, wk.v.II. *lament, sigh;* pret. 3p. seofodon, S 10.

seofon, num. adj. *seven;* npm. —e, B 30.

seolfor, n. *silver;* dis. seolfre, R 77.

ġe-sēon, contr.v.5. *see;* pres. 3s. ġe-siehþ, W 46; pret. 1s. ġeseah, R 14, 21, 33, 36, 51; 3p. ġesāwon,

M 84, 203; 1s. subj. ġesāwe, R 4. [SĒON (*SEHWAN), SEAH, SĀWON, SEWEN.]

ġe-set, n. *seat;* np. ġesetu, W 93.

setl, n. *seat;* ds. —e, B 17.

ġe-settan, wk.v.I. *set, seat, place;* pret. 3p. ġesetton, R 67; pp. ġeseted, nsn. R 141. [SETTAN, SETTE. SETED; cf. a-settan, sittan.]

sē-þe, see sē.

sīde, wk.f. *side;* ds. sīdan, R 49.

sīde, adv. *widely;* wīde and sīde, *far and wide,* R 81.

sīe, see bēon-wesan.

ġe-siehþ, see ġe-sēon.

sīen, f. i-stem. *sight, spectacle.* See wǣfer-sīen, and cf. an-sīen.

ġe-sīene, adj. ja-stem, *visible;* npn. R 46. [Cf. ġe-sēon.]

ġe-sierwed, pp. adj. *armed;* nsm. M 159. [As from ġe-SIERWAN, wk.v.I, unrecorded in other forms; base-word SEARU, f. wō-stem. *equipment.*]

sīgan, v.l. *sink;* pret. 3s. sāg, B 17. [SĪGAN, SĀG, SIGON, SIĠEN.]

siġe, m. i-stem. *victory.* siġe-bēam, m. *tree of victory* (the cross); ns. R 13; as. R 127.

sigor, m. *victory;* gp. —a, R 67.

sigor-fæst, adj. *victorious;* nsm. R 150.

ġe-sihþ, f. jō-stem. *sight, vision;* ds. —e, R 21, 41, 66; as. —e, R 96.

simble, adv. *ever, always;* S 68.

sinc, n. *treasure;* as. M 59; gs. —es, W 25; ds. —e, R 23. sinc-ġiefa, wk. m. *giver of treasure, bountiful lord;* as. —n, M 278. sinc-þegu, f. *receiving of treasure;* as. —þeġe, W 34.

sind, sindon, see bēon-wesan.

sin-gāl, adj. *ever-living, perpetual;* nsf. R 141. [sin-, *always* (Lat.

SEMPER, OE sim-ble), gāl, *lusty,* hence *vigorous, alive;* hardly felt as a compound; cf. gāl, wīn-gāl.]

singan, v.3. *sing;* pres. part. sing-ende, asm. uninfl., S 22; pres. 3s. singeþ, S 54; pret. 3s. sang, M 284. [SINGAN, SANG, SUNGON, SUNGEN.]

sinu, f. wō-stem. *sinew.* sinu-bend, f. jō-stem. *sinew-bond* (a bond made by cutting a sinew, ham-stringing); ap. —a, D 6.

sittan, v.5. *sit;* pres. 3s. siteþ, D 28; pret. 3s. sæt, D 24. [SITTAN, SÆT, SǢTON, SETEN.]

ġe-sittan, v.5. *sit;* pret. 3s. ġe-sæt, W 111.

sīþ, m. *journey, voyage, venture;* ds. —e, S 51; *experience, trial,* ap. —as, S 2. sīþ-fæt, m. *expedition;* ds. —e, R 150. [Cf. bealu-sīþ.]

ġe-sīþ, m. *companion;* ds. —e, D 3.

sīðian, wk.v.II. *travel, journey, pass;* inf. R 68; M 177; pres. 1s. subj. sīðie, M 251.

siþþan, adv. *afterwards,* R 142; S 78; —conj. *after,* B 13, 69; R 3, 49, 71 (MS.; emended to stefn, q.v.); W 22; D 5.

slǣp, m. *sleep;* ns. W 39; is. slǣp' for slǣpe, D 16.

slāt, see slītan.

sleaht, m. or n. (var. of slieht, i-stem) , *slaughter.* See wæl-sleaht, and cf. bill-ġe-slieht.

slēan, contr.v.6. *strike;* pret. 3s. slōg, M 163, 285; 3s. subj. slōge, M 117. [SLĒAN (*SLEAHAN), SLŌG, SLŌGON, SLÆĠEN; cf. be-slēan.]

ġe-slēan, contr.v.6. *obtain by striking, win;* pret. 3p. ġeslōgon, B 4.

ġe-slieht, m. or n. i-stem. *slaughter.* See bill-ġeslieht, and cf. sleaht and slēan.

slītan, v.1. *lacerate, tear, rend;* pret.

3s. **slāt**, S 11. [SLĪTAN, SLĀT, SLITON, SLITEN.]

**slīðen**, adj. *cruel, dire, fierce;* nsf. W 30.

**slōg, slōge**, ġe-slōgon, see **slēan**, ġe-slēan.

**smiþ**, m. *smith;* see **wīġ-smiþ**.

**snāw**, m. *snow;* as. W 48.

**snell**, adj. *keen, bold;* np. —e, M 29.

**snīwan**, v.1, with wk. pret. *snow;* pret. 3s. **snīwde**, S 31.

**snottor**, adj. *wise, discerning;* nsm. W 111 (as noun). [Both **snotor** and **snottor** appear to be metrically substantiated in different poems.]

**sōfte**, adv. *easily;* M 59. [Cf. the mutated **sēft**-.]

**sōht-**, ġe-sōht-, see **sēċan**, ġe-sēċan.

**sorg**, f. *sorrow;* ns. W 30, 39, 50; as. —e, S 42 (*anxiety?*) , 54; D 3; gp. —a, R 80; dip. —um, R 20, 59; D 24. **sorg-ċeariġ**, adj. *troubled by sorrow, sorrowful;* nsm. D 28 (as noun, or modifying indef. "someone" understood). **sorg-lēoþ**, n. *song of sorrow, dirge;* as. R 67. **sorg-lufu**, f. *sorrowful love;* ns. D 16.

**sōþ**, n. *truth;* ds. —e, W 11 (to **s.**, *for a truth, indeed*) . **sōþ-ġiedd**, n. ja-stem. *lay of truth* (as opposed to legendary matter) ; as. S 1.

ġe-**spann**, n. *fastening, joint.* See **eaxl-ġespann**.

**spēdan**, wk.v.I. *be prosperous, be wealthy;* pres. 2p. **spēdaþ**, M 34 (**ġif ġē s. to þām**, *if you have that much wealth, if you are good for the necessary amount*—see Gordon's note). [Base-word SPĒD, f. i-stem (from *SPŌDI-) , *success, wealth*.]

**spēdiġ**, adj. *successful;* nsm. R 151.

**spell**, n. *message;* as. M 50.

**spere**, n. i-stem. *spear;* as. M 137 (*spear-head*); ap. **speru**, M 108. [Cf. **wæl-spere**.]

**spillan**, wk.v.I. *destroy;* inf. M 34 (**ūs spillan**, *slaughter each other*).

**sprang**, see **springan**.

**sprecan**, v.5, intrans. or trans. *speak;* with a clause, *say;* inf. R 27; pres. 3s. **spriċeþ**, W 70; pret. 3s. **spræc**, M 211, 274; 1p. **sprǣcon**, M 212; 3p. M 200. [SPRECAN, SPRÆC, SPRÆCON, SPRECEN.]

**spreṅgan**, wk.v.I. *cause to spring or quiver;* pret. 3s. **spreṅġde**, M 137 (the subject may be **se sceaft** rather than **Byrhtnōþ**). [Based on SPRANG, 2nd grade of **springan**.]

**springan**, v.3. *spring;* pret. 3s. **sprang**, M 137. [SPRINGAN, SPRANG, SPRUNGON, SPRUNGEN.]

**stæf**, m. *sign, letter of the alphabet; verbal formula.* See **glēo-stafas**.

**stæþ**, n. *bank, shore;* ds. —e, M 25. [Cf. **ēa-stæþ**.]

ġe-**stāg**, see ġe-**stīgan**.

**stān**, m. *stone;* ds. —e, R 66. **stān-clif**, n. *rocky cliff, crag;* ap. —u, S 23. **stān-hliþ**, n. *rocky slope; stone declivity;* ap. —u, W 101 (fig. for high stone walls, or transition from image of a ruined citadel to weatherbeaten cliffs of the earth itself?).

**standan**, v.6. *stand, remain, endure;* inf. R 43, 62; M 19; pres. 3s. **stent**, M 51; **standeþ**, W 74, 97, 115; 3p. **standaþ**, W 76; S 67; pret. ls. **stōd**, R 38; 3s. **stōd**, M 25, 28, 145, 152, 273; 1p. **stōdon**, R 71; 3p. **stōdon**, R 7; M 72, 79, 100, 127, 182, 301; W 87; 3p. subj. **stōden**, M 63. [STANDAN, STŌD, STŌDON, STANDEN; cf. be-, wiþ-standan.]

ġe-standan, v.6. *stand, stand up;* inf.
M 171; pret. 3p. ġestōdon, R 63
(w. refl. dat., *took their stand?—*
see note).

stang, see stingan.

-stapa, wk.m. *stepper, treader.* See
eard-stapa.

staðol, m. *(fixed) position; founda-
tion;* ds. —e, R 71; dp. —um, S
109 (healdan on s., *keep in place,
control*—Mrs. Gordon).

ġe-staðolian, wk.v.II. *establish, con-
firm, make steadfast;* pres. 3s.
ġestaðolaþ, S 108; pret. 3s. ġe-
staðolode, S 104.

steall, m. *standing-place.* See weall-
steall.

ġe-steall, n. *foundation, resting
place?* ns. W 110 (eorðan g.,
*earthly resting place, habitation?*)

stēam, m. *moisture, blood;* dis. —e,
R 62.

stearn, m. *tern* (perhaps not the
modern tern or sea-swallow but a
small species of seagull—see Mrs.
Gordon's note); ns. S 23.

stede, m. i-stem. *place, position;* as.
M 19. stede-fæst, adj. *steadfast,
unyielding;* npm. —e, M 127, 249.
[Cf. camp-, folc-, mæðel-stede.]

stefn, m. i-stem. *stem.* (a) *prow or
stern of a ship;* ds. —e, B 34; (b)
*trunk of a tree;* ds. —e, R 30.

stefn, f. *voice;* ns. R 71 (not in MS.,
which has *siþþan*) .

stefna, wk.m. *stem of ship, prow or
stern;* ds. —n, S 7 (prow, as the
place for a look-out, or stern,
where one steers?).

stefnettan, wk.v.I, *stand firm;* pret.
3p. stefnetton, M 122.

stellan, wk.v.I. *place.* See a- and on-
stellan.

stent, see standan.

steppan, v.6. *step, go, advance;* pret.
3s. stōp, M 8, 78, 131. [STEPPAN,
or STÆPPAN, STŌP, STŌPON, STAPEN.]

stīeran, wk.v.I, w. dat. *steer, control;*
inf. S 109.

ġe-stīgan, v.1. *climb up, mount,
ascend;* inf. R 34; pret. 3s. ġe-stāg,
R 40. [STĪGAN, STĀG, STIGON,
STIĠEN; cf. a-stigan.]

stihtan, wk.v.I. *direct;* pret. 3s. stihte,
M 127.

stingan, v.3. *stab, pierce;* pret. 3s.
stang, M 138. [STINGAN, STANG,
STUNGON, STUNGEN.]

stīþ, adj. *hard, firm, stubborn,
severe;* nsn. M 301; apm. —e, S
104. stīþ-hycgende, pres. part. adj.
ja-stem. *firm of purpose, resolute;*
npm. M 122. stīþ-mōd, adj. *brave,
unflinching;* nsm. R 40.

stīþlīċe, adv. *sternly, harshly;* M 25.

stōd, stōden, stōdon, see standan.

ġe-stōdon, see ġe-standan.

stōl, m. *seat, high-seat, throne.* See
ġief-stōl.

stōp, see steppan.

storm, m. *storm;* np. —as, W 101;
S 23.

stōw, f. *place.* See wæl-stōw.

strǣl, m. or f. *arrow;* dip. —um, R
62.

strang, adj. *strong;* nsm. R 40; dsn.
—um, S 109 *(headstrong)*; npm.
—e, R 30.

strēam, m. *stream;* as. M 68; in pl.,
*seas, ocean;* ap. —as, S 34. [Cf.
lagu-strēam.]

strēġan, wk.v.I. *strew, spread;* inf. S
97. [A non-West-Saxon form oc-
curring only here. Related W-S
forms are STREWIAN and
STRĒAWIAN, wk.II.]

**stund,** f. *a time, (short) while;* as. —e, M 271. See **ymb.**

**styrian,** wk.v.I. *stir, move.* See **a-styrian.**

**sum,** pron. and adj. (a) pron., *one, a certain one;* w. part. gen., nsm. M 149, 164; nsn. S 68; asn. M 285; —without gen., in a series of singulars, *one . . . another,* etc.; asm. —ne, W 81, 82, 83; —in pl., *some, a number;* apm. —e, W 80 (preceding the series of singulars; understatement for "many"?); dp. —um, D 34; *certain ones,* npm. —e, S 56 (þā sume, *those particular ones*—not *some of those;* see Mrs. Gordon's note) . (b) adj. *some,* a; asf. —e, M 271.

**sumor,** m. (here a-stem; sometimes u-stem) . *summer;* gs. —es, S 54.

**sundor,** adv. *separately, apart;* him sundor, *by himself,* W 111.

**sunne,** wk. f. *sun;* ns. B 13.

**sunu,** m. u-stem. *son;* ns. R 150; M 76, 115, 298; as. B 42.

**sūðerne,** adj. ja-stem. *southern;* asm. (-rne for -rnne) , M 134 (*of southern make*) .

**swā,** adv. *so; in such manner; in like manner; accordingly;* M 33, 59, 122, 132, 198, 209, 243, 280, 319, 320, 323; W 6, 19, 62, 85, 111; S 51; D 7, 13, 17, 20, 27, 42; correl. w. the conj., *so, as,* D 9a; —conj. *as,* C 3; B 7; R 92, 108, 114; M 290; W 14, 43, 75; S 90; correl. w. the adv., D 9b; w. subj., *as if,* W 96.

**swǣs,** adj. *dear, beloved;* asm. —ne, W 50 (as noun, *loved one*) .

**swǣtan,** wk.v.I. *bleed;* inf. R 20. [Base-word swāt, m. *blood.*]

**swancor,** adj. *supple;* apf. **swancre,** D 6.

**swāt,** m. *blood;* gs. —es, R 23; dis. —e, B 13.

**sweart,** adj. *dark, black;* asm.wk. —an, B 61.

**swebban,** wk.v.I. *put to sleep; kill.* See **a-swebban.**

**swefn,** n. *(sleep,) dream, vision;* gp. —a, R 1.

**swēġ,** m. i-stem. *sound;* (bird's) *song* or *cry;* as. S 21.

**swelċ,** rel. pron. *such as;* np. —e, S 83. [swā plus līċ.]

**swelċe,** conj. adv. *likewise, and also;* B 19, 30, 37, 57; R 8; S 53. **swelċe swā,** conj. *just as,* R 92.

**swelgan,** v.3. *swallow;* see **for-swelgan.**

**sweltan,** v.3. *die, perish;* inf. M 293. [SWELTAN, SWEALT, SWULTON, SWOLTEN.]

**sweng,** m. i-stem. *blow, stroke;* gs. —es, M 118.

**sweorcan,** v.3. *become gloomy;* pres. 3s. **sweorceþ,** D 29. [SWEORCAN, SWEARC, SWURCON, SWORCEN.]

**ġe-sweorcan,** v.3. *grow dark, gloomy;* pres. 3s. subj. **ġesweorce,** W 59.

**sweord,** n. *sword;* ns. M 166; as. M 15, 161, 237; gs. —es, B 68; ds. —e, M 118; ap. sweord, M 47; gp.—a, B 4; dip. —um, B 30.

**sweostor,** f. r-stem. *sister;* gs. M 115.

**sweotule,** adv. *clearly,* W 11.

**swēte,** adj. ja-stem. *sweet;* asn. S 95 (as noun). [Cf. unmutated swōt, *sweet.*]

**swican,** v.1. *deceive, fail, desert.* See **be-swican.**

**swillan,** wk.v.I. *wash.* See **be-swillan.**

**swimman,** v.3. *swim;* pres. 3p. **swimmaþ,** W 53 (fig. ?—or partly literal, the spirits of the vision fading into sea-birds?). [SWIMMAN, SWAMM, SWUMMON, SWUMMEN.]

**ġe-swinċ,** n. i-stem. *toil.* **ġe-swinċ-**

dagas, m.pl. *days of toil or hardship;* dip. —**dagum,** S 2.

swiþ, adj. *strong;* comp. **swiðre,** nsf. S 115; asf. in **on þā swiðran healfe,** *on the right (the stronger) side,* R 20.

swiðe, adv. *greatly, very; fiercely, severely;* M 115, 118, 282; W 56.

symbel, n. *feast, banquet;* ds. **symble,** R 141; gp. **symbla,** W 93.

synn, f. jō-stem. *sin;* gp. —**a,** S 100; dp. —**um,** R 99, 146; dip. —**um,** R 13.

## T

tǣċan, wk.v.I. *show, direct, teach;* pret. 3s. **tǣhte,** M 18. [TǢCAN, TǢHTE, TǢHT; cf. TĀCN, n. *token, sign.*]

tǣsan, wk.v.I. *lacerate, rive;* pret. 3s. **tǣsde,** M 270.

tēoġan, wk.v.II (contr.). *adorn, prepare, create;* pret. 3s. **tēode,** C 8. [The inf. is conjectural; apparently from *TEHOJAN, then *TEOHOJAN, contr. to TĒOJAN; pret. TĒODE, pp. TĒOD.]

tīd, f. i-stem. *time, hour; period of time;* ns. M 104; as. S 124; *lifetime,* in **tīd-dæġ,** m. *last day of one's life, final hour,* ds. —**e,** S 69 (Grein's emendation for MS. *tide ge;* **tīd-dæġ** is recorded only in *Genesis* 1165, where it may mean either *last day* or *life-span*). [Cf. **ǣfen-, morgen-tīd.**]

til, adj. *good;* asm. —**ne,** D 38; *praiseworthy, commendable,* nsm. W 112.

til, prep. w. dat. *for,* C 6 (Moore MS.—the rest have **to**).

tilian, wk.v.II. *strive, endeavor;* pres. 1p. subj. **tilien,** S 119.

tīr, m. *glory;* ns. M 104; as. B 3.

tō or **to,** prep. w. dat., instr., rarely gen., *to, for, at,* etc.

1. w. dat. or instr. (a) where the meaning is still expressed by "to" (in various senses), B 17, 28, 34; R 42, etc. (9 times); M 8, etc. (20 times); W 36; S 51, 61; **to þām,** *to that extent,* M 34; **to hwon** (instr.), *to what (end, service, fate),* S 43; —(b) marking purpose, function, service, value, effect: *for, as,* C 6; R 31, 102, 153; M 46, 131, 197, 245; W 11, 30; S 20, 69 (**to twēon,** *as an occasion for uncertainty*), 101; D 3; —(c) marking sphere of action or juxtaposition: *at, in,* R 141, M 12; —(d) marking object of thought: *on, of,* M 4 (twice), 128; *(thought) for, (delight) in,* S 44 (twice), 45 (twice); —(e) marking object inspiring awe or desire: *toward, of, for,* R 86, 129; —(f) marking source of help: *from,* W 115; —(g) marking time: *at, toward,* R 2; **to ealdre,** *for ever,* S 79; —(h) **fōn to** (*take to,*) *seize upon, take up,* M 10.

2. w. uninflected inf. (often dat.), *to,* S 37.

3. w. gen., **to þæs,** *to that extent,* S. 40, 41 (twice).

tō, prep. as adv. *thither, to that place;* S 119.

tō, adv. *too* (w. adj. or adv., denoting excess); M 55, 66, 90, 150, 164; W 66 (twice), 67 (twice), 68 (3 times), 69, 112.

to-berstan, v.3. *burst asunder, be shattered;* pret. 3s. **tobærst,** M 136, 144. [Cf. **berstan.**]

to-brecan, v.4. *break apart, break through;* pp. **tobrocen,** nsf. M 242. [Cf. **brecan.**]

to-gædere, adv. *together,* M 67. [Cf. æt-gædere.]

to-ġēanes, prep. w. dat. *against;* S 76 (postpos.)

ġe-toht, n. *battle;* ds. —e, M 104.

torn, n. *passion, anger;* as. W 112.

to-twǣman, wk.v.I. *divide, split in two;* pp. totwǣmed, nsn. M 241. [Base-word TWĀM, dat. of twēġen, q.v.]

trem, m. or n. *step, space;* as. M 247 (adverbial acc., marking extent).

trēo, n. wa-stem. *tree, cross;* as. R 4, 14, 17, 25. [Cf. ġealg-trēo.]

trēow, f. wō-stem. *good faith, pledge, agreement;* as. —e, W 112.

trymian or trymman, wk.v.I. *make firm, encourage; put in order, marshal, array;* inf. trymian, M 17; pret. 3p. trymedon, M 305. [Base-word TRUM, adj. *firm, strong.*]

ġe-trymian, wk.v.I. same as preceding; pp. ġetrymed, M 22 (perhaps both *drawn up in order* and *encouraged: arrayed for battle*). [MS. getrymmed is irregular but perhaps intended for meter.]

tū, see bū-tū and twēġen.

tungol, n. *star;* ns. B 14.

twǣman, wk.v.I. *divide;* see to-twǣman.

twēġen, m., twā, f., tū, n. *two;* nom. twēġen, M 80; gen. twēġa, M 207. [Cf. bū-tū.]

twēo, wk. m. *doubt, uncertainty;* ds. —n, S 69 (to twēon weorðeþ, *becomes an occasion for uncertainty*).

## þ

þā, adv. and conj.—(a) as adv., *then, after that, next;* C 7; R 27, etc. (10 times); M 2, etc. (35 times);

—(b) as rel. conj., *when,* R 36, 41, 42, 68, 151, 155; M 5, 10, 16, 22, 84, 121, 165, 199, 239, 276. þā-ġiet, adv. *still,* M 168, 273.

þā, dem. adj., def. art. and pron., see sē.

þǣr, adv. and conj.—(a) as adv., *there,* B 17, 32, 37; R 8, etc. (17 times); M 17, etc. (19 times); W 54; S 18, 23a; (perhaps) *thereupon, then,* R 30, 31, 32, 57, 60; —(b) as rel. conj., *where,* R 123, 139, 140, 141, 142, 156; M 23, 24, 28; W 115; S 6, 23b, 121; — (vaguely logical) *whereas, while,* S 10. þǣr-on, adv. *therein,* R 67.

þǣre, þǣs, þǣs-þe, see sē.

þæt, conj. *that.* — (a) in substantive clauses (subject, object, appositive), B 8; R 4, etc. (7 times); M 6, etc. (20 times); W 12, 13, 41; S 67, 77 (explaining þæt, pron., 74), 123 (explaining þæs, pron.); D 10, 11, 14 (introducing clause as obj. of ġefrugnon), 26, 30, 31, 36; —(b) in apposition with a noun signifying a time: *that, when,* R 81; M 105; — (c) in causal clauses: *in that, for, because;* B 48; R 19, 34, 107; M 221, 243, 251; — (d) the clause equivalent to a noun in gen. governed by a noun or adj. in the main clause: *that,* M 176, 180; —(e) the clause stating what is urged or asked; *that,* M 229, 257, 263, 307; — (f) in a clause of purpose: *that, in order that,* M 177; S 34, 37, 119; — (g) in clauses of result or manner: *that, so that,* M 63, 119, 135, 136, 137, 142, 144, 150, 157, 226, 227, 286; S 42; D 16.

þæt, dem. adj., def. art., and pron., see sē.

þām, þām-þe, see sē.

þanan, adv. *thence,* W 23.

þanc, m. and n., w. gen. *thanks (for);* ns. S 122; as. M 120, 147.

ġe-þanc, m. or n. *thought;* as. M 13 (gōd ġ., *an unflinching spirit*). [Cf. mod-geþanc.]

ġe-þancian, wk.v.II, w. dat. of person. *thank, give thanks to;* pres. 1s. ġeþancie, M 173.

þāra, see sē.

þās, see þēs.

þe, þē, indecl. particle, serving as rel. pron., any case, number, or gender. *who, which, that,* etc.; R 111, 118, 137; M 36, etc. (19 times; at 190, obj. of on understood); S 57, 100; þe . . . him, dsm. *to whom,* W 10; S 13; in þā hwīle þe, conj. *while* (lit. *the time in which*), M 14, 83, 235, 272. [Also in combination with þēah, q.v., and with the dem. pron.: see sē. In the MSS. also isn. of the dem. pron., here normalized as þȳ; see sē.]

þē, pers. pron., see þū.

ġe-þeah, see ġe-þicgan.

þēah, adv. *though, however,* M 289.

þēah-þe, conj. *though,* W 2; S 97, 113.

þearf, f. (a) *need;* ns. M 233; as. —e, M 175; —(b) *(time of) need, distress;* ds. —e, M 201, 307; —(c) *what is needful, morally requisite or desirable;* ds. —e, M 232 (*our good, what we must do*).

þearf, see þurfan.

þearle, adv. *severely, sorely, grievously;* B 23; R 52; M 158.

þēaw, m. *custom, habit;* ns. W 12.

þeġn, m. *servant, minister;* esp. *a (noble) retainer;* as. M 151; np. —as, R 75 (*the Lord's servants*); M 205, 220; ap. —as, M 232; gp.

—a, S 68 (MS. þinga). [Cf. bur-, magu-þeġn.]

þeġnlīċe, adv. *as befitting a þeġn; loyally, nobly,* M 294.

-þegu, f. *receipt, receiving.* See hring-, sinc-þegu, and cf. ġe-þicgan.

þenċan, wk.v.I. *think;* inf. S 96; pres. 3p. þenċaþ, R 115; —w. inf., *purpose, intend, desire (to);* pres. 1s. þenċe, M 319; 3s. þenċeþ, R 121; M 258, 316; S 51. [PENĊAN, ÞŌHTE, ÞŌHT; base-word þanc, *thought;* cf. ġeond-þenċan.]

ġe-þenċan, wk.v.I. *think, determine, reflect, consider;* —w. indirect question, *think why* or *how,* inf. W 58; S 118; D 12; w. subst. clause, *reflect that,* inf. D 31.

þenden, conj. *while,* S 102.

þenian or þennan, wk.v.I. *stretch out;* inf. þenian, R 52 (w. **God** as object and unstated subject; equivalent to passive, *stretched out,* w. **God** as subject).

þēod, f. *people;* ds. —e, M 90, 220; gp. —a, M 173; dp. —um, B 22.

þēoden, m. *prince, lord;* ns. M 120, 232; vs. M 178; as. M 158; ds. þēodne, R 69; M 294; gs. þēodnes, W 95.

þēodiġ, adj. combining-form. *of a people or country.* See el-þēodiġ.

þēs or þes, þēos, þis, dem. adj. and pron. *this;* — (a) as adj., þes, nsm. W 62; þēos, nsf. R 12, 82; S 86; þis, nsn. M 45; W 110; S 65; asn. W 89; þisne, asm. R 104; M 32, 52; W 75, 85, 88; þās, asf. R 96; W 58; S 87; D 31; ap. M 298; W 91, 101; þisse, gsf. W 74; dsf. M 221; þissum, dsn. R 83, 109, 138; þȳs, ism. M 316; isn. B 66. (b) as pron., þisses, gsn. (*as to this, with respect to this*), D 7, 13, 17, 20,

27, 42; þissum, dsn. B 67 (this, the present time).

ge-þicgan, v.5. receive; pret. 3s. geþeah, D 40 (MS. geþah). [ÞICGAN, ÞEAH (occas. ÞAH), ÞǢGON, ÞEGEN.]

þider, adv. thither, S 118.

þīestre, n. ja-stem. darkness; often pl., shades of night; np. þīestru, R 52. [An alternate þīESTRU, f. īn-stem, is also found and cannot always be distinguished from the neuter.]

þīn, poss. adj. thy, thine; asn. M 178; apm. —e, M 37; dp. —um, M 50.

þing, n. (thing,) state, condition; affair, trouble; ns. D 9; circumstance, gp. —a, S 68 (MS. þinga gehwylce, emended to þegna gehwelcum. See note.)

þingan, wk.v.I. determine. See un-þinged.

þis, þisne, þisse, þisses, þissum, see þēs.

ge-þōht, m. thought; as. D 22; is. —e, W 88; np. —as, S 34.

þolian, wk.v.II. (a) trans., suffer, undergo, endure; pret. 3p. þolodon, R 149; (b) intrans. endure, hold out; inf. M 201, 307. [Cf. for-þolian.]

ge-þolian, wk.v.II, trans. endure, put up with; inf. M 6.

þon, pron., ism. and isn., see sē, pron., for, for-þon, ǣr-þon.

þone, þone-þe, see sē.

þonne, adv. and conj. —(a) as adv., then (temporal), R 107, 115, 117, 139, 142; W 45, 49; S 94a, 118, 119; D 31; then (consequential), therefore, W 88; —(b) as rel. conj., when, M 213; W 39, 51, 60, 70, 74, 103; S 8, 84, 94b (correl.), 102;

—(c) conj. w. comp., than, R 128; M 33, 195; S 65, 116.

þorfte, þorfton, see þurfan.

þrāg, f. (period of) time; ns. W 95.

ge-þrang, n. throng, press; ds. —e, M 299.

þrīe, m., þrēo, f. and n. pl. three; gen. þrēora, M 299; S 68 (w. sum, one of three things).

ge-þringan, v.3. press, constrict; pp. geþrungen, npm. uninflected (for geþrungne), S 8 (pinched). [ÞRINGAN, ÞRANG, ÞRUNGON, ÞRUN-GEN; cf. oþ-þringan.]

þrīste, adv. resolutely, unflinchingly, D 12.

þrītig, num. thirty; as subst. w. part. gen., acc. (extent of time), D 18.

þrōwian, wk.v.II. suffer; intrans., pret. 3s. þrōwode, R 84, 98, 145; trans., suffer, endure, pret. 1s. þrōwode, S 3.

ge-þrungen, see ge-þringan.

þrymm, m. ja-stem. glory, majesty; ns. W 95. þrymm-fæst, adj. glorious; nsm. R 84.

þrȳþ, f. i-stem. strength, power; often in plural w. reference to the powers of inanimate things, as here of spears: np. —e, W 99.

þū, pron. 2d pers. sg. thou; ns. R 78, 96; M 30, 36, 37, 45, 176, 231; þē, ds. M 29, 30, 177, 179; as. R 95; M 173. [See þīn, poss. adj., and gē.]

pūhte, see þyncan.

þurfan, pret.-pres. v. need, have reason to (w. inf.); pres. 3s. þearf, R 117; 1p. þurfe (wē), M 34; 3p. þurfon, M 249; pret. 3s. þorfte, B 39, 44; 3p. þorfton, B 47. [ÞURFAN, ÞEARF, ÞURFON, ÞORFTE.]

þurh, prep. w. acc. through; — (a) of motion: through, R 18; M 141, 145, 151; — (b) expressing cause or agency: *through, by, by reason of, by means of;* R 10, 119; M 71; S 88.

þurh-drīfan, v.l. *drive through, pierce;* pret. 3p. þurhdrifon, R 46. [DRĪFAN, DRĀF, DRIFON, DRIFEN.]

þurh-wadan, v.6. *pass through, pierce;* pret. 3s. þurhwōd, M 296. [Cf. wadan.]

þus, adv. *thus,* M 57.

þȳ, see sē.

ġe-þyldiġ, adj. *patient;* nsm. W 65.

þynċan, wk.v.I, impers. w. dat. of person. *seem;* pres. 3s. þynċeþ, M 55; W 41; D 29; pret. 3s. þūhte, R 4; M 66. [ÞYNĊAN, ÞŪHTE, ÞŪHT; based on þunc-, passive grade of the ablaut series *þINC-, *þANC-; *þUNC-; cf. þenċan.]

þȳs, see þēs.

# U

ūhta, wk.m. *period before daybreak, early morning;* gp. ūhtna, W 8.

un-befohten, adj. *unopposed, without a fight;* npm. unbefohtne, M 57. [Cf. feohtan.]

unc, see wit.

under, prep. *beneath, under;* w. dat., R 55, 85; W 107; w. acc. (after a verb implying motion), W 96.

un-earg, adj. *undaunted, unflinching:* npm. —e, M 206.

un-forcūþ, adj. *undisgraced, reputable;* nsm. M 51.

un-forht, adj. *unafraid, undaunted;* nsm. R 110; npm. —e, M 79. [MS. has *unforht* at R 117, but with opposite meaning; see an-forht.]

ġe-unnan, pret.-pres. v., w. gen. *grant;* pres. subj. 2s. ġeunne, M 176. [UNNAN, ANN, UNNON, ŪÐE.]

un-orne, adj. ja-stem. *unpretentious, simple, humble;* nsm. M 256. [Cf. orne.]

un-rīm, n. *countless number;* ns. B 31 (w. part. gen.). [RĪM, n. *number.*]

un-þinged, adj. *unprepared for, unexpected;* nsm. S 106. [ÞINĠAN, wk.v.I, *invite, determine upon.*]

un-wāclīċe, adv. *without weakening;* M 308. [Cf. wāc, wācian.]

un-wearnum, adv. *irresistibly;* S 63. [wearn, f. *hindrance;* q.v.]

un-weaxen, adj. *not fully grown;* nsm. M 152. [weaxan, v.7, *grow.*]

upp, adv. *up;* B 13, 70; R 71; M 130.

upp-gang, m. *passage up on land, passage to shore;* as. M 87. upp-rodor, m. *high heaven, the heavens above;* as. S 105.

uppe, adv. *up,* R 9.

ūre, poss. adj. *our;* nsm. M 232, 240, 314; nsn. M 313; ūrne, asm. M 58; ūrum, dp. M 56. [For the pron. see wē.]

ūriġ, adj. *dewy.* ūriġ-feðra, wk.m. *dewy-feathered one;* ns. S 25. [A valid word though in a seemingly corrupt passage; a wk. noun or wk. adj. with subst. function, from strong adj. *ŪRIĠ-FEÐER, *dewy-feathered;* see -feðra.]

ūs, ūsiċ, see wē.

ūt, adv. *out;* B 35; M 72.

ūþ-wita, wk.m. *wise man;* np. —n, B 69. [The stressed prefix is intensive; it may once have meant *beyond.* Cf. wita.]

# W

wāc, adj. *weak* (morally or physically); nsm. W 67 (wāc wīga, *weak in battles*) ; asm. —ne, M 43 (of a

spear-shaft vigorously shaken): *pli-
ant, slender*); comp. **wācra**, npm.
—**n**, as noun, *the inferior, degen-
erate,* S 87. [Implies moral weak-
ness in **un-wācliċe**, q.v.]
**wācian**, wk.v.II. *weaken, prove soft;*
inf. M 10.
**wacu**, f. *watch.* See **niht-wacu.**
**wadan**, v.6. (a) intrans., *pass, pro-
ceed, advance;* inf. M 140; pret.
1s. **wōd**, W 24; 3s. M 130, 253; 3p.
**wōdon**, M 96, 295; —(b) trans.,
*tread, traverse;* inf. W 5. [WADAN,
WŌD, WŌDON, WADEN; cf. **þurh-
wadan.**]
**ġe-wadan**, v.6. *go, pass (all the way)* ;
pret. 3s. **ġewōd**, M 157.
**wæcnan**, v.6 (irreg.). *awake.* See **on-
wæcnan.**
**wǣd**, f. (or **wǣde**, n. ja-stem). *cloth-
ing, an article of clothing, cover-
ing;* dp. —**um**, R 15, 22 (the alter-
nating vesture of the cross, now
precious ornaments, possibly in-
cluding silken streamers, now
blood).
**wǣfer-sīen**, f. i-stem. *spectacle, show;*
ds. —**e**, R 31. [**wǣfer** does not oc-
cur alone but is used in several
compounds referring to theatri-
cal exhibitions and is probably
related to WĀFIAN, wk.v.II, *marvel
at, gaze at.* Cf. **ġe-siene, an-sīen,**
and **ġe-sēon.**]
**wǣġ**, m. i-stem. *wave, surf;* as. S 19;
ap. —**as**, W 46.
**wǣgon**, see **wegan.**
**wæl**, n. *slaughter; the slain collec-
tively, number of slain;* in com-
pounds often translatable by
*battle,* ns. B 65; M 126, 303;
ds. —**e**, M 279, 300. **wæl-feld**, m.
u-stem. *battlefield;* ds. —**a**, B 51.
**wæl-ġifre**, adj. *greedy for slaugh-
ter;* npn. —**ġifru**, W 100. **wæl-rest,**

f. *a resting-place among the slain;*
as. —**e**, M 113. **wæl-sleaht**, n. (or
m.) *deadly combat;* gp. —**a**, W 7,
91. **wæl-spere**, n. i-stem. *deadly
spear;* as. M 322. **wæl-stōw**, f.
*place of slaughter, battlefield;* gs.
—**e**, M 95; ds. —**e**, B 43; M 293.
**wæl-wulf**, m. *death-dealing wolf;*
np. —**as**, M 96 (epithet for the
vikings).
**wǣpen**, n. *weapon;* ns. M 252; as.
M 130, 235; np. W 100; gs. **wǣp-
nes**, M 168; ds. **wǣpne**, M 228; gp.
**wǣpna**, M 83, 272, 308; dp. **wǣp-
num**, M 10, 126. **wǣpen-ġewrixl,**
n. *weapon-exchange, trading of
blows;* gs. —**es**, B 51.
**wǣr**, f. *covenant, pledge;* dip. —**um**,
S 110 (ġewiss wǣrum, *unfailing in
its* [the mind's] *pledges;* MS.
*werum* can also be taken as dp.
of wer: *constant toward men;* but
see note).
**wǣre, wǣron, wæs,** see **bēon-wesan.**
**wǣta**, wk.m. *moisture, blood;* ds.
—**n**, R 22.
**wæter**, n. *water;* as. B 55; M 91, 98;
ds. —**e**, M 64, 96.
**wamm**, m. *blemish, iniquity;* dp. —
um, R 14.
**wan**, adj. *lacking, wanting* (general-
ly as first member of a com-
pound). **wan-hyġdiġ**, adj. *heedless,
reckless, imprudent;* nsm. W 67.
**wand**, see **windan.**
**wandian**, wk.v.II. *turn aside, waver,
flinch;* inf. M 258; pret. 3s. **wan-
dode**, M 268. [Cf. **windan.**]
**wang**, m. *field, meadow;* ap. —**as**, S
49 (less probably np.) .
**wann**, adj. *dark;* nsm. W 103; nsf.
R 55.
**-ware**, m.pl. (orig. f.pl. of WARU,
*people*), *inhabitants, people.* See
**bealu-, burg-ware.**

**warian,** wk.v.II. *guard, take charge of; attend* (as a guardian or ruling spirit); pres. 3s. **waraþ,** W 32.

**wāt,** see **witan.**

**ġe-wāt,** see **ġe-witan.**

**waðum,** m. *wave, stream, sea;* gp. —**a,** W 24, 57. (MS. *waðena, waþema.*)

**wāwan,** v.7. *blow, be blown about in the wind.* See **be-wāwan.**

**wē,** pron. 1st pers. pl. *we;* nom. C 1 (var.); R 70; M 33, 34, 35, 40, 61, 212, 213; S 117 (twice), 118, 119 (twice); D 14, 21; **ūre,** gen. M 234 (w. **ǣġhwelċ**); **ūs,** dat. B 68; R 147b; M 39, 40, 93, 233; W 115; acc. R 73, 75, 147a; M 34 (refl., *each other*), 60, 237. **ūsiċ,** acc. S 123. [See **iċ, wit,** and **ūre,** poss. adj.]

**wēa,** wk.m. *woe, misery;* as. —**n,** D 4; gs. —**n,** D 25; gp. —**na,** D 34.

**ġe-wealc,** n. *rolling, tossing;* as. S 6, 46.

**weald,** m. u-stem. *forest, woodland;* ds. —**a,** B 65.

**ġe-weald,** n. *control, prerogative, power;* as. R 107; M 178.

**wealdan,** v.7., w. gen. *wield;* inf. M 83, 168, 272; *hold, be master of,* inf. M 95. [WEALDAN, WĒOLD, WĒOLDON, WEALDEN.]

**wealdend,** m. nd-stem. *ruler;* esp. *the Lord;* ns. R 111, 155; vs. M 173 (w. gen.); as. R 67 (w. gen.); gs. —**es,** R 17, 53; ds. —**e,** R 121; in the secular sense, np. W 78.

**weall,** m. *wall;* ns. W 98; ds. —**e,** W 80; np. —**as,** W 76. **weall-steall,** m. *site of a wall, wall-stead, foundation;* as. W 88. [Cf. **bord-weall.**]

**weard,** m. *guardian, lord;* w. defining gen., (a) *God:* **heofon-rīċes w.,** as. C 1; **mann-cynnes w.,** ns. C 7;

(b) *the cuckoo:* **sumeres w.,** ns. S 54. [Cf. **brycg-weard.**]

**wearg,** m. *criminal;* ap. —**as,** R 31.

**wearn,** f. *hindrance;* dp. —**um,** D 1 (**be wearnum,** *by hindrances,* an emendation for MS. *be wurman:* see note). [Cf. **un-wearnum.**]

**wearþ,** see **weorðan.**

**weaxan,** v.7. *grow, increase.* See **un-weaxen.** [WEAXAN, WĒOX, WĒOXON, WEAXEN.]

**weġ,** m. *way, path, road;* as. R 88. [Cf. **eorþ-, flōd-, forþ-, hwæl-weġ,** and **on-weġ,** adv. under **on.**]

**wegan,** v.5. *carry, bear;* pret. 3p. **wæġon,** M 98. [WEGAN, WÆĠ, WÆGON, WEĠEN; cf. **for-wegan.**]

**wēl,** adv. *well, fully;* R 129, 143; as quasi-adj., **wēl biþ,** *it will be well, turn out well,* W 114.

**wela,** wk.m. *wealth;* ns. W 74. [Cf. **eorþ-wela.**]

**wēman,** wk.v.I. *allure, entertain;* inf. W 29.

**wēn,** f. i-stem. *expectation;* dp. —**um,** D 25.

**wēnan,** wk.v.I. (a) *believe, suppose;* **wēnde,** pret. 3s. M 239 (w. gen. **þæs,** and explanatory clause); (b) *expect, hope, look forward to;* pres. 1s. **wēne,** R 135 (w. refl. pron. dat. and clause).

**wendan,** wk.v.I. *turn;* (a) *change;* inf. R 22; (b) *go (away); go about;* inf. M 316; pres. 3s. **wendeþ,** D 32; 1s. subj. **wende,** M 252; pret. 3p. **wendon,** M 193; (c) w. **forþ,** *go forth, advance;* pret. 3p. **wendon,** M 205. [WENDAN, WENDE, WENDED; base-word WAND, corresponding to pret. of **windan,** q.v.; cf. **on-wendan.**]

**wenian** or **wennan,** wk.v.I. *accustom* (mod. "wean" with wider application); pret. 3s. .**wenede,** W 36 (w.

to wiste, *accustomed him to the feast, was ever feasting him*). [Related to wunian, q.v.]

wēop, see wēpan.

weorc, n. *work; pain;* as. R 79 (*work or pain*); ap. C 3 (*works;* or as. *work*). [Cf. beadu-, dæġ-weorc.]

ġe-weorc, n. *a piece of construction, a work;* np. W 87.

weorod, n. *band of men, host, company;* ns. M 64, 97; as. M 102; ds. —e, R 152; M 51; is. —e, B 34; R 69, 124; gp. —a, R 51. [Cf. heorþ-weorod.]

weorold, f. i-stem. *world;* ns. S 49; as. W 58, 107; S 87; D 31; gs. —e, R 133; W 74; ds. —e, M 174; S 45.

weorold-ġesǣliġ, adj. *blessed with this world's goods, prosperous;* nsm. M 219. weorold-rīċe, n. *kingdom of the world;* ds. W 65. [wer, *man;* ELD, *age, lifetime,* later supplanted by -old, -uld.]

weorðan, v.3. *become, be;* —(a) as independent verb: inf. W 64; pres. 3s. weorðeþ, W 110; S 69; pret. 3s. wearþ, M 113, 186 (w. on flēame, *took to flight;* E's transcript has pl. *wurdon*), 295 (*came to pass, there was*); 3p. wurdon, B 48 (beteran w., *were the better, had the better of it*); D 15; —(b) as auxiliary w. past part., forming passive, pret. 3s. wearþ, B 32, 65; M 106, 114, 116, 135, 138, 241, 288; 3s. subj. wurde, M 1; forming pluperfect, pret. 3s. wearþ, M 202. [WEORÐAN, WEARþ, WURDON, WORDEN.]

ġe-weorðan, v.3. *become;* pp. ġeworden, nsm. R 87.

weorðian, wk.v.II. *honor, adore;* inf. R 129; pres. 3p. weorðiaþ, R 81.

ġe-weorðian, wk.v.II. *honor, exalt;* pret. 3s. ġeweorðode, R 90, 94; S

123; *adorn,* pp. ġeweorðod, asm. R 15.

weorþlīċe, adv. *splendidly, worthily, honorably;* R 17; M 279.

wēpan, v.7. *weep;* pret. 3s. wēop, R 55. [WĒPAN, WĒOP, WĒOPON, WŌPEN.]

wer, m. *man;* ns. W 64; gp. —a, S 21; dp. —um, S 110 (alt. reading: see wǣr).

werian, wk.v.I. *defend;* pret. 3p. weredon (w. refl. pron.), M 82, 283.

wēriġ, adj. *weary, exhausted, afflicted;* nsm. B 20; S 29; asm. —ne, W 57; npm. wērġe, M 303. wēriġmōd, adj. *weary in spirit, dejected;* nsm. as noun, W 15. (Can be taken separately, *a weary spirit,* but the compound improves the sense. See note.) [Cf. lim-, mere-wēriġ.]

wesan, see bēon-wesan.

west, adv. *west(ward),* M 97.

wēste, adj. ja-stem. *waste;* nsm. W 74.

wicg, n. ja-stem. *horse, steed;* ds. —e, M 240.

wīċing, m. *pirate, viking;* as. M 139; ap. —as, M 322; gp. —a, M 26, 73, 97; dp. —um, M 116. [Perhaps so called because the earliest pirates lived along the shores of bays: OE wīċ.]

wīde, adv. *widely, far;* S 60; D 22; wīde and sīde, *far and wide,* R 81; superl. widost, *farthest, most widely,* S 57.

wiernan, wk.v.I. w. gen. of thing. *refuse, deny, withhold;* pret. 3s. wiernde, M 118; 3p. wierndon, B 24 (w. dat. of pers.). [Base-word wearn, f. *hindrance,* q.v.]

wīf, n. *woman;* ds. —e, S 45; gp. —a, R 94.

wiġ, n. *war, battle;* ns. W 80; gs.
—es, B 20, 59; M 73, 130; ds. —e,
M 10, 128, 193, 235, 252; gp. —a,
W. 67. **wiġ-haga**, wk.m. *battle-hedge* (shield-wall); as. —n, M 102.
**wīġ-heard**, adj. *hardy in battle;*
asm. —ne, M 75. **wiġ-pleʒa**, wk.m.
*play of battle;* ds. —n, M 268; is.
—n, M 316. **wiġ-smiþ**, m. *war-smith* (kenning for warrior); np.
—as, B 72.

**wiga**, wk.m. *warrior;* ns. M 210; as.
—n, M 75, 235; ds. —n, M 126;
np. —n, M 79, 302; gp. **wiġena**,
M 135. [Cf. **byrn-wiga**.]

**wiġend**, m. nd-stem. *warrior;* np.
M 302.

**willa**, wk.m. *desire;* ns. R 129.

**willan**, anom. v. *be willing, desire,
will* (w. inf. except as noted);
pres. 1s. R 1; M 216, 247, 317
(**fram ne w.**, *will not go away*); D
35; 3s. **wile**, R 107; M 52; 1p.
**willaþ**, M 35, 40; 3p. **willaþ**, M 46;
1s. subj. **wille**, M 221; 2s. subj. **wille**,
M 37; 3s. subj. **wille**, W 14
(**hycgan** understood), 72; S 43, 97,
113; pret. 3s. **wolde**, R 34, 41, 113
(or subj.); M 11, 129, 160; 3s. subj.
**wolde**, W 28; pret. 3p. **woldon**, R
68; M 207.

**win**, n. *wine*. **win-gāl**, adj. *gay, or
wanton, with wine;* nsm. S 29.
**wīn-sæl**, n. *wine-hall;* np. —salu,
W 78.

**wind**, m. *wind;* dis. —e, W 76.

**windan**, v.3. *wind;* —(a) intrans.,
*fly, speed; circle round;* inf. M
322; pret. 3p. **wundon**, M 106;
—(b) trans., *wave, brandish;* pret.
3s. **wand**, M 43. [WINDAN, WAND,
WUNDON, WUNDEN; cf. **be-windan**
and **wunden**.]

**wine**, m. i-stem (treated as a-stem).
*friend, loved-one, comrade, pa-tron;* ns. M 250; as. S 115; ap.

winas, M 228. **wine-dryhten**, m.
*lord and friend, patron;* as. M
248, 263; gs. —dryhtnes, W 37.
**wine-lēas**, adj. *friendless, lordless;*
nsm. W 45. **wine-mǣġ**, m. *beloved
kinsman;* ap. —māgas, M 306; gp.
—māga, W 7; dip. —māgum, S 16.
[Cf. **ġeō-**, *gold-wine*.]

ġe-**winn**, n. *battle, struggle, agony;*
as. M 214; ds. —e, R 65; M 248;
302. [Cf. **ǣr-ġewinn**.]

ġe-**winnan**, v.3, trans. *win* (by
fighting), *conquer;* inf. M 125.
[WINNAN, WANN, WUNNON,
WUNNEN.]

**winter**, m. (elsewhere with u-stem
forms), *winter;* as. S 15 (as adv.,
*in winter*); gs. —es, W 103; pl.,
in reckoning age, *years:* gp.
**wintra**, W 65; D 18, 38; dip.
**wintrum**, M 210. **winter-ċeald**, adj.
*winter-cold;* asf. —e, D 4. **winter-ċeariġ**, adj. *winter-sad;* nsm. W 24.

**wis**, adj. *wise;* nsm. M 219; W 64;
ism. —e, W 88.

**wise**, wk.f. *manner, way* (*of behav-ing*); dip. **wīsum**, S 110.

**wīsian**, wk.v.II. *guide, direct;* pret.
3s. **wisode**, M 141.

**wislīċ**, adj. *certain, assured;* asm.
—ne, D 34. [Cf. next word.]

ġe-**wiss**, adj. *trustworthy, unfailing;*
asn. S 110.

**wisse**, see **witan**.

**wist**, f. *means of subsistence, food,
feast;* ds. —e, W 36.

**wit**, pron. 1st pers. dual, *we two,*
acc. **unc**, R 48. [See **iċ, wē**.]

**wita**, wk.m. *wise man, counselor;* ns.
W 65.

**witan**, pret.-pres. v. *know, have
knowledge* es. 1s. **wāt**, W 11;
3s. **wāt**, M 94; W 29, 37; S 12, 55,
92; pret. 3s. **wisse**, M 24; subj. W
27 (**mīne wisse**, *might know about*

*my people;* for the traditional emendation, see **myne**). [WITAN, WĀT, WITON, WISSE, or WISTE.]

ġe-**witan**, v.1. *go, depart;* —(a) w. limiting adv. or prep. (for**þ**, **upp**, **ūt**, **þurh**, etc.); inf. S 52; pret. 3s. ġe**wāt**, B 35; R 71; M 72, 150; W 95; 3p. ġe**witon**, R 133; —(b) w. inf. specifying the manner of going or attendant action; pret. 3p. ġe**witon**, B 53 (w. refl. dat.); —(c) unmodified: pp. ġe**witen**, *departed;* npm. —**e**, S 80, 86. [WĪTAN, WĀT, WITON, WITEN; cf. ÆTWĪTAN, with different semantic development.]

**wite**, n. ja-stem. *punishment, torment, torture;* ds. R 61; gp. **wita**, R 87.

**witiġ**, adj. *wise;* nsm. D 32 (w. **dryhten**, *God in his wisdom*— Malone).

**wiþ**, prep. *with, against, towards,* etc. (a) w. gen., *towards,* M 8, 131; — (b) w. dat. *against,* M 103; *in exchange for,* M 31, 35, 39; — (c) w. acc. *against,* B 9, 52; M 82, 277, 298; S 75; *toward,* S 112 (twice); — (d) w. acc. or dat. *(in friendly rivalry) with,* M 290.

**wiðer-lēan**, n. *requital;* ns. M 116.

**wiþ-standan**, v.6. w. dat. *withstand;* inf. W 15. [Cf. **standan**.]

**wlanc**, adj. *proud, high-spirited, bold, lusty;* nsm. S 29; nsf. W 80; asm. —**ne**, M 139; dsn.wk. —**an**, M 240 (of a horse: *spirited,* or *proud, splendid?*); npm. —**e**, B 72; M 205. [Cf. **mōd-wlanc**.]

**wlītan**, v.1. *look;* pret. 3s. **wlāt**, M 172. [WLĪTAN, WLĀT, WLITON, WLITEN.]

**wlitiġian**, wk.v.II. *make beautiful, brighten;* pres. 3p. **wlitiġiaþ**, S 49.

(Less probably, *become beautiful.*) [WLITIĠ, adj., *beautiful.*]

**wōd, wōdon**, ġe-**wōd**, see **wadan**, ġe-**wadan**.

**wolcen**, m. or n. *cloud, sky;* dp. **wolcnum**, R 53, 55.

**wolde, woldon**, see **willan**.

**wōma**, wk.m. *noise, tumult* (or *proclaimer, herald?*) ; ns. W 103.

**word**, n. *word, speech, command;* as. R 35; M 168; ap. R 27; W 91; ds. —**e**, R 111; dip. —**um**, (as formal indication of speech: *with, in words*), R 97; M 26, 43, 210, 250, 306. [Cf. **ġielp-, lāst-word**.]

ġe-**worden**, see ġe-**weorðan**.

ġe-**worhtne**, ġe-**worhton**, see ġe-**wyrċan**.

**wōrian**, wk.v.II. *wander, go astray;* fig., *degenerate, go to ruin;* pres. 3p. **wōriaþ**, W 78 (*totter?*—Bosworth-Toller).

**worn**, m. *a great number, multitude;* as., w. part. gen., W 91.

**wracu**, f. *misery;* as. **wræce**, D 4.

**wræc**, n. *persecution, exile;* gs. —**es**, D 1. **wræc-lāst**, m. *path or track of exile;* ns. W 32; ap. —**as**, W 5; S 57 (w. **lecgaþ**, *lay tracks of exile: direct their exiled steps, travel*— Mrs. Gordon).

**wræc, wræce**, verb-forms, see **wrecan**.

**wrāþ**, adj. *hostile, cruel, angry;* gp. —**ra**, R 51; W 7.

**wrecan**, v.5. (a) w. acc. of person, *avenge* (someone); inf. M 248, 258; pret. 3s. **wræc**, M 279; 3s. subj. **wræce**, M 257; —(b) *utter, recite;* inf. S 1. [WRECAN, WRÆC, WRÆCON, WRECEN.]

ġe-**wrecan**, v.5, w. acc. of person. *avenge* (someone); inf. M 208, 263.

**wreċċa**, wk.m. *an exile;* gs. —**n**, S 15.

wrēon, contr.v.I. *cover.* See **be-, on-wrēon.**

ġe-**wrixl,** n. *exchange.* See **wǣpen-ġewrixl.**

**wudu,** m. u-stem. *wood, forest;* ns. R 27; as. M 193. [Cf. **holt-wudu.**]

**wuldor,** n. *glory; the realm of glory, heaven;* gs. **wuldres,** R 14, 90, 97, 133; S 123; ds. **wuldre,** R 135, 143, 155. **wuldor-fæder,** m. r-stem. *glorious or heavenly Father,* gs. C 3.

**wulf,** m. *wolf;* ns. W 82; as. B 65. [Cf. **wæl-wulf.**]

**wund,** f. *wound;* as. —**e,** M 139, 271; dip. —**um,** B 43; M 293, 303.

**wund,** adj. *wounded;* nsm. M 113, 144.

**wunden,** pp. adj. *wound, twisted;* **wunden gold,** *twisted gold* (i.e. gold rings, ornamental gold, the traditional gift of the lord to his retainers); nsn. W 32. [Cf. **windan,** v.3.]

ġe-**wundian,** wk.v.II. *wound;* pp. ġe-**wundod,** nsm. M 135. [Cf. **for-wundian.**]

**wundon,** see **windan.**

**wundor,** n. *wonder;* gp. **wundra,** C 3; dip. **wundrum,** as adv. *wondrously,* W 98.

**wunian,** wk.v.II. (a) intrans., *dwell, live, remain;* inf. R 121, 143; pres. 3p. **wuniaþ,** R 135; S 87 (*remain*); pret. 3p. **wunodon,** R 155; —(b) trans., *remain on, dwell in;* pret. 1s. **wunode,** S 15; *occupy, be in,* pret. 3p. **wunodon,** R 3 (**reste w.,** *were in bed*). [Related to **wenian,** q.v.]

**wurde, wurdon,** see **weorðan.**

**wurman** (D 1, according to the MS.), see **wyrm.**

**wuton** or **uton,** hortatory auxiliary. *let us* (pres. 1p. subj., originally of **witan**); S 117.

**wylfen,** adj. *wolfish;* asm. —**ne,** D 22.

**wynn,** f. i-stem. *joy, delight, pleasure;* ns. W 36; S 45; as. S 27; dip. —**um,** R 15 (as adv., *beautifully*); W 29; gp. —**a,** M 174.

**wyrċan,** wk.v.I. *make, form;* inf. R 65; M 102.

ġe-**wyrċan,** wk.v.I. (a) *make, form;* pret. 3p. ġe**worhton,** R 31 (acc. **mē** *understood*); pp. ġe**worht,** asm. —**ne,** S 115 (**his ġ. wine,** *the friend he has made*); —(b) *bring about, work, accomplish;* inf. M 264; pres. 3s. subj. ġe**wyrċe,** S 74 (*let him bring it about*); —(c) **flēam** ġe**wyrċan,** lit. *make flight: take to flight;* inf. M 81.

**wyrd,** f. i-stem. *fate, destiny;* ns. R 74; W 5, 100 (personified, **wyrd sēo mǣre,** *Wyrd the renowned, Wyrd the mighty*); S 115; ds. —**e,** W 15; gp. —**a,** R 51; W 107. [Related to \***wurd-,** grade of **weorðan,** *become;* hence, *that which comes to pass.* Perhaps anciently regarded as a goddess.]

-**wyrde,** adjectival combining-form, ja-stem. *-worded, -spoken;* see **hræd-wyrde.** [Based on **word,** n., prehist. \***wurd-.**]

ġe-**wyrht,** f. i-stem (or n.). *deed.* See **eald-ġewyrht,** and cf. **wyrċan.**

**wyrm,** m. i-stem. *worm, snake, serpent;* dp. —**um,** D 1 (usual normalization of MS. *wurman,* here emended to **wearnum**). [Malone suggests that **be wurman** may refer to snake rings, gold rings made by Weland and coveted by Niþhad, or to swords with serpentine markings, instruments of the hamstringing.] **wyrm-līca,** wk. m. *likeness of a serpent;* dip. —**līcum,** W 98 (probably alluding to serpentine ornamentation such as was practiced by the Roman builders).

**wȳscan,** wk.v.I. *wish;* pret. 3s. **wȳscte,** D 25. [Gmc. *WUNSCJAN; cf. Germ. WUNSCH, WÜNSCHEN.]

# Y

**yfel,** n. *evil, harm;* gs. —**es,** M 133 (dep. on **hogode.)**

**ymb,** or **ymbe,** prep. w. acc. — (a) *about, near, round about;* **ymbe,** B 5; M 249; **ymb,** S 11. (b) *about, concerning;* **ymbe,** M 214; S 46a; **ymb,** S 46b; D 12. (c) governing words for periods of time: *after;* **æfre ymbe stunde,** *ever after a while, ever and anon,* M 271.

**ymb-clyppan,** wk.v.I. *embrace;* pret. 3s. **ymbclypte,** R 42. [Cf. **clyppan.**]

**ȳþ,** f. jō-stem. *sea-wave;* gp. —**a,** S 6, 46. [Cf. **sealt-ȳþ.**]

# Proper Names

Most personal names among the Germanic peoples were compounds made of recognizable elements of the language and at least vaguely significant when put together. Such names in the list below are separated into their elements by hyphens, but no systematic effort has been made to expound their meaning. Sometimes the two elements in a name were selected in honor of different relatives, and only a vague propriety was demanded of the combination. Sometimes the entire name was that of an ancestor or ancient hero. Spellings in the manuscripts show that both elements in names, especially the weakly stressed second element, were subject to slurring, with loss of identity as words. In poetry, these elements could be given a restored dignity and treated like members of ordinary compounds, with strong secondary stress on the second member, particularly when it was followed by an inflectional syllable, as in *Byrht-nōðes*. Sometimes, however, even in such an ancient poem as *Beowulf,* the second member receives much less stress than it would be entitled to in an ordinary compound and ranks with syllables of the weakest grade.

The historical and legendary names in *Brunanburh, Maldon,* and *Deor* are summarily treated here. For several of them much fuller discussion is provided by the editions of Campbell, Gordon, and Malone respectively. For *Deor* Malone's later articles should also be consulted.

---

Ādam, Adam; gs. —es, R 100.

Ælf-here, one of the three defenders of the ford at Maldon; ns. M 80.

Ælf-nōþ, one of two retainers who fell beside Byrhtnoþ when he died; ns. M 183.

Ælf-riċ, father of Ælfwine, probably the ealdorman of Mercia who was banished in 985 or 986; gs. —es, M 209. See Gordon's ed.

Ælf-wine, scion of a distinguished Mercian family: kinsman of Byrhtnoþ, son of Ælfric, grandson of Ealhhelm. See Gordon's ed.

He sets the pattern of sacrifice after Byrhtnoþ's death. ns. M 211; vs. M 231.

**Æsc-ferhþ**, son of Ecglaf, a Northumbrian of noble family, a hostage in Byrhtnoþ's household; ns. M 267.

**Æðel-gār**, father of the virtuous Godric; gs. —es, M 320.

**Æðel-rēd**, Ethelred II, King of England 978–1016 ("the Unready," i.e. unwise or "Redeless"); gs. —es, M 53, 151, 203. [The second element of the name is R.ĒD, *advice, counsel,* which figures also in the traditional epithets.]

**Æðel-rīċ**, retainer of Byrhtnoþ and brother of Sigebyrht, cited for valiant conduct in the last phase of the battle; ns. M 280. [On the possibility that he survived the battle, see Gordon's ed.]

**Æðel-stān**, Athelstan, King of England 924–939; ns. B 1.

**Anlāf**, leader of the Vikings from Dublin at Brunanburh; ns. B 46; gs. —es, B 31; ds. —e, B 26. [Early form of Old Norse Ólaf; on his identity see Campbell's edition.]

**Beadu-hild**, daughter of Niþhad, mother of the famous Widia by Weland; ds. —e, D 8.

**Briten**, f. Britain; as. —e, B 71. [The spelling of this name, ultimately from Lat. BRITANNIA, varies greatly; e.g. also BRYTEN, BRITON, BREOTON.]

**Brūnan-burh**, unidentified site of the battle of A.D. 937; as. B 5. [The second element is certainly BURG, f. cons.-stem, *fortress,* etc.; the first may be gs. of BRŪNA, wk.m., pr. name, Brown.]

**Byrht-helm**, father of Byrhtnoþ; gs. —es, M 92.

**Byrht-nōþ**, earl or ealdorman of Essex, A.D. 956–991. Gordon thinks he was born about 926, so that he was about 65 when he was killed at Maldon. See Gordon's introduction. ns. M 17, 42, 101, 127, 162; as. M 257; gs. —es, M 114. [BYRHT, var. of BEORHT, adj. *bright;* NŌÞ, f. *daring.*]

**Byrht-wold**, the old retainer of Byrhtnoþ whose prescription for courage in defeat opens the last speech of the incomplete poem, 312 ff.; ns. M 309. [WOLD, half-stress form of WEALD, WALD, *power.*]

**Ċēola**, father of the Wulfstan who led the defence of the ford at Maldon; gs. —n, M 76.

**Constantinus**, Constantine III, King of the united Picts and Scots at Brunanburh; ns. B 38.

**Dene**, m. i-stem pl. Danes (a name often applied to Scandinavians in general) ; dp. **Denum**, M 129 (chiefly Norwegians).

**Dēor**, known only as speaker of the poem of that name, who says he was formerly the scop of the Hedenings; ns. D 37.

**Dinges Mere**, the otherwise unknown name of some part of the sea off the coast of Britain, probably an estuary between northern England and Ireland; (less probably ds.), B 54. [See **mere** in the main glossary.]

**Dunnere**, a simple freeman at Maldon. ns. M 255.

**Dyflin**, Dublin, where Anlaf ruled a Norse kingdom at the time of the battle of Brunanburh; as. B 55.

**Ēad-mund,** Prince Edmund, younger brother of Athelstan, who ruled after him, 939–946; ns. B 3.

**Ēad-rīċ,** a retainer of Byrhtnoþ's; ns. M 11.

**Ēad-weard,** (1) Edward the Elder, King of Wessex 899–924, son of Alfred and father of Athelstan; gs. —es, B 7, 52. (2) a retainer of Byrhtnoþ's; ns. M 117. (3) **Ēad-weard se langa,** the Tall, a retainer of Byrhtnoþ's, perhaps the same as 2; ns. M 273.

**Ēad-wold,** a retainer of Byrhtnoþ's, brother of Oswold; ns. M 304.

**Eahl-helm,** grandfather of Ælfwine, father-in-law of Ælfric; ealdorman of Mercia ca. 940–950; ns. M 218. [EALH, m. *temple.*]

**Ēast-Seaxe,** m. i-stem pl. the East Saxons, centered in Essex; gp. **Ēast-Seaxna,** M 69.

**Ecg-lāf,** a Northumbrian nobleman, father of Æscferhþ; gs. —es, M 267.

**Engle,** m. i-stem pl. the Angli, Angles as contrasted with Saxons; np. B 70.

**Eorman-rīċ,** the Ermanaric of history, ruler of the Goths in the third quarter of the fourth century, who died ca. 375 when the Huns invaded his empire, centered near the mouth of the Danube. Known in legend as a violent man, and eventually as a tyrant who meted out savage punishment for imagined crimes; gs. —es, D 21.

**Gadd,** kinsman of Offa; gs. —es, M 287.

**Ġēat,** legendary hero, perhaps originally a god, lover of Mæþhild; gs. —es, D 15.

**God-rīċ,** (1) son of Odda; leader of the flight from the battle of Maldon; ns. M 187, 237, 325. (2) son of Æðelgar; a retainer of Byrhtnoþ's who, unlike the preceding, fought to the last; ns. M 321.

**God-wiġ,** son of Odda; a fugitive with his brothers Godric (1) and Godwine; ns. M 192.

**God-wine,** son of Odda; a fugitive with his brothers Godric (1) and Godwig; ns. M 192. (E's transcript calls him *Godrine.*)

**Gotan,** wk.m.pl. the Goths; in the time of Ermanaric they had not yet separated into Ostrogoths and Visigoths; gp. **Gotena,** D 23.

**Hedeningas,** m.pl. the people ruled by Heden, a legendary Germanic king, wooer of Hagen's daughter, Hild, and once the lord of Deor; gp. —a, D 36.

**Heorrenda,** a scop of Heden, celebrated in one of the versions of the Hild saga; according to Deor, his successful rival; ns. D 39.

**Īras,** m.pl. the Irish; gp. **Īra,** B 56.

**Lēof-sunu,** retainer of Byrhtnoþ, probably from Sturmer in Essex; the third to speak after Byrhtnoþ's death; ns. M 244.

**Maccus,** one of the three defenders of the ford at Maldon; ns. M 80.

**Mǣringas,** m.pl. an unidentified people ruled by the unidentified Þeodric; gp. **Mǣringa,** D 19.

**Mǣþ-hild,** a legendary lady, beloved by Ġēat; probably the one who was threatened with rape by a river demon; gs. —e, D 14.

**Māria,** the Virgin Mary; as. —n, R 92.

**Mierce,** m. i-stem pl. the Mercians; np. B 24; dp. **Miercum,** M 217.

**Niþ-hād,** legendary king, persecutor of Weland; ns. D 5.

**Norþ-Hymbre,** m. i-stem pl. the Northumbrians; dp. —**Hymbrum,** M 266.

**Norþ-mann,** m. cons.-stem, Norseman; np. **Norþ-menn,** B 53; gp. **-manna,** B 33.

**Odda,** father of the fugitives, Godric (1), Godwig and Godwine; gs. —**n,** M 186, 238. [See Gordon's glossary for the possible origin of the name, Scandinavian or English.]

**Offa,** an officer of Byrhtnoþ's, apparently second in command under him; his speech after B's death, M 231 ff., seems to indicate that he is now the leader; ns. M 198, 230, 286, 288; gs. —**n,** M 5.

**Ōs-wold,** a retainer of Byrhtnoþ's, brother of Eadwold; ns. M 304.

**Pante,** wk.f. the river near Maldon, in Essex, now called Blackwater, though the old name Pant (pron. Pont) survives for the part below Maldon. See Gordon's glossary. gs. **Pantan,** M 68; as. **Pantan,** M 97.

**Scottas,** m.pl. the Scots; gp. **Scotta,** B 11, 32. [The spelling *Sceotta* in MS. A suggests that at least in the South the *sc* was palatalized; but perhaps only by a few.]

**Scyttisc,** pr. adj. Scottish; nsm. B 19.

**Seaxe,** m. i-stem pl. the Saxons, as distinguished from the Angles; np. B 70. [The reference is to the invasion of the fifth century as recounted by Bede and the Anglo-Saxon Chronicle.]

**Sige-byrht,** brother of Æðelric, one of Byrhtnoþ's retainers. It is not definitely stated that Sigebyrht was present at the battle; gs. —**es,** M 282.

**Stūr-mere,** a pool (mere) in the river Stour in Essex, from which the village of Sturmer takes its name. (See Gordon's glossary.) as. M 249.

**Þēod-rīc,** a ruler of uncertain identity; held by some to be Theodoric the Ostrogoth, in later legend Dietrich von Bern; by others, including Malone, to be the king of the Franks, the Hug-Dietrich, father of Wolf-Dietrich, of later legend. Perhaps he is neither. ns. D 18.

**Þur-stān,** father of Wistan; gs. —**es,** M 298. [The name is adapted, according to Gordon, from OE Scand. ÞURSTÆIN; the first element may be ÞŪR, OE variant of ÞUNOR, Old Norse ÞÓR, the god.]

**Wealh,** m. a Welshman (originally a foreigner), Briton; ap. **Wēalas,** B 72.

**Wēland,** legendary smith; ns. D 1.

**West-Seaxe,** m. i-stem pl. the West-Saxons; np. B 20; gp. **West-Seaxna,** B 59.

**Wīg-helm,** father of an unidentified warrior at Maldon; gs. —**es,** M 300. [Gordon suggests that **Wīg-helmes bearn** is Offa, but this seems unlikely. Perhaps we should read **mǣg** for **bearn** and conclude that Wistan was not only the son of Þurstan but a nephew or grandson of Wighelm.]

**Wī-stān,** one of Byrhtnoþ's retainers, son of Þurstan; ns. M 297. [Gordon suggests that the first element may be either wīġ, *war,* or, by way of Scandinavian, wīh, wēoh, *idol, shrine;* if he was named for Wiġhelm, q.v., the element is wīġ.]

**Wulf-mǣr,** (1) son of Byrhtnoþ's sister; ns. M 113. (2) **Wulfmǣr se** Ġeonga, W. the Young, a retainer of Byrhtnoþ's, son of Wulfstan; ns. M 155, 183.

**Wulf-stān,** chief defender of the ford at Maldon, son of Ceola, father of Wulfmǣr (2); ns. M 75; gs. **—es,** M 155; ds. **—e,** M 79.

# SUPPLEMENT

Since the first edition of 1966, all seven poems have received
critical attention, and some have received new editions. Only a
few of the critical essays, those that require or suggest modifica-
tions of the commentary on the five most complex and problemat-
ical poems (*The Dream of the Rood, The Battle of Maldon, The
Wanderer, The Seafarer,* and *Deor*), are included below under
the headings of the several poems. Three more inclusive works,
to which I shall refer by the abbreviations in the left-hand
column, are the following:

Whitelock 1967

*Sweet's Anglo-Saxon Reader in Prose
and Verse,* 15th edition, revised through-
out by Dorothy Whitelock (Oxford:
Clarendon Press, 1967). Both texts and
commentary have been revised. Among
the poems are all those here edited ex-
cept *Deor. Cædmon's Hymn* appears in
two versions: the West Saxon, pp. 46–
47, and the Northumbrian, pp. 181–182.
Following Sweet's example, the main
text of *The Seafarer* ends at line 108,
the remainder (lines 109–124) being
printed without annotation in the
notes.

Shippey 1972

T. A. Shippey, *Old English Verse* (Lon-
don: Hutchinson, 1972). Much stimu-
lating comment on Old English verse
in general. Chapter 3 discusses *The
Wanderer, The Seafarer, and Deor* in
the context of other elegies and poems
of wisdom.

Nicholson-Frese 1975

*Anglo-Saxon Poetry: Essays in Appre-
ciation, for John C. McGalliard,* ed. by

215

Lewis E. Nicholson and Dolores War-
wick Frese (Notre Dame: The Univer-
sity Press, 1975). Includes essays on
*The Dream of the Rood, The Wan-
derer, The Seafarer,* and *Deor.* Three
of these are mentioned below under
the relevant headings.

In quotations of Old English words in the following com-
mentary I omit, as needless, marks of vowel length and the
palatalized pronunciation of *c* and *g*.

# The Dream of the Rood

A new edition by Michael Swanton (Manchester: The Univer-
sity Press; New York: Barnes and Noble, 1970) reconsiders all
aspects of the poem and the fragment on the Ruthwell Cross.
It has many valuable insights, though the text retains some
very improbable scribal readings. The text of Whitelock 1967
does greater justice to the poet. Among many critical articles
of value, the most comprehensive in its explication of the text
is that of Alvin A. Lee, "Toward a Critique of *The Dream of
the Rood,*" Nicholson-Frere 1975, pp. 163–91. Two essays that
shed great light on the background of Anglo-Saxon, especially
Northumbrian monasticism with its partly Irish tradition of
contemplation of the Christian mysteries, are John V. Fleming,
"*The Dream of the Rood* and Anglo-Saxon Monasticism,"
*Traditio* XXII (1966), 43-72, and Robert B. Burlin, "The Ruth-
well Cross, *The Dream of the Rood,* and the Vita Contemplativa,"
the very depth and intensity of contemplation cultivated within
*Studies in Philology,* LXV (1968), 22–43. Burlin suggests that
the early monastic tradition could lead to the universal human
understanding that distinguishes the poet's vision.

## Notes

19. *earmra ær-gewinn.* Swanton's revival and elaboration of Cook's interpretation of these words as referring (though with dreamlike vagueness) to the former strife of the wretches who were Christ's enemies have convinced me that this is the superior interpretation, leading directly to the precisely significant vision of the bleeding on the right side.

91. *ofer holt-wudu.* I cannot approve of the efforts by Swanton and others to justify the scribe's *ofer holmwudu* (where *ofer holm* ends a manuscript line). Ingenious exegetical interpretations of *holm-wudu* cannot be reconciled with the simple logic of the superlative assertion and its parallel with the superlative exaltation of Mary. The scribe could very well have absent-mindedly substituted the phrase *ofer holm* (in itself intelligible) without attending to its impropriety in conjunction with *wudu* and the logic of the passage.

125. *ealra.* Swanton, in agreement with Dickins and Ross, glosses this as "in all," a meaning well attested when *ealles* or *eallra* accompanies a numeral. Here the idiom seems to be extended to the indefinite *fela*, which then governs *langung-hwila* separately. Bernard Huppé, who includes text, translation, and critical analysis of *The Dream of the Rood* in *The Web of Words* (Albany: State University of New York Press, 1970), Part II, pp. 64–112, translates *fela ealra* with judicious freedom as "full many."

# The Battle of Maldon

For a convenient summary of recent controversy about the meaning of *ofermod* in line 89 and its bearing on the poet's view of Byrhtnoþ, see D. G. Scragg's *Supplement* to the reprint of *The Battle of Maldon*, ed. E. V. Gordon (Manchester: The Univer-

sity Press, 1976). Scragg brings the bibliography up to date and
gives a sensible review of important articles, including those on
the *ofermod* passage by George Clark (1968), J. E. Cross (1974),
and Helmut Gneuss (1976). Although Gneuss (*Studies in Phi-
lology*, LXXIII, 117–137) makes an exhaustive study of the oc-
currences and meanings of the word in Old English prose and
verse, it cannot be said that the meaning of *ofermod* in this
passage has been settled, because, as Gneuss admits, its definition
as *superbia* or "pride" in the ecclesiastical sense, one of the deadly
sins, depends on occurrences in religious and ecclesiastical con-
texts. Its appearance here in a secular, military context is unique.
In a second, more recent article by George Clark, "The Hero of
*Maldon*: Vir pius et strenuus," *Speculum*, LIV (1979), 257–282,
the author scores an important point when he quotes (p. 274) a
passage from Alfred's *Boethius* (ed. Sedgefield, p. 62) in which
Alfred, without warrant from the Latin, adds to the definition
of a hypothetical wise (and therefore worthy) man the notion
of his having *swiðe gooda oferhyda* (where the plural *oferhyda*
might perhaps be rendered "high-spirited thoughts"). Since
*oferhygd*, like *ofermod*, usually signifies pride in a bad sense,
and is so used by Alfred himself in his translation of Gregory's
*Pastoral Care* (ed. Sweet, p. 111, line 22), where the reference is
to the pride of Lucifer himself, it is clear that Alfred's qualifica-
tion, *swiðe gooda*, "very good," shows his awareness of an admir-
able kind of pride or high-mindedness. Thus, the fact that the
poet blames Byrhtnoþ's *ofermod* for a fateful decision is no proof
that he regards this *ofermod* as in itself unequivocally bad. It
may be noticed that the poet uses the possessive *his* in the verse
*for his ofermode*, where, in contrast to a simple *for ofermode*, he
is pointing to an ingrained characteristic of the man rather than
a momentary access of passion. Surely this is the very characteris-
tic that appears in a good light in Byrhtnoþ's reply to the Viking
messenger (lines 45–61). The poet seems to feel that the Vikings
are trading on his characteristic when they ask permission to
cross the ford unhindered, but he attributes Byrhtnoþ's response,
not to any beguilement, but to the settled characteristic of a

heroic nature, the *ofermod* that makes him choose the hazard of a fight to the finish. Qualities normally considered admirable can prove fatal. Compare Edmund's boast in *King Lear*, that Edgar's nobility, as well as Gloucester's credulity, allows his villainous practices to ride easy.

Two essays by Fred C. Robinson are notable for bringing to notice other aspects of the art and spiritual power of the poem. In one, "Some Aspects of the *Maldon* Poet's Artistry," *Journal of English and Germanic Philology*, LXXV (1976), 25–40, he calls attention to many features commonly overlooked, some of which are mentioned in the notes below. In the other, "God, Death, and Loyalty in *The Battle of Maldon*," in *J. R. R. Tolkien . . . Essays in Memoriam*, ed. Mary Salu and Robert T. Farrell (Ithaca: Cornell University Press, 1979), 76–98, he brings out eloquently the spiritual depth and range of the poem, especially in its treatment of the heroic retainers.

## Notes

11. *gelæstan.* The glossary gives "support, help" for this instance, but in view of *to gefeohte* in the next line it is better to substitute "follow (in support)," as one follows a leader. (See Bosworth-Toller, *gelæstan*, II.) The meaning of *to* in line 12 thus falls under 1 (a) in the glossary rather than 1 (c).

29–41. See Robinson, "Some Aspects" (1976) for evidence that the speech of the Viking messenger is colored by Scandinavian vocabulary and idiom. May not the poet have been familiar with Danelaw idiom?

53. Robinson (*ibid.*) suggests that Byrhtnoþ's determination to defend *Æðelrædes eard,* though primarily stressing his loyalty to the king, would have seemed ironic to early audiences in view of Æðelred's reputation as "unready" (an epithet later attached to him because he was said to have been inclined toward *unræd,* "bad counsel") and his policy of paying tribute to the Danes instead of resisting them. Whether the poet was conscious of or intended such irony depends in part on where and when he com-

posed the poem. For important qualifications of the retrospective criticism of Æðelred in the *Anglo-Saxon Chronicle*, see Simon Keynes, *The Diplomas of King Æthelred 'the Unready,'* 978–1016 (Cambridge University Press, 1980), especially pp. 202 and 231. Æðelred was a young man in his middle twenties in 991 and Keynes suggests that the decade of the nineties was the least ill-counseled part of his reign. As for the date of composition of the poem, an attempt by John McKinnell, "On the Date of *The Battle of Maldon*," *Medium Ævum*, XLIV (1975), 121–136, to prove that the application to Byrhtnoþ of the title *eorl* rather than *ealdorman* points to a date as late as 1020 in the reign of Cnut, though it is carefully documented, conflicts with responsible older opinion (e.g. that of Whitelock 1967) that the poem was composed within a few years of the battle, and overlooks the connection of Byrhtnoþ with areas in and near the Danelaw (not merely Essex), where *eorl* may have been applied popularly to Byrhtnoþ long before the title (an adaptation of Old Norse *jarl*) became general.

86–90. On the overgrown controversies concerning this passage see the introductory comments above.

130. Robinson, "Some Aspects" (1976), suggests that a line or two may have been lost before 130, introducing the Viking there described as *wiges heard*.

212. Robinson (*ibid.*) has ably defended the form *Gemunu* in Elphinstone's transcript of the lost manuscript as a first person singular, "I remember" (a variant of the more ancient form *geman*), with the personal pronoun understood. The ninth-century gloss to the Vespasian Psalter renders *si non meminero tui* (Psalm 136. 6) by *gif ic ne gemunu ðin*, and *ic gemune* (apparently the normal late West Saxon form) translates Latin *recordor* in Ælfric's *Grammar* (ed. Zupitza, p. 146). The first person singular allows Ælfwine's speech to correspond, as the personal response of one individual, with all the rest of the speeches, except for Offa's, which properly applies Ælfwine's example to all the company because, as Byrhtnoþ's chief officer, he has become the leader after Byrhtnoþ's death. Probably the emendation of *þa* to *þara* is wise, since *mæla* is more easily ex-

plained as genitive plural than as accusative plural. *Gemunan* can take either accusative or genitive, but here the partitive aspect of the genitive seems proper.

# The Wanderer

Besides the edition of R. F. Leslie (Manchester: The University Press, 1966), which is mentioned above, p. 80, as having appeared too late to be of service in the preparation of the first edition, an important, differently conceived edition by T. P. Dunning and A. J. Bliss (London: Methuen, 1969) should also now be consulted. Both editions deal intelligently with the problems of interpretation, about which, as one would expect, they sometimes disagree. Dunning and Bliss have much that is new to say about the connotations of individual words and about syntactical difficulties. Both agree (and Leslie argues) that the poem is not a dialogue: the shift of emphasis and range at line 59 implies a new development, but there are enough links between the two parts to justify the traditional assumption that there is but one speaker: the *eardstapa* is shown by the second part of the poem to be entitled to be called *snottor on mode*. Although I now agree with this assumption (as I have stated in "Second Thoughts on the Interpretation of *The Seafarer*," to which there is particular reference below, p.224), I have allowed the dialogue punctuation in the text to stand, as it corresponds to the original commentary and merely exaggerates the difference between the two parts.

Among the many recent essays on *The Wanderer*, all of which treat the main speech as a monologue, that of Rosemary Woolf, "*The Wanderer, The Seafarer,* and the Genre of *Planctus*," Nicholson-Frese 1975, pp. 192–207, is notable for its fresh perspective. She suggests incidentally (p. 197) that the modern use of quotation marks is too precise. She would take lines 1–5 and

112–115 as merging the sentiments of the poet with those of his fictional speaker, a possibility suggested to me some time ago by one of my students, and one that accords well with the conditions of writing and recitation of the period. Shippey 1972, Chapter III, treats *The Wanderer* perceptively in the context of other "elegies" and the larger category of Old English poems of wisdom. An important essay by Peter Clemoes is mentioned below in the note on lines 50–57.

## Notes

1-5. These lines, as suggested in Rosemary Woolf's essay, are probably best taken as the narrator's statement of a generalization with which the *eardstapa*, as suggested by line 6, agrees. Thus they provide an introduction for the poem and also for the direct discourse that begins formally at line 8.

50–57. Dunning and Bliss, in their edition of 1969, pp. 21–23, give a different interpretation of the syntax and meaning of these lines from that of previous editors. Among other differences, Dunning and Bliss regard *mod* 51 as the subject of *geondhweorfeþ* and *gemynd* as the object, thus making *geondhweorfeþ*, *greteþ*, and *geondsceawaþ* a consecutive series, all with *mod* as subject. The same construction (though not all else advocated by Dunning and Bliss) was independently proposed at almost the same time by Peter Clemoes in the course of his essay, *"Mens absentia cogitans* in *The Seafarer* and *The Wanderer,"* in *Medieval Literature and Civilization: Studies in Memory of G. N. Garmonsway,* ed. by D. A. Pearsall and R. A. Waldron (London: The Athlone Press, 1969), pp. 62–77. He proposes this construction in part because it is more in accord with the principal argument of his essay, that the psychology of the passage (and of *The Seafarer* 58–64) had been influenced by discussions of the powers of the soul in Christian Latin literature: specifically, for the passage in *The Wanderer*, by a passage in Ambrose's *Hexaemeron* (which he quotes, p. 66) in which Ambrose speaks of the soul's power to be united with persons it knows when they are absent: in Clemoes's translation, "we speak to them when they are separated, even when they are dead we revive them to talk to, and we embrace and hold them as we would living people and accord them the courtesies and usage of life." The resemblance is striking and the influence surely possible. But although I prefer Clemoes's interpretation of the passage as a whole to that of Dunning and Bliss, I still prefer the traditional assumption that *gemynd* is the subject of *geondhweorfeþ* ("sorrow is renewed when the memory of kinsmen roves through the mind"), and that either *mod* or an implicit *he* is the subject of the two verbs that follow. This interpretation is indicated by my punctuation (and that of other editors), with semicolon after *geondhweorfeð*. I prefer to take *gemynd* as subject of the first verb because it seems proper to suggest that the memory of kinsmen comes into and roves through the mind involuntarily, just as the dream of homage to the lord had done. The mind, not fully awake, is thus momentarily under the illusion that the seabirds are kinsmen and comrades. Only then does it take command by the actions of greeting and seeking to recognize.

87. *enta geweorc*. See P. J. Frankis, "The Thematic Significance of *enta geweorc* and Related Imagery in *The Wanderer*," *Anglo-Saxon England*, 2 (1973), 253-269. Frankis presses the imprecise imagery of the poem so far as to suggest (what is not in itself impossible) that the poet was familiar not only with Roman ruins in England but with learned references to Rome, Babylon, and the tower of Babel as the work of post-diluvian giants.

98. *wyrm-licum fag*. Tony Millns, commenting on line 98 in *The Review of English Studies*, n.s. 28 (1977), 431–8, argues cogently that the poet is referring to herring-bone masonry in the shape of serpents such as can still be seen in the remains of Roman buildings in Britain and in some later imitations. He suggests (less compellingly) that the reference to serpents may also have been taken as an appropriate memorial to those who died by the wall.

# The Seafarer

As with *The Wanderer*, I have allowed the indications of dialogue
and the explanations of them in the original commentary to
stand, but I have since concluded that what, following Rieger, I
took for evidence of a second speaker is too uncertain to warrant
rejection of the prevailing view that the poem is a monologue.
In "Second Thoughts on the Interpretation of *The Seafarer*,"
*Anglo-Saxon England,* 3 (1974), 75–86, I proposed to return
in most respects to Dorothy Whitelock's interpretation (de-
scribed above, p. 86), and suggested that the troublesome *sylf*
of line 35 (here normalized as *self*) may mean "by myself,"
"alone." Meanwhile Stanley B. Greenfield, in *"Min, Sylf,* and
'Dramatic Voices in *The Wanderer* and *The Seafarer*'," *Journal
of English and Germanic Philology*, LXVIII (1969), 212–220,
had not only opposed my earlier interpretation of both poems
as dialogues, but had interpreted *sylf* as "of my own accord" and
taken the earlier voyages of lines 1–33a as obligatory penance,
the voyage contemplated in the ensuing lines as for the first time
a voluntary one. In the article of 1974 I expressed doubts about
this interpretation, and Greenfield himself has now modified
these views, while proposing others of interest, in *"Sylf,* Seasons,
Structure and Genre," *Anglo-Saxon England,* 9 (1981 for 1980),
199–224. He rejects my interpretation of *sylf* and proposes a new
one, "for myself," which requires lengthy explication and leaves
me still in doubt. Perhaps we have both worried too much about
*sylf*, as suggested below in the note on line 35. For help with a
different problem, the characterization of the speaker, I am at-
tracted by Rosemary Woolf's suggestion that in the second half
of the poem one can suppose a gradual merging of the dramati-
cally conceived seafarer with the sermonizing poet. (See p. 205
of her essay in Nicholson Frese, to which I refer particularly
above, p. 221.)

# Notes

33. *For-þon.* The transition from lines 1–33a to what follows, supposing no change of speaker, would be eased if we could take *for-þon* in this instance as at least mildly adversative ("as for that," "but yet," as suggested in the glossary). Modern "for all that," though not strictly parallel, suggests the possibility of an adversative sense, for which plausible instances in Old English were assembled by Marjorie Daunt, "Some Difficulties of *The Seafarer* Reconsidered," *Modern Language Review*, XIII (1918), 474 ff.

35. *self.* See the general commentary above for recent interpretations of this word, which many earlier editors and translators have passed over (forgivably and perhaps rightly) as untranslatable, a mere alliterating iteration of *ic*, at most enforcing the idea of the speaker's bold confrontation of the high seas.

58–64. Peter Clemoes, "*Mens absentia cogitans* in *The Seafarer* and *The Wanderer* (see the note above on *The Wanderer* 50–57) quotes two passages from Alcuin's *De animae ratione* (one in prose, the other in verse) which expatiate on the mind's power to travel, in imagination, far from the body, and to fly, as the verse has it, "across sea, lands and lofty sky," and argues that they are likely to have provided a psychological basis for these lines. He admits, of course, that much else lies behind the poet's total concept and his brilliantly imaginative expression of it.

# Deor

Some important modifications of older interpretations of the poem, as represented by Kemp Malone's editions and articles (see above, p. 91) have been brought together by James L. Boren, "The Design of the Old English *Deor*," in Nicholson-Frese 1975, pp. 264–276. The most significant of these, each of which, as Boren notes, had been proposed earlier, are mentioned below in the notes on lines 18 and 42.

## Notes

7. *þæs þofereode, þisses swa mæg.* Jon Erickson, "The *Deor* Genitives," *Archivum Linguisticum*, VI (1975), 77–84, argues that the grammar (though not the essential meaning) of the refrain, and also that of *þæs ofercumen wære* 26, has been misunderstood. He contends that *þæs* and *þisses* are not genitives of respect, a classification otherwise unsupported for the genitive case. Rather they are dependent on a deleted subject of vague import. In the refrain he suggests "result" as the suppressed noun: "the result of that passed over; so may the result of this." More appropriate than "result," perhaps, would be Wardale's "sorrow" (to which Erickson refers with approval of its grammatical understanding), if it were not for the possibility that a period of good fortune is referred to by *þæs* in the final refrain. (See below on line 42.) According to this interpretation of the genitives, *ofereode* has a suppressed subject, not the impersonal "it." Similarly, Erickson suggests, for *þæs ofercumen wære* 26, "[the ruler] of that were overcome." Morton Bloomfield, in "The Form of *Deor*," *Publications of the Modern Language Association*, LXXIX (1964), 534–541, properly enough insists that *mæg* means "is able to" and must be translated as "can," not the more equivocal modern English "may." Even "can," though more positive than "may," is short of the certainty of "will," which has sometimes been proposed.

18. *þeodric.* Boren approves the argument of P. J. Frankis on pp. 162–64 of his article, *"Deor* and *Wulf and Eadwacer*: Some Conjectures," *Medium Ævum*, XXXI (1962), 161–175, that the reference is to Theodoric the Ostrogoth, not as an exile among the Huns but as the tyrannical ruler of Italy in Ravenna, a rule that approximated thirty years (actually thirty-three, 493–526) and was regarded in the England of King Alfred's day (as

shown most clearly by Alfred's version of the *Consolatio Philosophiae* of Boethius) as oppressive because Theodoric was held responsible for the deaths of Boethius, Symmachus, and Pope John. Frankis suggests that *Mæringa* 19 may refer, not to the Visigoths, as Malone had suggested, but simply to the Goths, in this instance the Ostrogoths. Hence *Mæringa burg* may point to Ravenna. This interpretation accords better than the earlier ones (where the thirty winters were taken as a period of exile, whether for the Frankish or the Ostrogothic Theodoric) with the normal sense of *ahte*, "possessed." It links *þeodric*, not with previous sufferers of misfortune, but with the still more notoriously tyrannical *Eormanric*.

42. *þæs.* Boren approves, and elaborates, a suggestion made independently by two scholars at almost the same time: Murray F. Markland, in *"Deor: þæs ofereode þisses swa mæg,"* *American Notes and Queries*, XI (1972), 35–36, and Shippey 1972, pp. 77–78. They contend that in the final refrain *þæs* refers, not to the misfortune of Deor's having been supplanted by Heorrenda, but to the fortunate period when Deor was the *scop* of the Hedenings. Hence *þisses* refers, not to whatever misfortune may be suffered by anyone in Deor's audience (as Malone maintained) but to Deor's present misfortune in having been supplanted. This interpretation is perhaps best defended by Shippey, who urges that the previous stanza, in lines 32–34, allows one to recognize that both kinds of fortune are changeable. The use of *nu* in line 39 may indeed seem to imply that Deor's misfortune is a present one, to which *þisses* should refer. Yet *nu* may be taken to indicate Heorrenda's present possession of the position and the *land-riht*, not to the moment when Deor was supplanted and driven into exile. According to Malone's interpretation, Deor has already found some measure of consolation for that misfortune, and *þisses* refers, as before, to whatever may be troubling anyone now. On the whole I find Malone's interpretation superior, since it does not require a sudden alteration of the meaning of *þæs*, for which I think lines 32–34 do not adequately prepare us.